# Mac® for Seniors

Studio Visual Steps

# Mac®
# for Seniors

*Learn step by step how to work with Mac OS X*

*www.visualsteps.com*

This book has been written using the Visual Steps™ method.
Cover design by Studio Willemien Haagsma bNO

© 2012 Visual Steps
With the assistance of Yvette Huijsman
Edited by Jolanda Ligthart, Rilana Groot and Mara Kok
Translated by Irene Venditti, *i-write* translation services and Chris Hollingsworth, *1ˢᵗ Resources*.
Printed in Canada.

First printing: February 2012
ISBN 978 90 5905 008 2

**Resources used**: A number of definitions and explanations of computer terminology are taken over from the *Mac User Guide*.

**Do you have questions or suggestions?**
**E-mail: info@visualsteps.com**

**Would you like more information?**
**www.visualsteps.com**

**Website for this book:**
**www.visualsteps.com/mac**
Here you can register your book.

**Subscribe to the free Visual Steps Newsletter:**
**www.visualsteps.com/newsletter**

# Table of Contents

# Bonus Chapters

On the website accompanying this book you will find the bonus chapters. In *Appendix B Opening Bonus Chapters* you will read how to open these bonus chapters.

**Bonus Chapter 8. Basic Text Editing Operations**
**Bonus Chapter 9. Downloading Apps**

# Foreword

For a number of years, the *Mac* notebooks and desktop computers have increased in popularity among a growing group of users. In this book, you will learn how to use the *Mac*, step by step.

You will learn how to use the *TextEdit* application to handle you basic writing needs, such as creating letter, notes and memos. The *Finder* app allows you to work with the folders and files stored on your computer. You can delete, copy, move and rename your files with the *Finder* app.

You can use the *Safari* Internet browser to surf the web. This program comes with some very useful functions, such as *Top Sites*. This feature keeps track of the websites you visit most often, and allows you to open these websites with just a single mouse click. The e-mail program that is included in the *Mac* software package is called *Mail*. You can use this program to quickly and easily send and receive e-mail messages.

Did you know that the *Mac* also has built-in programs for working with photos, videos and music? This book will help you get acquainted with *iPhoto* and *iTunes*. You will learn how to edit a photo, transfer a music CD to your computer and play video files and DVDs with *QuickTime Player* and *DVD Player*.

Furthermore, you will learn how to adapt the settings according to your own preferences. For example, you can change and adjust the mouse or trackpad settings to suit your own working method. You can also change the size of the icons, as well as the sound settings.

I wish you lots of fun while working with your *Mac*!

Yvette Huijsman
Studio Visual Steps

PS We welcome your comments and suggestions.
Our e-mail address is: mail@visualsteps.com

# Visual Steps Newsletter

All Visual Steps books follow the same methodology: clear and concise step-by-step instructions with screen shots to demonstrate each task. A complete list of all our books can be found on our website **www.visualsteps.com** You can also sign up to receive our **free Visual Steps Newsletter**.
In this Newsletter you will receive periodic information by e-mail regarding:
- the latest titles and previously released books;
- special offers, supplemental chapters, tips and free informative booklets.
Also, our Newsletter subscribers may download any of the documents listed on the web pages **www.visualsteps.com/info_downloads**

When you subscribe to our Newsletter you can be assured that we will never use your e-mail address for any purpose other than sending you the information as previously described. We will not share this address with any third-party. Each Newsletter also contains a one-click link to unsubscribe.

# Introduction to Visual Steps™

The Visual Steps handbooks and manuals are the best instructional materials available for learning how to work with computers and computer programs. Nowhere else will you find better support for getting to know the *Mac* computer, the iPad, the Internet, *Windows* or related software.

Properties of the Visual Steps books:
- **Comprehensible contents**
  Addresses the needs of the beginner or intermediate computer user for a manual written in simple, straight-forward English.
- **Clear structure**
  Precise, easy to follow instructions. The material is broken down into small enough segments to allow for easy absorption.
- **Screen shots of every step**
  Quickly compare what you see on your own computer screen with the screen shots in the book. Pointers and tips guide you when new windows are opened so you always know what to do next.
- **Get started right away**
  All you have to do is switch on your computer, place the book next to your keyboard, and begin at once.
- **Layout**
  The text is printed in a large size font. Even if you put the book next to your computer, this font will be clearly legible.

In short, I believe these manuals will be excellent guides for you.

dr. H. van der Meij

Faculty of Applied Education, Department of Instruction Technology, University of Twente, the Netherlands

# Register Your Book

When you can register your book, you will be kept informed of any important changes that are necessary to you as a user of the book. You can also take advantage of our periodic Newsletter informing you of our product releases, company news, tips & tricks, special offers, etcetera.

# What You Will Need

In order to work through this book, you will need to have a number of things:

The most important requirement is to have a *Mac* with *Mac OS X Lion* installed. This can be a desktop version including the Mac Mini, iMac and Mac Pro or the portable or notebook type of Mac including the Macbook, Macbook Pro and Macbook Air.

An active Internet connection.

Apple's Magic Mouse, or another type of computer mouse.

If you want, you can also use the trackpad on your notebook computer, or a mobile Magic Trackpad.

The following items can be very useful, but it is not absolutely necessary to own these items or devices. Just skip the exercises that make use of these things.

A USB stick (also called a USB memory stick or memory stick).

A printer.

A digital photo camera, an iPad, iPhone, or other portable device that is equipped with a built-in camera.

A music CD and a DVD.

# How to Use This Book

This book has been written using the Visual Steps™ method. The method is simple: just place the book next to your *Mac* and directly execute all the operations on your *Mac*, step by step. The clear instructions and the multitude of screen shots will tell you exactly what to do. The quickest way of learning how to use the *Mac*, is by working through the exercises.

In this Visual Steps™ book, you will see various icons. This is what they mean:

**Techniques**
These icons indicate an action to be carried out:

The mouse icon means you should do something on your *Mac* by using the mouse. Also, the mouse will regularly be used for operations where you can use a trackpad, as well as a mouse. In the first chapter you can read more about using the mouse.

The keyboard icon means you should type something on your *Mac*'s keyboard.

The index finger icon indicates you can do something on your notebook's trackpad, or on a mobile trackpad, for example, tapping something.

The hand icon means you should do something else, for example insert a USB stick into the computer. It is also used to remind you of something you have learned before.

In addition to these icons, in some areas of this book *extra assistance* is provided to help you successfully work through each chapter.

**Help**
These icons indicate that extra help is available:

 The arrow icon warns you about something.

 The bandage icon will help you if something has gone wrong.

 Have you forgotten how to do something? The number next to the footsteps tells you where to look it up at the end of the book in the appendix *How Do I Do That Again?*

In separate boxes you will find tips or additional, background information on the *Mac*.

**Extra information**
Information boxes are denoted by these icons:

The book icon gives you extra background information that you can read at your convenience. This extra information is not necessary for working through the book.

The light bulb icon indicates an extra tip for using the *Mac*.

# Website

On the website that accompanies this book, **www.visualsteps.com/mac**
Regularly check this website, to see if we have added any additional information or errata for this book. Also, you will find various bonus chapters on this website.

# Test Your Knowledge

Have you finished reading this book? Then test your knowledge with a test. Visit the website:
**www.ccforseniors.com**
This multiple-choice test will tell you how good your computer knowledge is. If you pass the test, you will receive your free *Computer Certificate* by e-mail.

# For Teachers

This book is designed as a self-study guide. It is also well suited for use in a group or a classroom setting. For this purpose, we offer a free teacher's manual containing information about how to prepare for the course (including didactic teaching methods) and testing materials. You can download this teacher's manual (PDF file) from the website which accompanies this book: **www.visualsteps.com/mac**

# The Screen Shots

The screen shots in this book were made on a computer running *Windows 7 Ultimate* edition. The screen shots used in this book indicate which button, folder, file or hyperlink you need to click on your computer screen. In the instruction text (in **bold** letters) you will see a small image of the item you need to click. The black line will point you to the right place on your screen.

The small screen shots that are printed in this book are not meant to be completely legible all the time. This is not necessary, as you will see these images on your own computer screen in real size and fully legible.

Here you see an example of an instruction text and a screen shot. The black line indicates where to find this item on your own computer screen:

**Click**
**Documents**

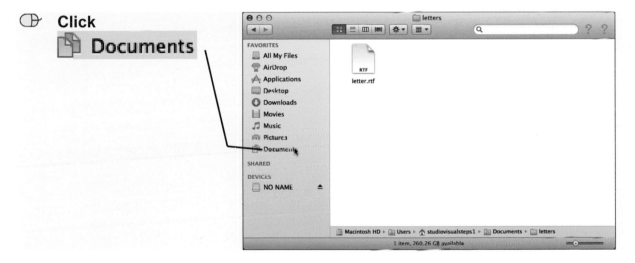

Sometimes the screen shot shows only a portion of a window. Here is an example:

At the bottom of the window:

**Click**

It really will **not be necessary** for you to read all the information in the screen shots in this book. Always use the screen shots in combination with the image you see on your own computer screen.

# 1. Start Working With the Mac

*Mac* is the abbreviation for *Macintosh*, the name of a series of desktop and notebook computers, manufactured and sold by the American company *Apple*. *Apple* also produces other devices, such as the iPod, iPhone and iPad.

The *Mac* uses the *OS X* operating system. This is the counterpart of the well-known *Windows* operating system, produced by the American company *Microsoft*.

The *Apple* products are famous for their beautiful design and user-friendly, intuitive interface. When you start to use a computer for the very first time, you will need to learn some basic operations. This may take a while, but afterwards, you will see that working with the *Mac* is quite easy. And if you have previously used a *Windows* computer, you will be surprised by the simplicity of the *Mac*.

In this chapter we will start with an overview of the main types of *Apple* computers. Next, you will get acquainted with your own *Mac*. We will cover all of the basic operations for using your *Mac*.

In this chapter you will learn how to:

- distinguish among the different types of *Macs*;
- turn on the *Mac*;
- use the mouse and/or the trackpad;
- open a program with *Launchpad*;
- use the *Dashboard*;
- view and move widgets;
- put the *Mac* into sleep mode;
- wake the *Mac* up from sleep mode;
- turn off the *Mac*.

# 1.1 The Different Types of Macs

*Apple* produces both desktop and notebook computers that use the *OS X* operating system. A desktop computer has a fixed place and usually resides on a desk or a table. A notebook computer can be used anywhere. You can set it on a table or desk as well as on your lap while sitting on a couch or bench (hence the name *laptop*). Below you will find an overview of the main models:

The *iMac* is an all-in-one desktop computer, where the computer and monitor are integrated as a single unit. This means you do not have a separate hard case or tower. You can operate the iMac with a keyboard or a mouse.

The iMac is currently available in a 21.5 inch screen or a 27 inch screen.

The *Mac mini* is the compact, portable and very quiet desktop computer produced by *Apple*. The Mac mini comes without a screen, keyboard, mouse or trackpad. You will need to buy these devices separately. They can be purchased from *Apple* as well as other hardware manufacturers.

The Mac mini is so tiny, it cannot fit a CD/DVD player or burner. But you can connect an external player or burner to it.

The *MacBook Pro* is an *Apple* notebook, specifically built for professional use. This notebook is available with a 13, 15 or 17 inch screen.

The *MacBook Air* is a very slim and lightweight *Apple* notebook. The thickest part is a mere 0.68 inches and the 11 inch model weighs only 2.38 pounds. The 13 inch model weighs just less than 3 pounds.

The MacBook Air is not equipped with a CD/DVD player.

It does not matter what type of *Mac* you use. You will be able to perform all the exercises in this book. But before you can use your *Mac* you need to turn it on. In the following section you can read how to do that.

# 1.2 Turn On the Mac

You turn on your *Mac* by using the power button. You will recognize this button by the ⏻ icon.

The power button of the MacBook Air is located on the keyboard, in the upper right corner:

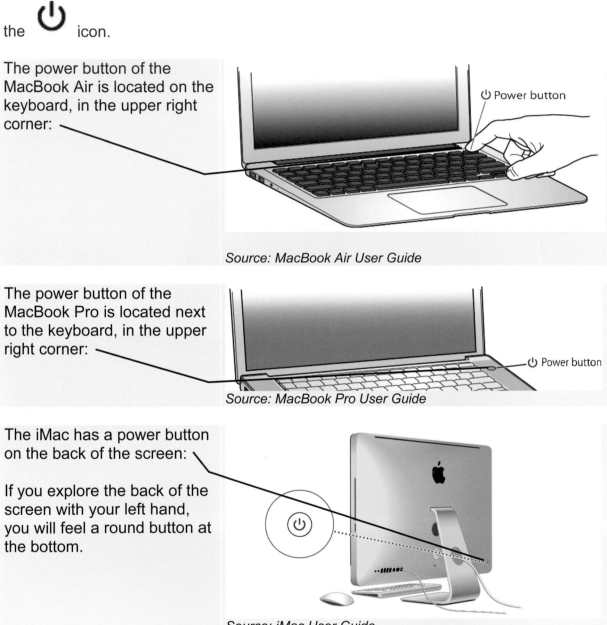

⏻ Power button

*Source: MacBook Air User Guide*

The power button of the MacBook Pro is located next to the keyboard, in the upper right corner:

⏻ Power button

*Source: MacBook Pro User Guide*

The iMac has a power button on the back of the screen:

If you explore the back of the screen with your left hand, you will feel a round button at the bottom.

*Source: iMac User Guide*

The Mac mini has a power button on the back of the unit:

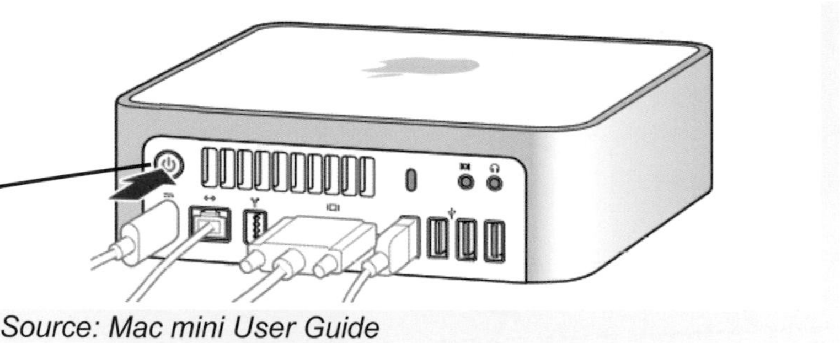

*Source: Mac mini User Guide*

### Please note:

If you are using a Mac mini, the screen will need to be turned on separately. The power button of the screen is usually located on the front of the screen.

When you turn on your *Mac* and the sound of your computer is turned on as well, you will hear a startup tone. The *OS X* will start up automatically.

You will see a grey screen with one or more icons (small pictures); below the icons their names are displayed:

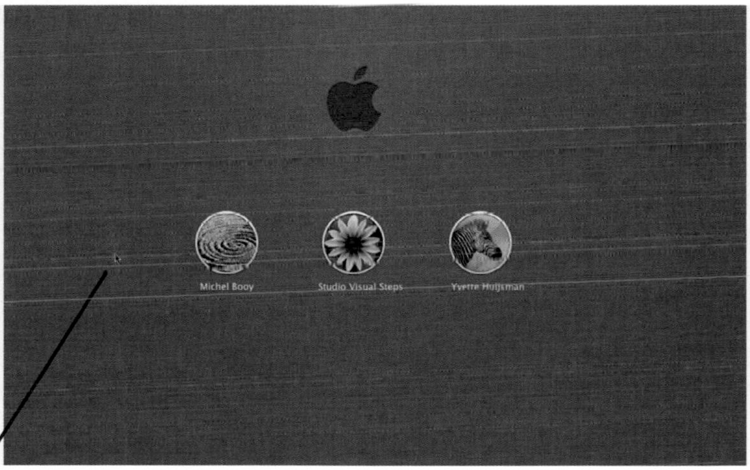


This is called the *login* screen.

Somewhere on this grey screen you will see a black arrow :

### HELP! I see a different screen.

Your *Mac* may be set up in such a way that you do not need to login with a password once you have turned it on. In this case, your desktop will display immediately:

On this screen you will also

see the black arrow :

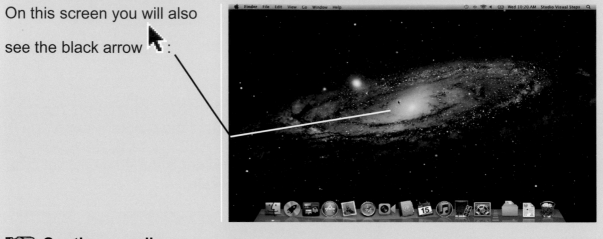

☞ **Continue reading**

This arrow is called the pointer. You can move this arrow with a mouse or a trackpad. In the following section you can read how to do this.

## 1.3 Mouse and Trackpad

You can move the pointer across the screen, in any direction you want, by using your mouse or trackpad. A trackpad, also called a touchpad, is a device used for moving a pointer. It consists of a special surface that is able to convert the movement of your fingers to an onscreen movement or command. Depending on the type of *Mac* you use, you can use one or more of the following devices:

The iMac always comes with a wireless *Magic Mouse*:

Put the mouse next to your keyboard, on a clean, smooth surface.

This may be a smooth table top, or a special mousepad.

Loosely lay your hand on the mouse. Keep your fingers relaxed and not stiff.

Allow your wrist and lower arm to rest on the table.

## 💡 Tip

**How do you hold your mouse?**

**Don't:**

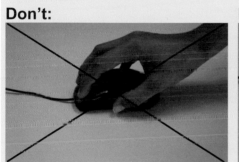

**Do:**

- Do not grip the mouse with just a few fingers, while sticking the other fingers in the air.
- Do not dangle your wrist over the table.
- Do not pinch or press.
- Do not lift the mouse.

- Loosely hold on to the mouse.
- Let the palm of your hand rest on the mouse.
- Your hand follows the shape of the mouse.
- Loosely rest your index finger on the left mouse button, let the other fingers relax beside your index finger.
- Put your thumb on the table, next to the mouse.
- Rest your wrist and lower arm on the table.
- Make sure the mouse buttons point away from you.

It is important to teach yourself how to hold the mouse in the correct position. By holding the mouse in the palm of your hand, in a relaxed and loose manner, you will be able to control the mouse.

This is how you move the pointer with a Magic Mouse:

 **Loosely place your hand on the mouse**

 **Move the mouse across the table**

You will see the pointer move: ———

## HELP! I see something on my screen.

If you see something appearing on your screen, move the pointer to a blank area on the screen and click this area.

The Mac mini does not come with a mouse. But you can connect almost any type of mouse to one of the USB ports located on the back:

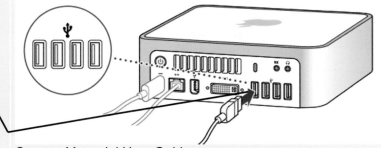

*Source: Mac mini User Guide*

You can also buy a Magic Mouse separately and connect it to your Mac mini through *Bluetooth* (this is a feature that sets up a wireless connection between different devices). Ask your computer supplier about this option, or read the Magic Mouse's manual for more information.

After you have connected a mouse to the USB port on your Mac mini, you can move the pointer in the same way as with the Magic Mouse:

 **Loosely place your hand on the mouse**

 **Move the mouse across the table**

The MacBook Air and Pro are equipped with a Multi-Touch trackpad. This is how you move the pointer with such a device:

☞ **Loosely drag the tip of your finger across the trackpad**

You will see the pointer move.

💡 **Tip**

**Use the mouse with a notebook**
You can also connect a mouse to one of the USB ports on your MacBook Pro or MacBook Air. If you are learning how to use a notebook computer for the first time, it is recommended to use a mouse in the beginning. You will be able to be more precise with your movements right away.

Do you own an iMac or a Mac mini and do you prefer to use a trackpad anyway? Then you can use the *Magic Trackpad.* This can be purchased separately:

The Magic Trackpad contains the same functionalities as the trackpad on the MacBook Pro and Air:

☞ **Practice moving the pointer across the screen for a while longer**

# 1.4 Clicking

You have just learned how to move the pointer across the screen. If you want to enter a command (an action that will do something), you need to click your mouse. In this section you can read how to do this on the various *Mac* devices. Then later, you can practice clicking with your own device. Here is how to click the Magic Mouse:

☞ **Position the pointer on a blank area of the screen**

☞ **Briefly press your index finger on the front side of the mouse**

You will hear a clicking sound.

If you have connected a different type of mouse to your Mac mini or MacBook, it will probably have two buttons.

☞ **Position the pointer on a blank area of the screen**

☞ **Briefly press your index finger on the <u>left</u> mouse button**

You will hear a clicking sound.

➥ **Please note:**

From this point on, if you come across the 'Click' command you will always need to click with the **left** mouse button, if you own a mouse with two buttons.

Clicking the trackpad of your MacBook Pro or Air works the same way as clicking a Magic Trackpad:

☞ **Position the pointer on an icon**

☞ **Briefly press the trackpad with one finger**

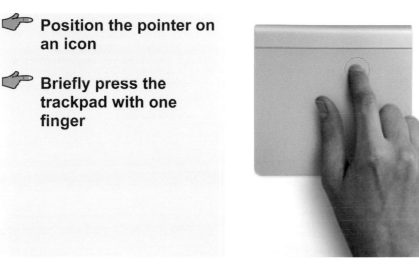

You will notice that there is not a lot of difference between working with the mouse and using the trackpad. While using a mouse you move the mouse, while using a trackpad you move your finger across the trackpad. You can click both devices with a single finger.

➥ **Please note:**

Whenever you see the ⬭ symbol in this book, it indicates that you need to do something with the mouse or the trackpad. If a certain action needs to be executed in a different way when using a trackpad, we will describe that action separately. In this case we will use the ☞ symbol.

Now you are going to try it yourself, by opening your user account:

⊕ **Position the pointer on the icon with your name, for example**

Studio Visual Steps

⊕ **Click the icon**

# HELP! I do not see an icon with my name on it.

If your screen does not display an icon with your name, you may already be viewing your desktop screen. In this case, you can practice clicking in the following way:

In the top left of the window:

☞ **Position the pointer on**

☞ **Click**

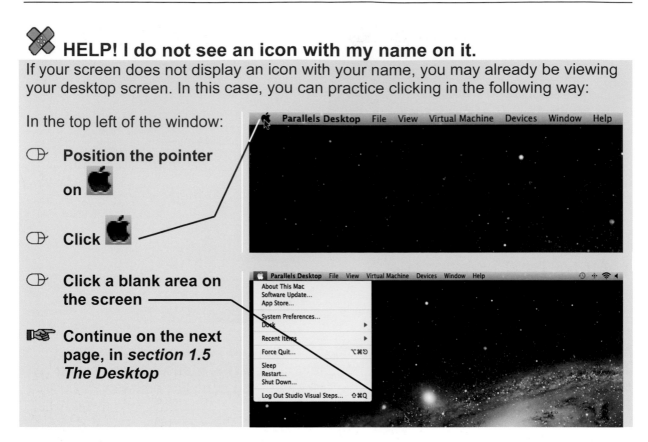

☞ **Click a blank area on the screen**

☞ **Continue on the next page, in *section 1.5 The Desktop***

In the next screen you will need a password in order to continue.

# HELP! I do not know the password.

If this is not your own computer, ask the owner to type the password for you.

⌨ **Type the password**

Instead of letters you will see small black dots:

This is a safety measure that prevents others from not being able to read your password.

**Position the pointer on**

**Click**

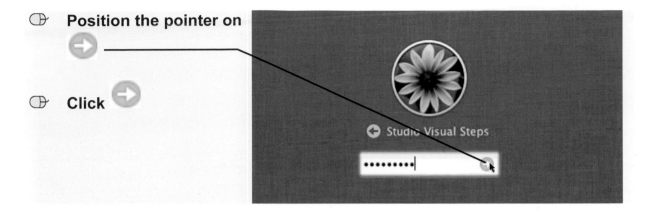

# 1.5 The Desktop

After you have logged in, the desktop will appear. Every action you carry out on your *Mac* begins from the desktop:

The default desktop picture on a *Mac* is a photo of the Andromeda Gallaxy:

You may see a different photo or a solid color on your desktop.

## Please note:

To display the screenshots in the rest of this book as clearly as possible, we use a simple, blue color for the desktop background. In the last chapter of this book you can read how to change the desktop picture to your own liking.

At the bottom of the screen you will see the *Dock*:

The *Dock* is one of the prominent features of the Mac. You will see a bar containing many icons. These icons are actually shortcuts for launching programs and opening folders.

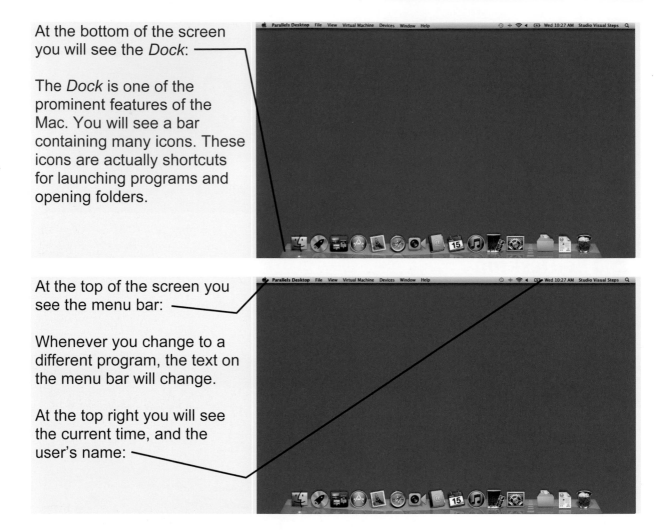

At the top of the screen you see the menu bar:

Whenever you change to a different program, the text on the menu bar will change.

At the top right you will see the current time, and the user's name:

Your *Mac* contains lots of other programs. However, there is not enough space on the *Dock* to display an icon for each one of them. In the next section you will take a look at the default set of programs.

# 1.6 Launchpad and Dashboard

In *Mac OS X Lion*, the *Dock* contains an [icon] icon for the *Launchpad*. The *Launchpad* is the place where you can view all the applications installed on your *Mac*.

On the *Dock*:

☞ **Position the pointer**

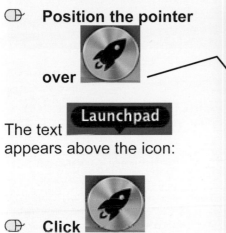

**over**

The text [Launchpad] appears above the icon:

☞ **Click**

Now the *Launchpad* is opened:

You will see various icons for the programs installed on your *Mac*:

You may see more or different icons on your own *Mac*.

You can use the icons for opening the corresponding programs. Just try this for the *Dashboard* program:

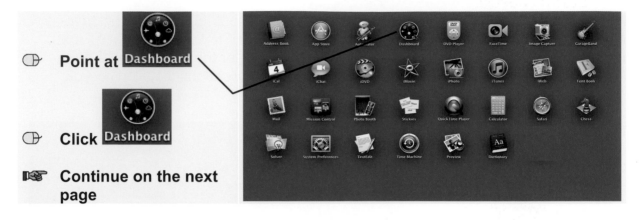

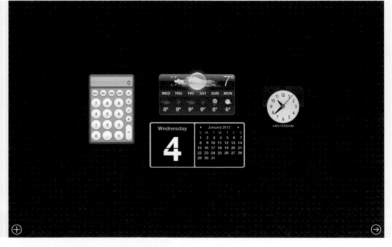

⊕  **Point at** Dashboard

⊕  **Click** Dashboard

☞  **Continue on the next page**

### ➥ **Please note:**

From this point on, the commands for ⊕  **Point at..., Point to... or** ⊕  **Position the pointer...** will be replaced by the shorter command ⊕  **Click...**

*Dashboard* is a program that provides access to all kinds of useful mini programs. These programs are called *widgets*.

Now you will see the *Dashboard* screen, containing the *Weather*, *World Clock*, *Calendar* and *Calculator* widgets:

If someone else has previously used your *Mac*, you may see other widgets.

### HELP! Dashboard has not opened and Launchpad has disappeared.

If you have not clicked the *Dashboard* icon accurately, but have clicked accidentally next to it, you may have caused the *Launchpad* application to close. You will then return to your desktop screen. Just give it a try once more:

CD Click

CD Click

This is how you calculate a sum with the *Calculator* widget:

CD Click

CD Click

CD Click

CD Click

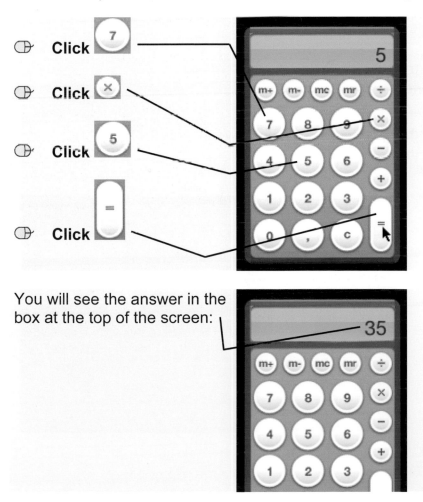

You will see the answer in the box at the top of the screen:

# 1.7 Dragging

The widgets do not have a fixed spot on the screen. You can move them across the screen by dragging them. This is how you drag an item with the Magic Mouse:

- **Position the pointer on the widget you want to move**
- **Press the mouse and keep it depressed**
- **Move the mouse**
- **Release the mouse when you have reached your destination**

This is how you drag an item using a mouse with two buttons:

- **Position the pointer on the widget you want to move**
- **Press the left mouse button and keep it depressed**
- **Move the mouse**
- **Release the mouse button when you have reached your destination**

This is how you drag an item using the trackpad:

- **Position the pointer on the widget you want to move**
- **Press the trackpad and keep pressing it**
- **Drag your finger across the trackpad**
- **Release the trackpad when you have reached your destination**

Now you are going to drag a widget:

- **Position the pointer on the *World Clock* widget**

- **Press the mouse button/trackpad and keep it depressed**

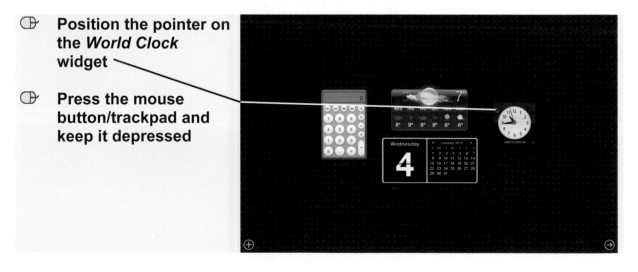

It is important to keep pressing the mouse button or the trackpad while you are dragging:

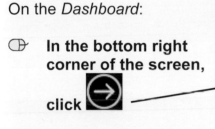 **Drag the clock to a position at the top right of your screen**

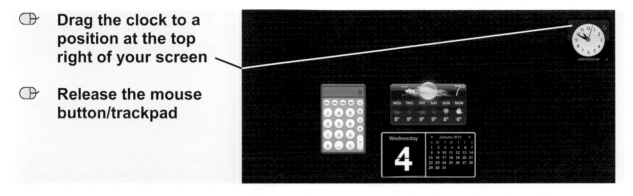

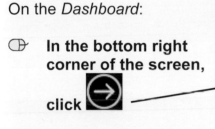 **Release the mouse button/trackpad**

This is how you return to your desktop, from the *Dashboard*:

On the *Dashboard*:

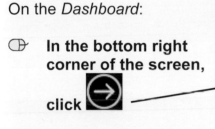 **In the bottom right corner of the screen, click** ⊘

You will see the desktop again:

# 1.8 Sleep Mode

If you have not used your *Mac* for a couple of minutes, it appears to turn off, all by itself. This is when the *Mac* reverts to *sleep mode*. In this mode the device will save energy. You can put the *Mac* into sleep mode yourself, if you do not need to use the computer for a while. To do this, you can use the menu bar:

In the top left of the desktop:

☞  **Click** 🍎

You will see a menu with various commands:

Put the *Mac* into sleep mode:

☞  **Click Sleep**

Now the screen will turn dark and the *Mac* will appear to be completely turned off. To wake the *Mac* up from sleep mode:

☞  **Press the mouse button or the trackpad**

Or:

⌨  **Press a random key on the keyboard**

Or:

☞  **Briefly press the power button**

## Tip

**Close the cover**
You can put your MacBook Pro or MacBook Air into sleep mode quickly by simply closing the screen cover. The MacBook will wake up when you open the cover again.

# 1.9 Turn Off the Mac

If you do not intend to use the *Mac* for a longer period of time, it is better to turn the power off altogether. With an iMac or Mac mini this will save energy. With a MacBook Pro or Air this will prevent the battery from going dead. This is how you turn off the *Mac*:

In the top left of the screen:

Click

You will again see the menu:

Click **Shut Down...**

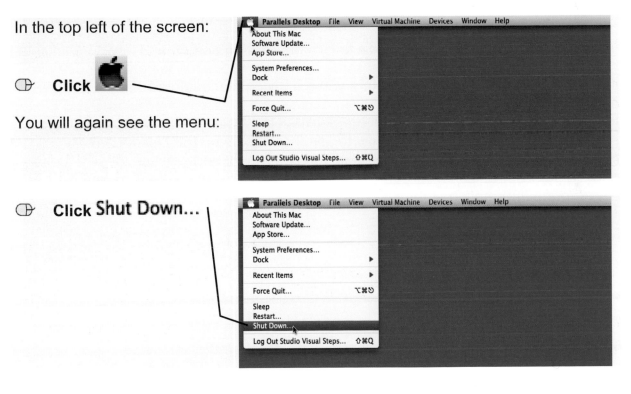

Now you will be asked if you are sure you want to shut down your computer. You will have a minute to think about this. Use the ⌈ **Cancel** ⌉ button to prevent the *Mac* from turning off the power. If you do not do anything, the *Mac* will turn off after 60 seconds. You can practice turning off the computer right now:

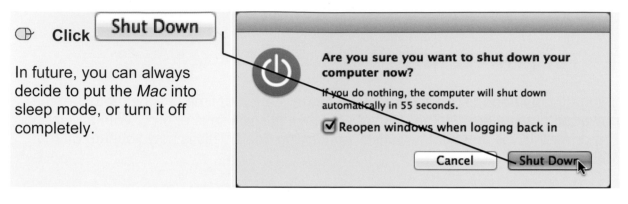

☞ **Click** ⌈ **Shut Down** ⌉

In future, you can always decide to put the *Mac* into sleep mode, or turn it off completely.

**Are you sure you want to shut down your computer now?**

If you do nothing, the computer will shut down automatically in 55 seconds.

☑ Reopen windows when logging back in

⌈ Cancel ⌉   ⌈ Shut Down ⌉

In this chapter you have learned how to turn the *Mac* on and off and how to put it into sleep mode. You have also learned some basic operations for using the mouse and the trackpad. In the following chapters you will become acquainted with some other actions, such as dragging files.

In addition, you have learned about the desktop, the *Dock*, the *Launchpad* and the *Dashboard* programs. You know how to use the widgets on the *Dashboard*. By following the exercises on the next page you can repeat and practice these actions once more. For additional information, be sure to take a look at the *Tips* and the *Background Information* at the end of this chapter.

# 1.10 Exercises

To be able to quickly apply the things you have learned, you can work through the following exercises. Have you forgotten how to do something? Use the numbers next to the footsteps 🐾[1] to look up the item in the appendix *How Do I Do That Again?* You will find this appendix at the back of this book.

## Exercise: Launchpad and Dashboard

☞ Turn on your *Mac* (and your screen, if necessary).

☞ If necessary, log in. 🐾[1]

☞ Open the *Dashboard* program. 🐾[101]

☞ Calculate this sum: `25 x 11` = with the *Calculator* widget. 🐾[3]

☞ Drag the *Calculator* widget to a position on the top left of the screen. 🐾[4]

☞ Go back to the desktop. 🐾[7]

## Exercise: Sleep mode and Turn Off

☞ Put your *Mac* into sleep mode. 🐾[8]

☞ Wake up the *Mac* again. 🐾[9]

☞ Turn off the *Mac*. 🐾[10]

# 1.11 Background Information

**Dictionary**

| | |
|---|---|
| **Apple** | *Apple Inc.* is a US-based company founded in 1976. Its headquarters are in Cupertino, California. Well known *Apple* products include the *Macintosh* personal computer, the portable iPod music player, the iPhone, the iPad tablet computer, the *Mac OS X* operating system and the *iLife* software, which includes the *iTunes* music program. |
| **Click** | Briefly press the mouse once (on a Magic Mouse), press the left mouse button (on a mouse with two buttons), or press the trackpad. By clicking something you can select this item or carry out a certain action or command. |
| **Dashboard** | A component of *Mac OS X* that contains mini software programs called *widgets*. |
| **Desktop** | The work area on a computer screen. When you open a program, it will appear on the desktop. |
| **Desktop computer** | A desktop computer is placed in a fixed spot on a table or on a desk. |
| **Dock** | A component of *Mac OS X* that lets you open various programs. The *Dock* is the bar of icons at the bottom of your screen. These icons actually represent shortcuts that will open folders or programs installed on the computer. |
| **Drag** | Move something on the screen by selecting the item and keeping the mouse button or trackpad depressed while you move the pointer. |
| **Icon** | A small picture indicating a file, folder or program. |
| **iMac** | A type of *Apple* desktop computer, where the computer and the screen are integrated as a single unit. The iMac was first introduced in 1998. |
| **iPad** | An *Apple* tablet computer. Instead of an actual keyboard or keypad, the iPad uses a Multi-Touch screen and a virtual keyboard with virtual keys and buttons. |

*- Continue on the next page -*

| | |
|---|---|
| **iPhone** | A combination of a cell phone, a multimedia player and a wireless Internet device, manufactured by *Apple*. Instead of a keyboard, the iPhone has a touchscreen that displays all the keys and buttons. |
| **iPod** | A series of mobile music players, made by *Apple*. |
| **Launchpad** | Component of *Mac OS X Lion* that provides instant access to your applications. *Launchpad* contains icons for all the programs installed on the *Mac.* Applications can be opened directly from the *Launchpad.* |
| **Lion** | The trade name for *Mac OS X* version 10.7. This is the eighth edition of the operating system for *Macintosh* computers. |
| **Mac** | An *Apple* computer, also called *Macintosh* computer. |
| **MacBook Air** | A very lightweight portable computer made by *Apple.* The first MacBook Air was introduced in 2008. This notebook computer is available with an 11 or 13 inch screen. |
| **MacBook Pro** | An *Apple* notebook, mainly intended for professional use. This notebook is available with a 13, 15 or 17 inch screen. |
| **Macintosh** | A type of personal computer made by *Apple* and first introduced in 1984. The *Macintosh* computer was the first commercially successful personal computer using a graphic user interface and a mouse, instead of the user having to type complicated commands. |
| **Mac mini** | A compact, portable and quiet desktop computer manufactured by *Apple.* The Mac mini is supplied without a monitor, keyboard, mouse or trackpad. These items must be purchased separately. |
| **Mac OS X** | The operating system for the *Macintosh* computers. Also called *OS X.* |
| **Magic Mouse** | The first Multi-Touch mouse in the world. With this mouse you not only can point and click, but also use various touch movements, such as swiping with two fingers. |
| **Magic Trackpad** | A separate trackpad made by *Apple* and equipped with the Multi-Touch technology. You can use the device by clicking it with your fingers or dragging your fingers across the device. |

*- Continue on the next page -*

| | |
|---|---|
| **Menu, menu bar** | A menu contains a list of options for a specific program. Menus will remain hidden until you click the titles on the menu bar. The menu bar is located in the top left of your screen. The menu bar will change and adjust itself according to the program that is currently active. |
| **Multi-Touch** | A method of interacting with a computer or another device by using a touch-sensitive surface. A trackpad, mouse or touchscreen that is equipped with the Multi-Touch technology will recognize multiple concurrent contacts made with the screen. Because of this technology you can operate such a device with multiple fingers at once. |
| **Notebook** | A notebook or laptop computer is a portable computer that you can use anywhere you want. You can set it on your lap for instance or place it on a table or desk. |
| **OS X** | The operating system for the *Macintosh* computers. Also called *Mac OS X*. |
| **Program** | A sequence of commands (instructions), used by a computer to execute a certain task is called a program. When you use a program, the computer will read the command you have typed and will execute it. |
| **Sleep mode** | A mode where the screen of the computer has turned black and the disk unit has been turned off. When you put your computer in sleep mode, it will still be turned on, but will consume less power. If you use sleep mode, it takes less time to start up the computer. |
| **Trackpad** | A trackpad is also called a touchpad. It is a pointing device that consists of a special surface that can transfer the movement and position of the user's fingers into an onscreen movement or command. |
| **USB port** | A narrow, rectangular connector on a computer, to which you can connect a USB (Universal Serial Bus) device, such as a mouse. |
| **Widget** | A mini program in *Dashboard*. Widgets can be used for a multitude of tasks, such as keeping track of the stock market, viewing the weather forecast, looking up words in a dictionary, etcetera. |

*Source: Apple Dictionary, www.apple.com*

# 1.12 Tips

### Tip

**Quickly open the Dashboard**

If you use the *Dashboard* often, there are several ways to open it more quickly. The first method is by using the keyboard:

 **Press the F4 key**

Depending on the type of keyboard you use it will look like this ⬚F4 or ⬚F4.

You can also use your Magic Mouse or trackpad and use your fingers. This is how you can use your Magic Mouse to switch from the desktop to the *Dashboard*:

👉 **Swipe two fingers across your Magic Mouse, from left to right**

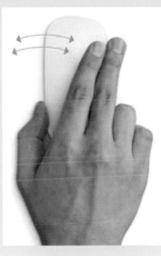

**Please note:** swiping is a very gentle movement. You do not need to press the mouse.

With the trackpad on your Macbook Pro or MacBook Air, and with the Magic Trackpad, it works like this:

👉 **Swipe three fingers across your trackpad, from left to right**

To return to the desktop you just need to repeat this movement, only this time from the right to the left.

## 💡 Tip

**Beach ball**

Do you see a spinning disk or 'beach ball' 🔘 instead of your regular pointer 🖱 ?
This means your *Mac* is busy executing a task.

☞ **Wait until the beach ball has disappeared**

Afterwards you can continue working.

## 💡 Tip

**Close the Launchpad**
If you open a program through the *Launchpad*, the *Launchpad* will automatically be
closed. But you can also close the *Launchpad* without opening a program:

☞ **Click a blank area on
the screen**

Now you will see the desktop
once again.

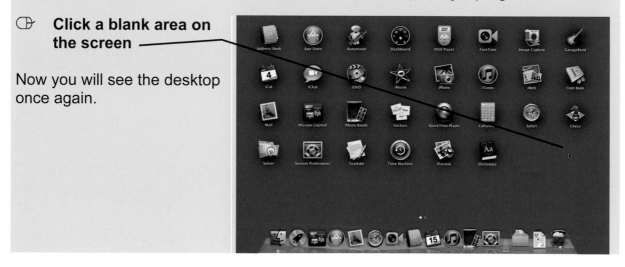

## 💡 Tip

**Add and delete widgets**
You can also add extra widgets to your *Dashboard*. This is how you do it:

☞ **In the bottom left
corner of the screen,**

**click** ⊕

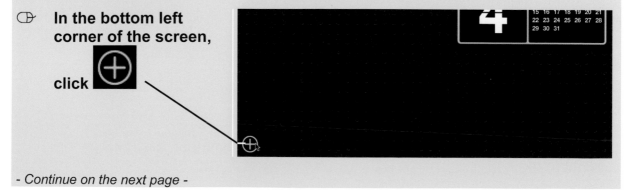

*- Continue on the next page -*

You will see a bar containing various widgets. You can practice adding a widget by adding the *Tile Game* widget:

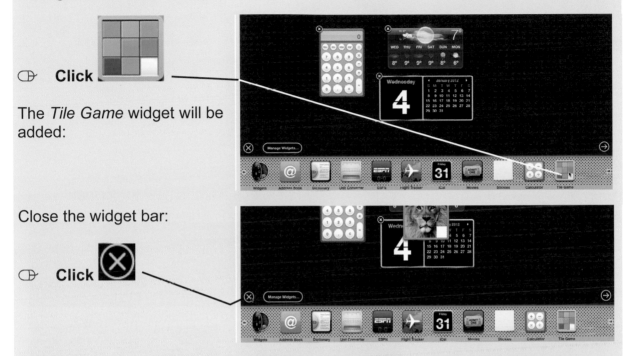

☞ **Click**

The *Tile Game* widget will be added:

Close the widget bar:

☞ **Click** ⊗

The *Tile Game* widget is a puzzle game. You will see an image in its completed form. First, shake the puzzle so the pieces are mixed up:

☞ **Click the puzzle**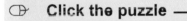

You will see the pieces of the puzzle move around. To stop them moving around:

☞ **Click the puzzle**

*- Continue on the next page -*

Now you can try to solve the puzzle by shifting around the pieces:

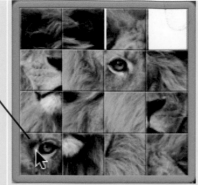

☞  **Click the piece you want to move** ⎯⎯

The block will move over to the blank area. This way you can solve the puzzle, step by step:

If you no longer want to use a widget, you can delete it. Here is how to do that:

☞  **In the bottom left corner of the screen, click ⊕**

You are going to remove the *Tile Game* widget:

☞  **At the top of the widget, click ⊗**

The widget will disappear:

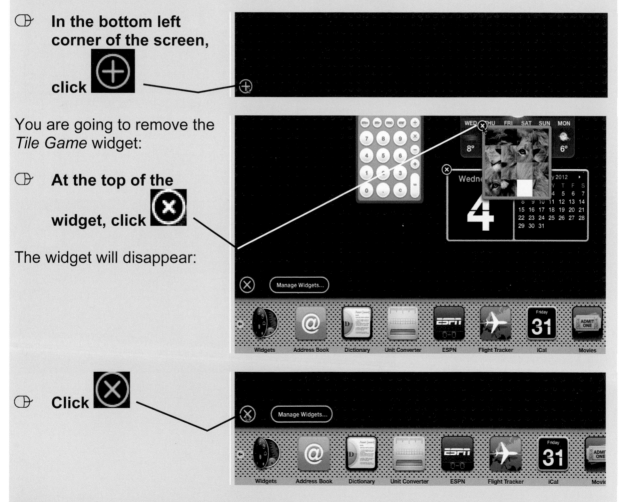

☞  **Click ⊗**

**Please note:** to use some of the widgets such as *Weather* and *Dictionary*, you will need to have an active Internet connection. If your computer is not connected to the Internet, you will see an error message when you try to use the widget or when the widget itself tries to retrieve new data.

# 2. Working with TextEdit

*TextEdit* is a simple and easy to use text editing program. It is one of the standard programs included in *OS X*. You can use this program for most of you writing needs such as creating a letter, note or memo. The handy thing about using a computer to type your letters or other documents is that you can keep improving them. With the old fashioned typewriter it was much harder to fix mistakes. Starting over with a fresh new piece of paper was often the only way to go. Now, you can simply save your text and in the meantime do something else. At a later time, you can resume your work and continue further with the text.

You can reuse documents that you have already created. With a few alterations you can change an existing letter and reuse it for a different situation.

Some of the things that you will learn in this chapter can also be used in several other programs, for instance, while you are writing an e-mail message. In this chapter you start by learning how to write a letter with the *TextEdit* program. Then you will learn how to save your documents and how to print them.

In this chapter you will learn how to:

- open the *TextEdit* program;
- minimize and maximize the window;
- write a letter;
- use bullets;
- save a letter;
- close *TextEdit* by using the menu bar;
- open a letter you saved by using the *Dock*;
- view the letter in print preview;
- print the text;
- save changes.

## 2.1 Opening TextEdit

In this example you are going to use the *Launchpad* to open the *TextEdit* program:

☞ **Open the *Launchpad* program** ✂️²

You will see the programs that are installed on your computer. This is how you open *TextEdit*:

The *TextEdit* program will be opened on the desktop, in a new window:

The name of the program, **TextEdit** will now appear on the menu bar:

This means that the commands you can execute with this menu, will be applied to the *TextEdit* program.

In the *Dock* you will see an icon for the *TextEdit* program:

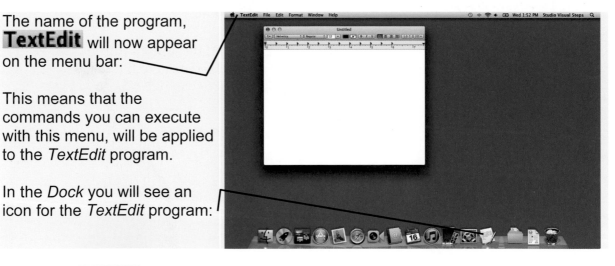

Below the ▢ icon you will see a luminous globe ▢. This indicates that the program is active. In this way, by looking at the *Dock,* you can always tell at a glance which programs are still opened.

The *TextEdit* window consists of various elements:

Buttons for closing,
minimizing and maximizing
the program:

The toolbar with all sorts of
tools for formatting the text:

The title bar:

The ruler:

The blank 'sheet' where you
can type your text:

The cursor:

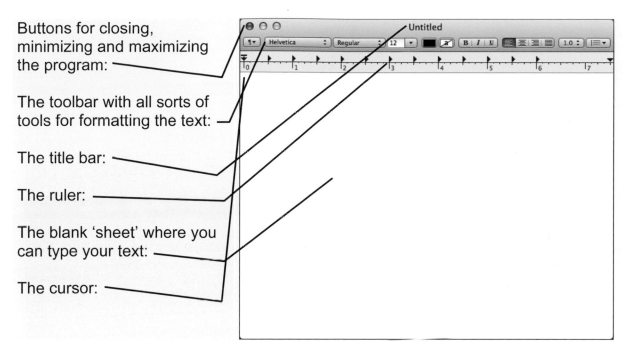

## 2.2 Maximizing and Minimizing a Window

In *OS X*, by default, a window will always be displayed in the optimum size that is
best suited to the program. But this does not mean that the size of the window is
fixed. If you think the window is too small, you can display the window on a full
screen, or 'maximize' it:

**Click**

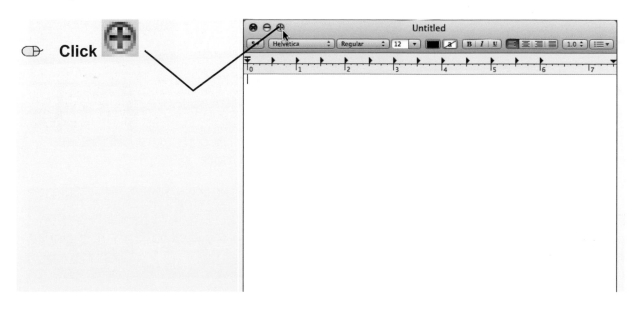

Now the *TextEdit* window will almost fill the entire screen:

By default, the *Dock* and the menu bar will always be visible when you maximize a window: ——

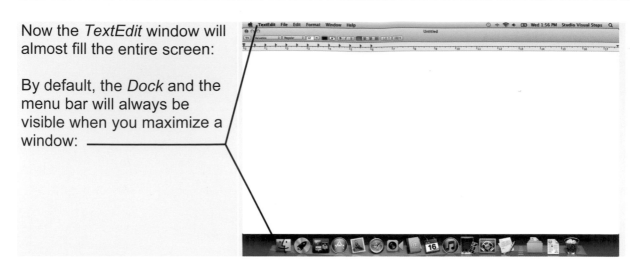

If you think this screen is too big, you can return to the default window size, like this:

⊕  **Click**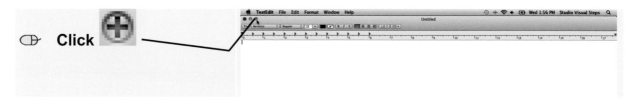

Now you will see the *TextEdit* program in its original window. You can also hide this window, without closing the program. This is called minimizing. It can be useful if you want to use a different program for a while and need working space on the desktop. Here is how to minimize a window:

⊕  **Click**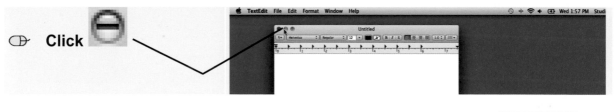

The *TextEdit* window will disappear. In the *Dock* you will see an extra icon. You can use this icon to display the window once more:

⊕  **Click**

## Tip

**Different icon**

You can also open this window by clicking the other *TextEdit* icon in the *Dock*.

Now you will see the *TextEdit* window once again. In the next section you are going to write a letter.

## Please note:

Be sure to perform the following tasks. This practice letter that you are about to make, will be used a number of times in later chapters of this book.

## 2.3 Writing a Letter

In this book we work on the assumption that you are already acquainted with the keyboard. You should be able to do the following things:

Type letters, blank spaces and digits.

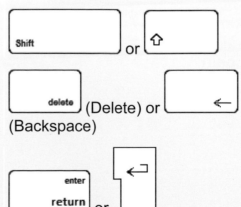

Type capital letters, punctuation marks and symbols with the Shift key.

Delete a typo with the Delete or Backspace keys.

Start a new paragraph with the Enter/Return key.

### ➥ Please note:

There are many different types of keyboards. Some keys, such as the Shift key, will have a text written on them while others may show an image of an arrow.

### ➥ Please note:

If you do not have a lot of experience using the keyboard, you can read the *Bonus Chapter Basic Text Editing Operations* and learn more about the basic operations. You can find this bonus chapter on the website that goes with this book:
**www.visualsteps.com/macseniors**
In *Appendix B Opening Bonus Chapters* you can read how to open the bonus chapter.

You are going to start by typing your own name and address information:

**Type your first and last name**

**Press (enter/return key)**

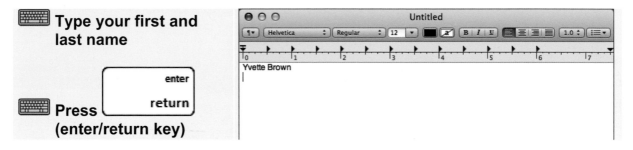

Now you can type your address:

**Type your address**

**Press**

**Type your city, state and the zip code (or postal code)**

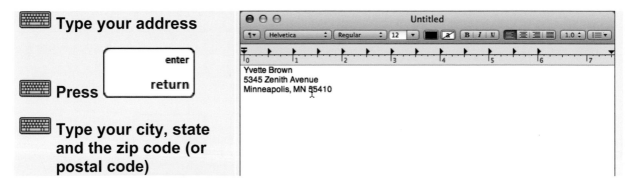

Continue and enter the place and date:

**Press twice** [enter return]

**For example, type:**
Minneapolis,
January 4, 2012

**Press twice** [enter return]

Yvette Brown
5345 Zenith Avenue
Minneapolis, MN 55410

Minneapolis, January 4, 2012

## ✖ HELP! I am not a very good typist.

If you do not yet have much experience with typing on a keyboard, typing the text may take up a lot of time. If you want, you can make up a shorter text to type.

You have started by typing the sender and the date. Now you can enter the name and address of the recipient, the subject and the introductory phrase or header:

**Type:**
William and Anne
Johnson
6455 Forestview Lane
Maple Grove, MN 55442

Subject: brunch

Dear William and Anne,

**Press twice** [enter return]

Yvette Brown
5345 Zenith Avenue
Minneapolis, MN 55410

Minneapolis, January 4, 2012

William and Anne Johnson
6455 Forestview Lane
Maple Grove, MN 55442

Subject: brunch

Dear William and Anne,

Now you are going to continue typing the rest of the letter:

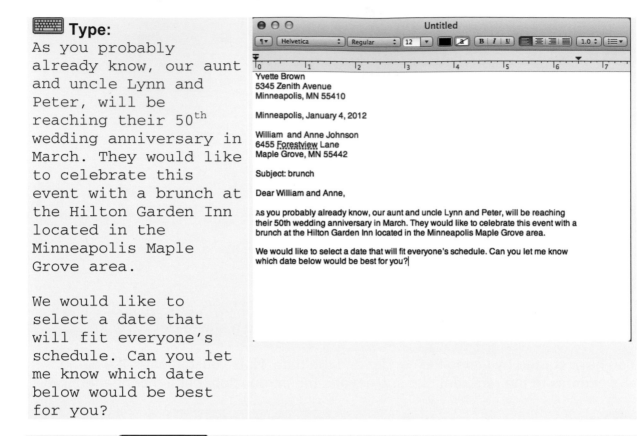

**Type:**

As you probably already know, our aunt and uncle Lynn and Peter, will be reaching their 50th wedding anniversary in March. They would like to celebrate this event with a brunch at the Hilton Garden Inn located in the Minneapolis Maple Grove area.

We would like to select a date that will fit everyone's schedule. Can you let me know which date below would be best for you?

**Press** enter / return **twice**

💡 **Tip**

**Type accents**

You can use the following methods for typing characters with accents, such as é:

**Press the** E **key for a bit longer than usual**

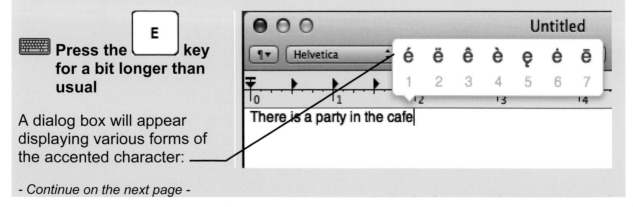

A dialog box will appear displaying various forms of the accented character: —

*- Continue on the next page -*

If you press the number of the desired accent on your keyboard, the letter with that accent will be inserted into the text. Number ⌷ stands for **é**:

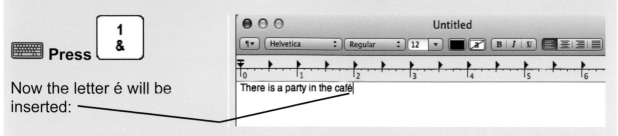

**Press** 1 &

Now the letter é will be inserted:

There is a party in the café

Do you want to know more about typing special characters? Then just read through the *Bonus Chapter Basic Text Editing Operations* and learn the basic operations. You can find this bonus chapter on the website that goes with this book:
**www.visualsteps.com/mac**
In *Appendix B Opening Bonus Chapters* you can read more about these bonus chapters.

## 2.4 Bullets

Now you can add a bulleted list of brunch dates:

**Click** ≣▼

You will see a menu with various bullet characters:

**Click** ✔

The first bullet will now appear in your letter:

**Type:** Saturday, March 7

enter / return

**Press** (enter/return)

You will see a new bullet character on the new line:

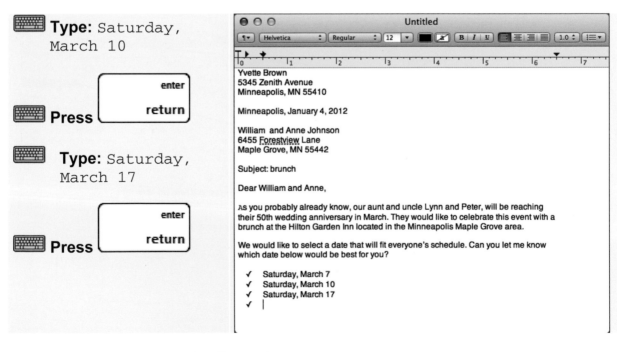

Now you can complete the list:

**Type:** Saturday, March 10

enter / return

**Press**

**Type:** Saturday, March 17

enter / return

**Press**

You have finished typing the list.

At the end of the list, a new bullet has been inserted. You do not need this bullet:

Press [enter return]

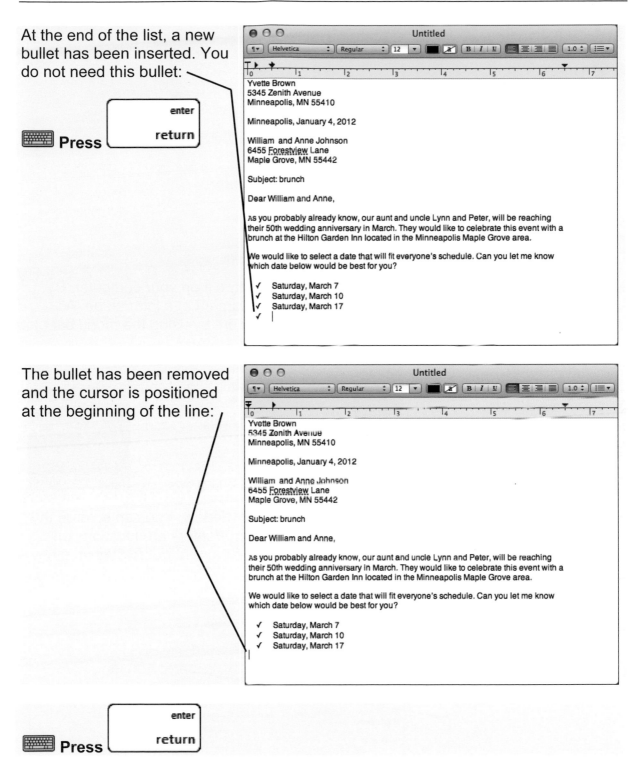

The bullet has been removed and the cursor is positioned at the beginning of the line:

Press [enter return]

Just finish the letter:

⌨ **Type:**

Many thanks for your quick response.

Best regards,
Yvette

In the next section you will save the letter to your computer.

## 2.5 Saving a Document

Now you are going to save the letter, in other words, store it on your computer. By saving the document, you can continue editing the document at a later stage. A document is also called a file. You can save the document by using the menu bar:

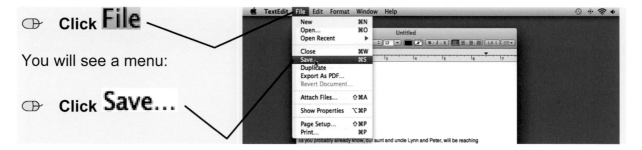

☞ **Click File**

You will see a menu:

☞ **Click Save...**

Now you will see a new window, on top of the *TextEdit* window. You can enlarge this window, in order to see all the folders on your computer. Folders are locations on your computer, where you can store files. You can read more about folders in *Chapter 3 Working with Folders and Files in Finder*.

When you save a file for the first time, you will see this small window:

☞ **Click** [▼]

Now you will see a larger window:

By default, *TextEdit* will add the file name *Untitled*:

You will see the file name in the box next to **Save As:**:

By default, a new document is saved in the **Documents** folder:

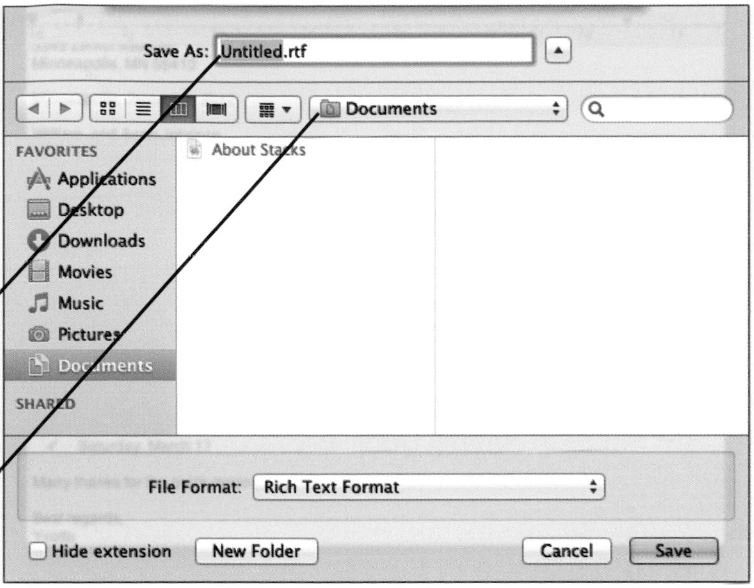

You are going to change the document's name:

**Type:** brunch letter

👉 **Click** **Save**

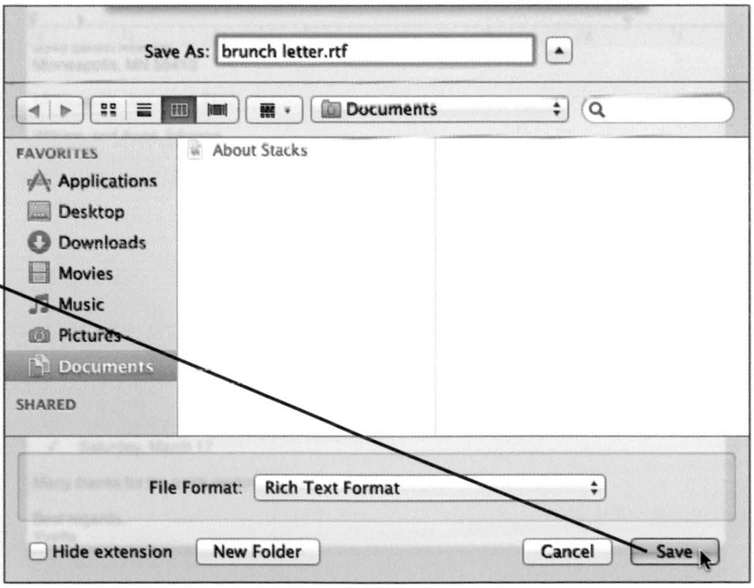

Now you will see the name of your letter on the title bar:

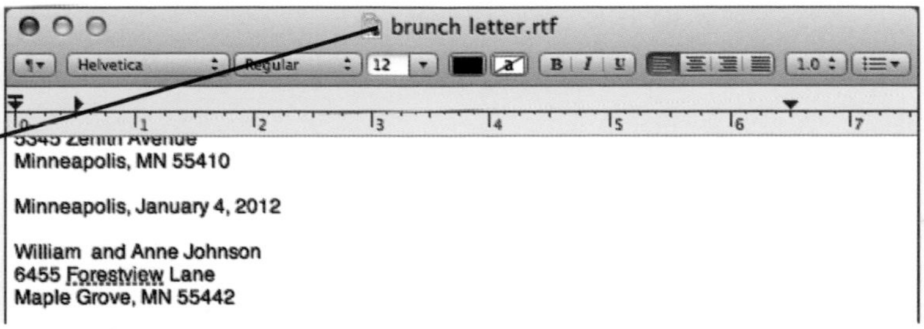

The letter has been saved in the *Documents* folder on your computer.

The *Dock* has an icon with which you can quickly gain access to the *Documents* folder. Your letter has been placed on top of the stack, as it were:

You can use this icon to open the letter later on, when you want to edit it a bit more. You are going to do this after you have closed the *TextEdit* window.

# 2.6 Closing TextEdit

In *OS X* you can close most of the program windows in this way:

☞ **Click**

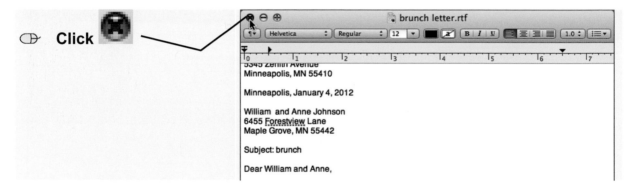

Now the *TextEdit* window has disappeared. But the program itself is still open:

You can still see the *TextEdit*

icon        in the *Dock*:

The luminous globe below the icon indicates that the program is still active:

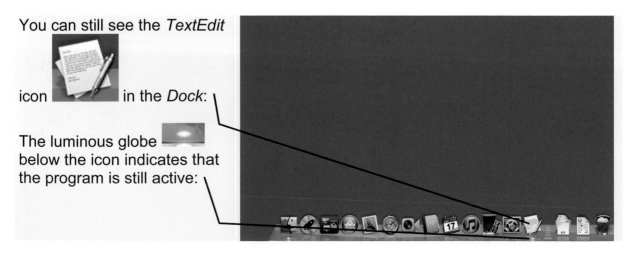

You can open the window again by clicking the icon:

☞ **Click**

Now the *TextEdit* window will be opened once again:

You will see a blank
document:

You can fully close the *TextEdit* program by using the menu bar:

☞ **Click TextEdit**

☞ **Click Quit TextEdit**

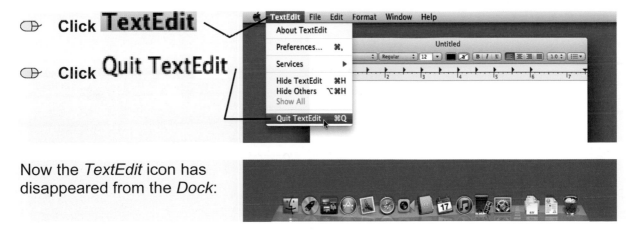

Now the *TextEdit* icon has
disappeared from the *Dock*:

You can quickly reopen your letter by clicking the icon of the *Documents* folder in the *Dock*:

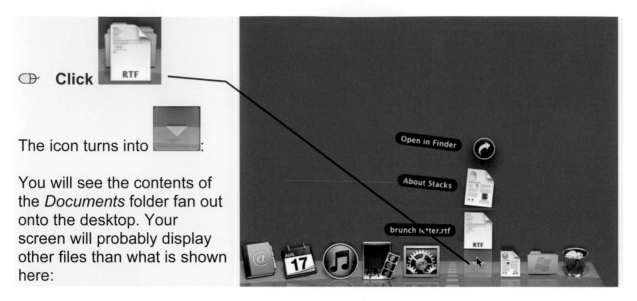

**Click** [RTF icon]

The icon turns into [icon] :

You will see the contents of the *Documents* folder fan out onto the desktop. Your screen will probably display other files than what is shown here:

You can quickly open a file by clicking the icon:

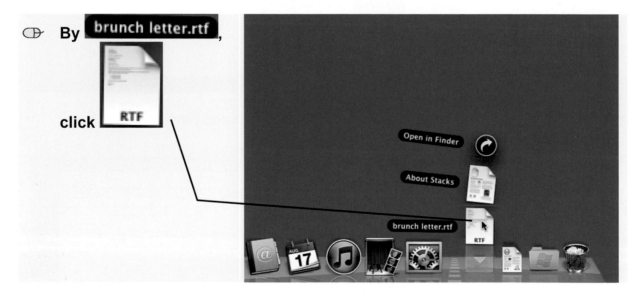

**By** `brunch letter.rtf`,

**click** [RTF icon]

The letter will be opened in *TextEdit*:

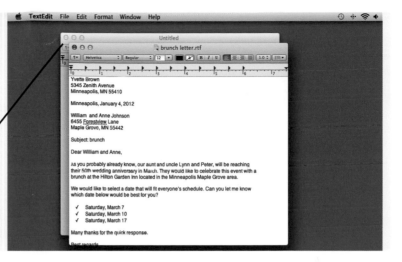

You may see a second window underneath the window containing the letter:

This is the window with the blank document that was still open when you decided to completely close *TextEdit* using the menu bar.

In the next section you will print the letter.

# 2.7 Printing a Letter

When you write a letter, most likely you will want to have it printed on paper. You can practice doing this now.

## ➥ Please note:

In order to complete the following tasks, you will need to have a printer connected to your *Mac*. If you do not have such a printer, just work through the next few steps until you reach the point where you actually need to print, on page 68. If you are using this book during a course, you can always ask your instructor for permission to print the document.

You can print the letter by using the option on the menu bar:

☞ **Click File**

☞ **Click Print...**

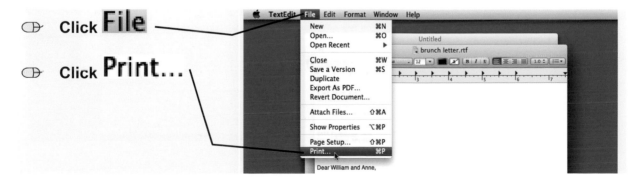

Now you will see a window with a *print preview*, a miniature rendering of how the printed version of the letter will look like:

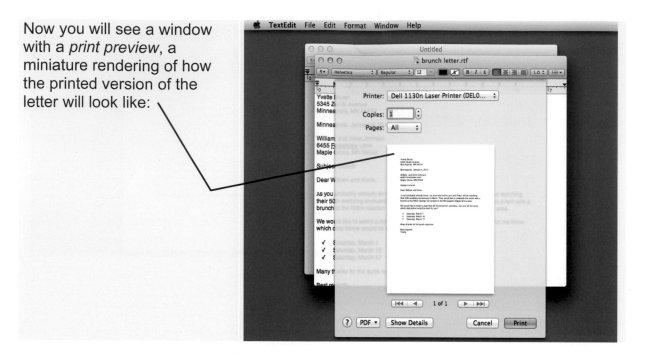

The text has not been evenly spaced across the length of the page. You can easily solve this problem by inserting some blank lines. First, you need to close this window:

☞ **Click** Cancel

You will see your letter again. Now you can insert a few blank lines:

⊕ **Click left next to your name**

The cursor should be blinking on the left side of the first letter:

⌨ **Press (enter/return) five times**

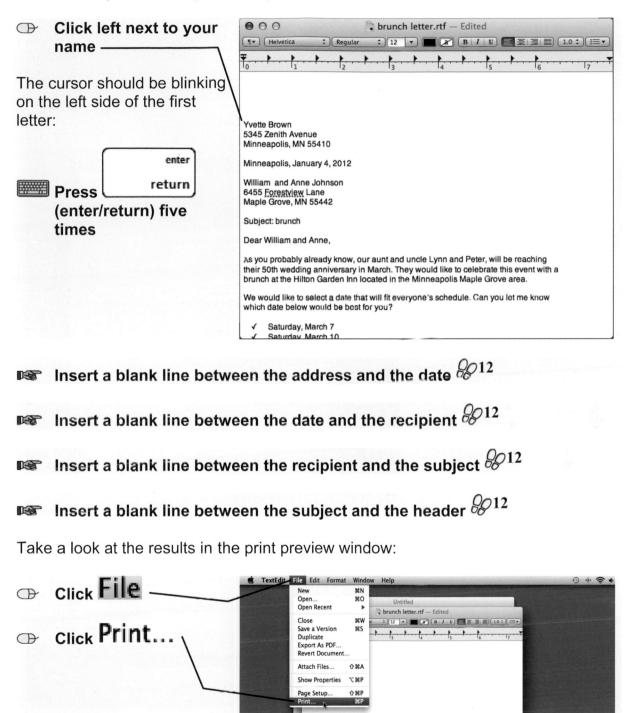

☞ **Insert a blank line between the address and the date** 👣12

☞ **Insert a blank line between the date and the recipient** 👣12

☞ **Insert a blank line between the recipient and the subject** 👣12

☞ **Insert a blank line between the subject and the header** 👣12

Take a look at the results in the print preview window:

⊕ Click **File**

⊕ Click **Print...**

Now the text of the letter has been evenly divided across the page. Before you enter the print command:

☞ **Check to make sure the printer is turned on**

☞ **Make sure the printer contains enough paper**

Is the printer ready? Then you can enter the print command:

If you really want to print the letter:

⊕ **Click** **Print**

If you do not want to print the letter:

⊕ **Click** **Cancel**

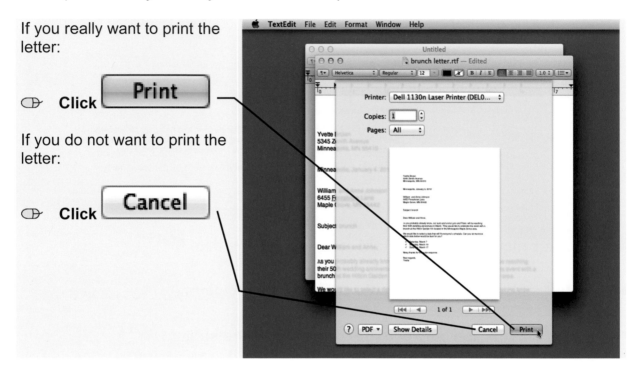

## 2.8 Save Changes

You have edited your letter in several places. If you need to work on your letter for a longer period of time, it is a good idea to save the document at regular intervals. Here is how to do that:

⊕ **Click File**

⊕ **Click Save a Version**

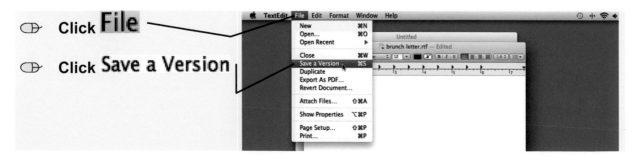

*OS X Lion* can also help you with the *Autosave* option: by default, the changes in your document are automatically saved every five minutes. When you close the *TextEdit* window, the final changes will also be saved. Now you are going to try this. First, add some text to the letter's subject:

☞ **Click next to the subject**

Now the cursor is blinking at the end of the word 'brunch':

⌨ **Type:** with uncle Pete and aunt Lynn

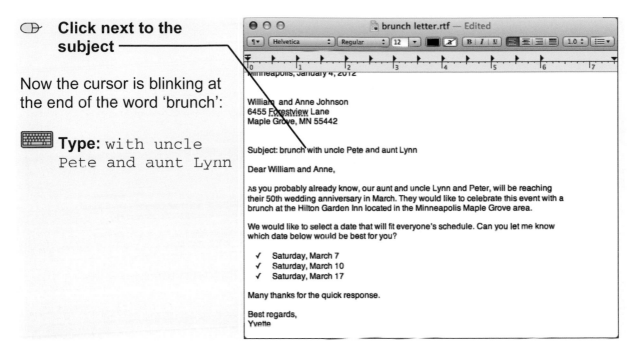

Now you are going to check whether the edited text is saved when you close the window:

☞ **Close the open *TextEdit* windows** 🐾¹³

☞ **Open the letter by clicking the *Documents* folder in the *Dock*** 🐾¹⁴

You will see that the final changes have been saved:

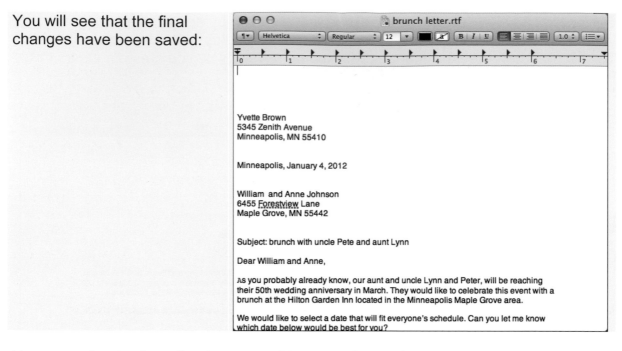

You are going to close the document. You can also do this with the menu bar:

⊕ Click **File**

⊕ Click **Close**

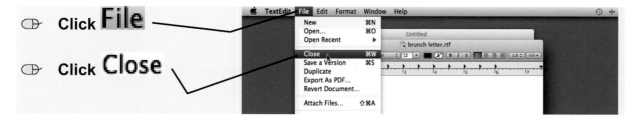

Now you can completely stop running the *TextEdit* program, that is, you can close the program:

⊕ Click **TextEdit**

⊕ Click **Quit TextEdit**

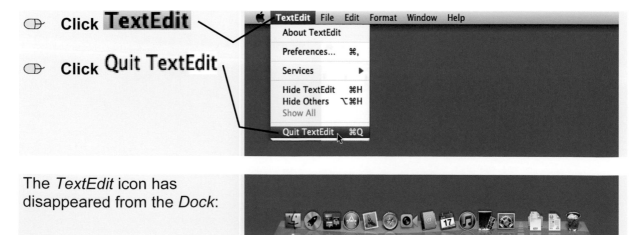

The *TextEdit* icon has disappeared from the *Dock*:

### Tip

**Continue where you left off**

Do you plan to edit the same document for days at a time? In that case, you do not need to close the document first, before quitting the *TextEdit* program through the menu bar. As soon as you open *TextEdit* again, you will immediately see the document you were working on.

This useful feature of *OS X Lion* goes even further: you can also decide not to close *TextEdit* when you turn your computer off. In this way, the program and the document that was open when you turned the computer off will both be open when you turn your computer on again.

Because *OS X Lion* automatically saves your work, you do not need to worry about losing the most recent changes you have made.

In the following exercises you can repeat the topics we have discussed in this chapter.

## 2.9 Exercises

To be able to quickly apply the things you have learned, you can work through these exercises. Have you forgotten how to do something? Use the numbers next to the footsteps $\mathscr{QO}^1$ to look up the item in the appendix *How Do I Do That Again?* You can find this appendix at the end of this book.

## Exercise: Minimize and Maximize

☞ Open the *TextEdit* program. $\mathscr{QO}^{11}$

☞ Minimize the window. $\mathscr{QO}^{15}$

☞ Open the minimized window through the *Dock*. $\mathscr{QO}^{16}$

☞ Maximize the window. $\mathscr{QO}^{17}$

☞ Restore the maximized window to its regular size. $\mathscr{QO}^{18}$

# Exercise: Write and Save a Letter

☞ Type your own name and address, one below the other.

☞ Type the following text. If you do not have a lot of typing experience, you can make up your own text:

Atlanta, September 30$^{th}$ 2011

Tim and Sandra Smith
1 Main Street
Atlanta GA 30507

Subject: garage sale

Dear Tim and Sandra,

On October 15$^{th}$ our local tennis club will hold its annual garage sale. This year, the proceeds will be donated to the Red Cross. Do you by any chance have any stuff for this garage sale? For instance:

☞ Start typing a bulleted list. 🦶**19**

☞ Type the list below. 🦶**20**

• books
• CDs
• toys
• old appliances

☞ Close the bulleted list. 🦶**21**

☞   Type the conclusion of the letter:

```
Please let me know if you have any goods we can use. I will
come and collect it.

Thank you very much!

Kind regards,

Your name
```

☞   Save the letter in the *Documents* folder and name the file *garage sale letter*.
    %22

# Exercise: Print a Letter

☞   View the print preview. %23

☞   If possible, print the letter. %24

# Exercise: Close and Stop

☞   Close the *TextEdit* window. %13

☞   Quit *TextEdit*. %25

# 2.10 Background Information

**Dictionary**

| | |
|---|---|
| **Autosave** | A function in *OS X Lion* that takes care of saving changes in a document automatically, at five minute intervals. |
| **Close** | If you close a window, you will only close the open window. The program itself will not be closed, it will stay active. You can tell this by looking at the *Dock*. |
| **Cursor** | The blinking vertical line that indicates where the text will be inserted. |
| **Documents** | A folder where you can save your text files. |
| **Hard disk** | A storage medium where you can store your programs and files. |
| **Maximize** | Making a program window bigger, so it is displayed on a full screen. In *OS X*, the *Dock* and the menu bar will still be visible after maximizing the window. |
| **Minimize** | Making a program window disappear from the screen, without quitting the program. |
| **Open** | A command for retrieving a document that is stored on a computer or other type of storage medium. |
| **Print** | A command for printing a document on paper, by means of a printer. |
| **Print preview** | A small preview of the letter, to show how it will look like on paper. |
| **Save** | A command for saving a document to the computer, or another type of storage medium. |
| **Stop** | Closing a program completely. |
| **TextEdit** | A text editing program that is part of the *OS X* operating system. |
| **Title bar** | The horizontal bar at the top of the desktop. The options on the title bar may change according to the program that is opened. In *TextEdit*, the title bar contains the name of the document you are editing. |

*Source: Apple Dictionary, www.apple.com*

## Printers

The printer most in use at home is the so-called *inkjet printer*.
This type of printer prints letters by spraying tiny droplets of ink onto the paper.

A lot of these printers can also print in color. Such a printer is equipped with a black ink cartridge, as well as a three-color cartridge. By mixing up these colors on paper, a huge variety of colors can be created.

The containers with the ink are called *cartridges*.
Each type of printer uses its own type of cartridges.

*Inkjet printer*

Inkjet printers can print on regular paper, but also on special types of paper, depending on the desired print quality. For example, you can buy special photographic paper for printing photos.

*Laser printers* operate according to a very different principle. A laser printer uses a very fine-grained powder, the so-called *toner*. The toner is used to melt the shape of the letters onto the paper, at very high temperatures.

The print quality of a laser printer is better than that of the inkjet. Laser printers are available as color printers or black and white printers.

*Laser printer*

*Photo printers* are printers that use a special process for printing digital photos on photographic paper.

According to the manufacturers, these printers can produce prints that approach the quality of professional printing services.

Most of these types of printers can be connected to the computer, but some models can also print photos directly from a digital camera's memory card.

The printer has a built-in cardreader, into which you can insert the camera's memory card. Some models are equipped with a CD drive, which will allow you to print photos from a photo-CD.

*Photo printer*

# 2.11 Tips

### 💡 Tip

**Revert to the last saved version**

Have you made changes to a document, but then decide you no longer want to keep them? You can easily undo the changes in programs where you have enabled the *Autosave* function.

As soon as you edit a document, you will see the word **Edited** in the title bar:

☞ Click **Edited**

☞ Click **Revert to Last Opened** ⟍

The document will be restored to the state it was in when you last opened it.

### 💡 Tip

**View different versions**

*OS X* does not just save the last opened version of a document, but you can retrieve all the versions that have been saved since the creation of the document. This is how you can retrieve previously saved versions:

If you have edited the document after opening it:

☞ Click **Edited**

If you have not yet edited the document after opening it:

☞ Click 🗎 **brunch letter.rtf**

☞ Click **Browse All Versions...**

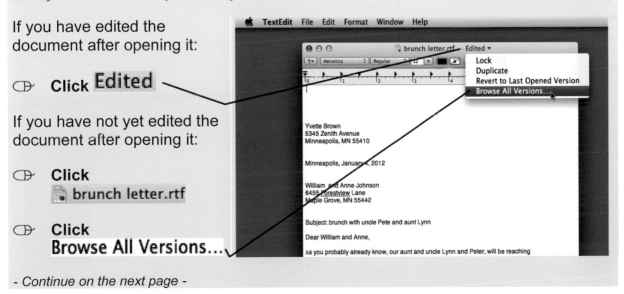

*- Continue on the next page -*

Here you see the document in its present state: ————

Here you see a stack of different versions of this document: ————

At the bottom of the version you will see the date and time of when the document was saved: ————

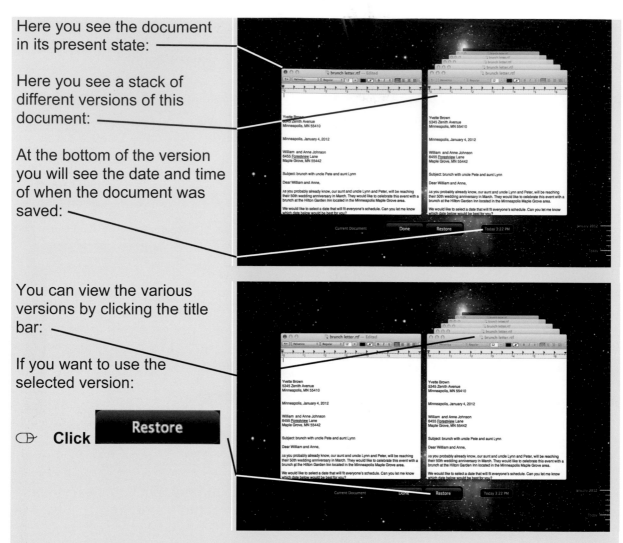

You can view the various versions by clicking the title bar: ————

If you want to use the selected version:

☞ **Click** Restore

If you want to keep using the current document:

☞ **Click** Done

You can also delete an older version you no longer use:

☞ **Click**
   📄 brunch letter.rtf

☞ **Click**
   **Delete This Version...**

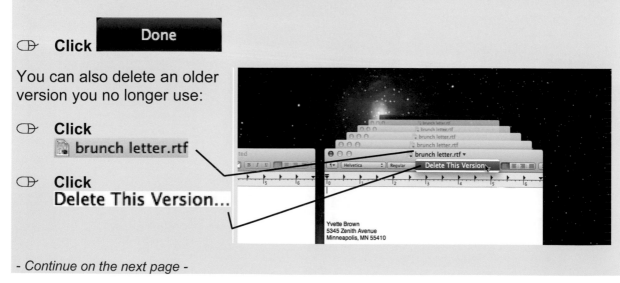

*- Continue on the next page -*

You will need to confirm this action:

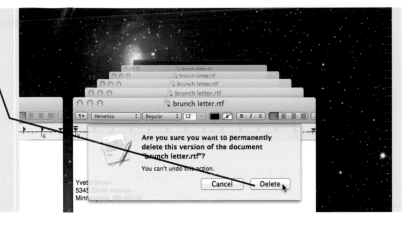

☞ **Click** | **Delete** |

Now this version has been permanently deleted.

## 💡 Tip
### Spell check

You may have noticed a dotted red line under some of the words. This means that the automatic spell checker has encountered a word that cannot be found in the *OS X* dictionary. It may be a misspelled word, or a name that is not recognized by *OS X*. With the *Show Spelling and Grammar* function you can check (possible) errors and correct them (or not). Here is how to do that:

☞ **Click Edit**

☞ **Click**
**Spelling and Grammar**

☞ **Click**
**Show Spelling and Gramm**

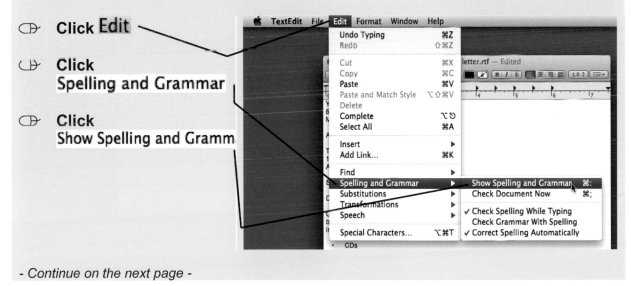

*- Continue on the next page -*

In this example, a typo is
found:

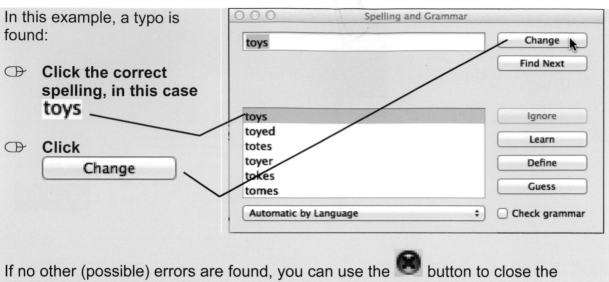

⊕  **Click the correct
    spelling, in this case
    toys**

⊕  **Click**
    **Change**

If no other (possible) errors are found, you can use the ⊗ button to close the
*Spelling and Grammar* window.

## 💡 Tip

**Open a document through the menu bar**
You can also open a document by using the menu bar. Here is how to do that:

☞  **Open** *TextEdit* ✇[11]

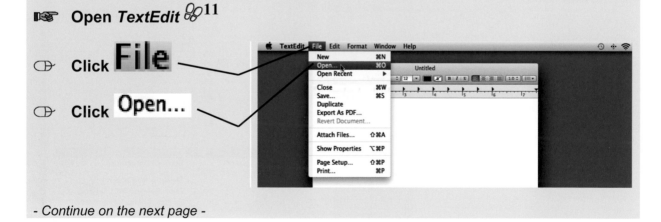

⊕  **Click** **File**

⊕  **Click** **Open...**

*- Continue on the next page -*

You will see the *Open* window:

The contents of the 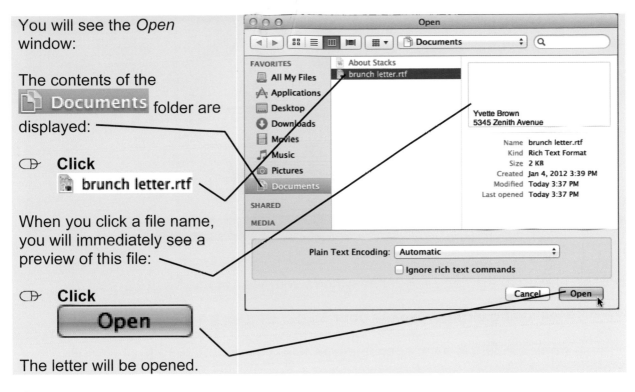 Documents folder are displayed:

⊕ **Click**

   📄 **brunch letter.rtf**

When you click a file name, you will immediately see a preview of this file:

⊕ **Click**

   **Open**

The letter will be opened.

## 💡 Tip

**Launchpad**

If there are more programs installed on your *Mac,* they may no longer fit in a single *Launchpad* window. A new window will be created automatically. Once a second *Launchpad* window has been created, you will see two dots at the bottom of the *Launchpad* window :

In this example, a second window is present. This is how you skip to the second *Launchpad* window:

⊕ **Click**

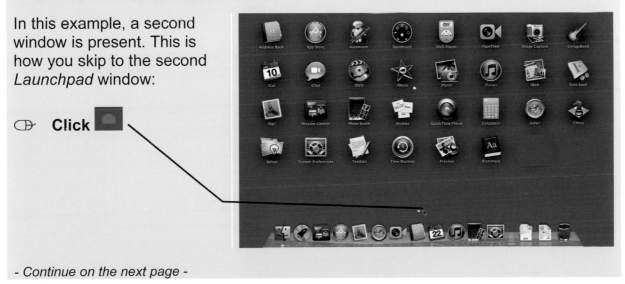

*- Continue on the next page -*

You can also use the arrow keys to switch between windows. Return to the previous window by using the left arrow key:

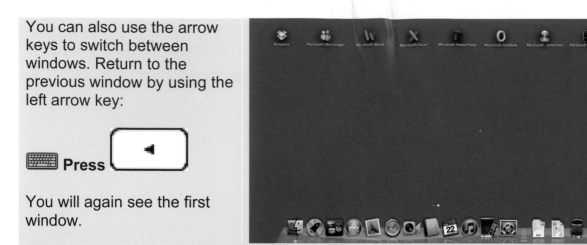

⌨ **Press** ◄

You will again see the first window.

You can also use the touch operations on your Magic Mouse or trackpad. This is how you return to the first *Launchpad* window with your Magic Mouse:

☞ **Swipe a single finger across your Magic Mouse, from left to right**

**Please note:** swiping is a very gentle movement; you do not need to press the mouse.

Here is how to do that with the trackpad on your Macbook Pro or MacBook Air, and with the Magic Trackpad:

☞ **Swipe two fingers across your trackpad, from left to right**

To go back to the second window you need to repeat this movement, but now do it from right to left.

💡 **Tip**

**Open programs**
In this book, you mainly will use *Launchpad* to open programs. But there is another method for opening programs:

☞ **Click** 

☞ **Click** 🄰 **Applications**

☞ **Double-click** 📝 **TextEdit**

# 3. Working with Folders and Files in Finder

In this chapter you will learn how to work with the *folders* and *files* stored on your computer. A file is a collective term for all the data stored on the computer. These files can be programs, your own text documents, or photos, for example. You can apply the operations you learn in this chapter to all types of files.

The files on your computer are arranged in *folders* (also called *directories*). Folders may not only contain files, they can also contain other folders. A folder that is stored within another folder is called a *subfolder*. You can create as many subfolders as you want, and store as many files and new subfolders within these subfolders.

Fortunately, on your *Mac*, you do not need to arrange all these things yourself. In *OS X*, a few folders have already been created for you. These standard folders include the *Documents*, *Downloads*, *Movies*, *Music* and *Pictures* folders. You can use these folders for arranging and ordering particular types of files. In the previous chapter you stored a file created with *TextEdit* in the *Documents* folder.

*Finder* is the name of the *OS X* program that can be used to manage the folders and files on your computer. In *Finder* you can delete, copy, rename and move files and folders. You will be using the *Finder* window for example, each time you want to copy a text file or a photo to a USB stick.

In this chapter you will learn how to:

- open *Finder*;
- change the view of the *Finder* window;
- create a new folder;
- copy and move a file to a different folder;
- change a file name;
- delete a file;
- empty the *Trash Bin*;
- copy a file to a USB stick;
- safely disconnect the USB stick.

# 3.1 Opening Finder

The *Finder* program has its own fixed place in the *Dock*. It is the only program that is always active. You cannot close *Finder*. You will always see a luminous globe  below the icon: . This is how you open the *Finder* window:

☞ **Click**

The *Finder* window will be opened:

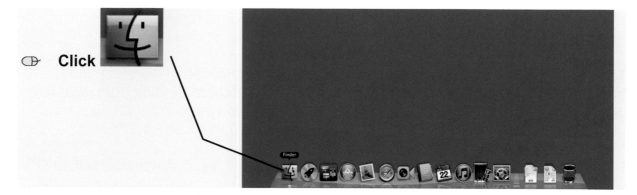

By default, the **All My Files** overview will be opened:

This is the place where *OS X* collects all your files. In the *Documents* folder you will find the documents you have saved in the previous chapter:

There are also two PDF files from *Apple*, **About Downloads** and **About Stacks** stored in the *Downloads* and *Documents* folders.

# 3.2 Changing the View for Finder

There are several ways of displaying the files and folders in *Finder*. Your screen may look a bit different at present.

In this example, the files are displayed as icons:

If you want to display the files in a list:

☞ **Click** ≡

You will see a list of all the files:

You can also display the files in columns:

☞ **Click** ⫴

Now the files are displayed in columns:

☞ **Click**
  🖹 **brunch letter.rtf**

The file has been selected. In the right-hand column you will see a preview of this file:

Beneath the preview, you will see additional information about this file:

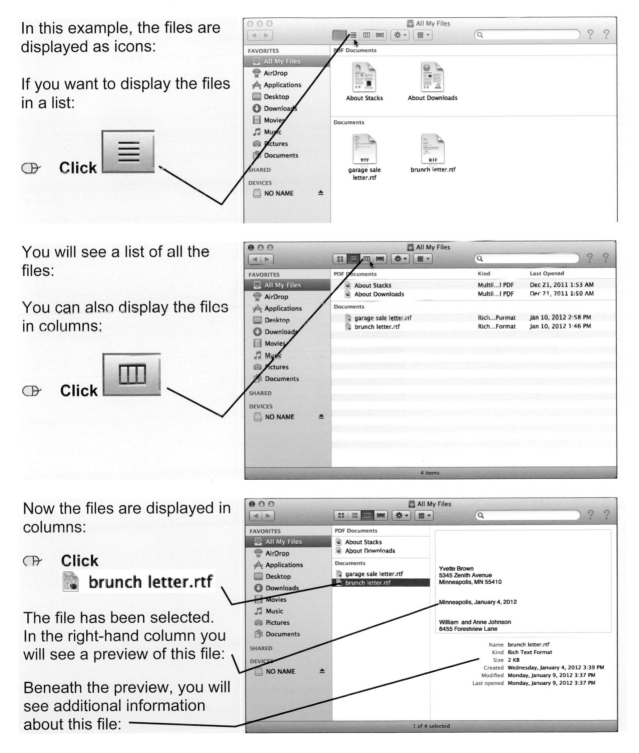

In the following examples, the *Symbols* view is used:

Click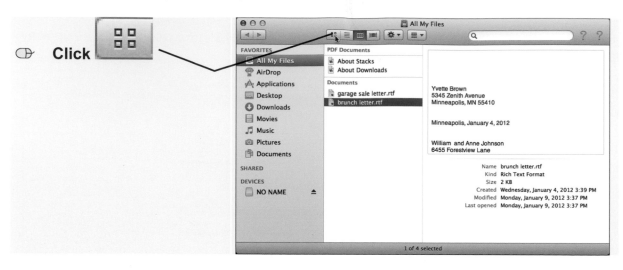

There are even more settings in which you can change the view of a window. For instance, you can display the *path bar* in the *Finder* window. Use the menu bar to do this:

Click **View**

Click **Show Path Bar**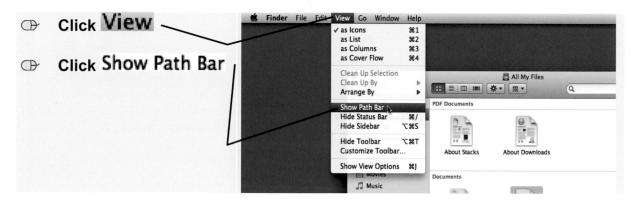

### ✖ HELP! I see a command called Hide Path Bar.

Does your menu contain an **Hide Path Bar** option? This means the path bar is already visible in *Finder*.

### ☞ Just continue reading

The path bar is displayed:

In the path bar, you can see at a glance in which folder a selected file or a selected

folder is stored: ⌂ **studiovisualsteps** ▸ 🗂 **Documents** ▸ 🗎 **brunch letter.rtf** .

This means that the *brunch letter* has been stored in the *Documents* folder. The *Documents* folder is stored in the personal folder of the user called *studiovisualsteps*. On your own computer, there will be a different name for this folder.

You are going to check if your computer has the same settings for the *Finder* view as in these examples:

☞ **Click View**

If you see the same menu options as here, your own *Finder* program has the correct settings:

**Hide Path Bar**

**Hide Status Bar**          ⌘/

**Hide Sidebar**          ⌥⌘S

**Hide Toolbar**          ⌥⌘T

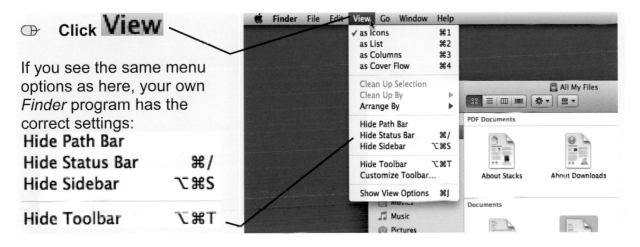

### 🩹 HELP! My menu has a Show... option instead of a Hide... option.

If you see **Show** in a menu option, it means the component is hidden by *Finder*.

☞ **For example, click Show Sidebar**

Now this component will be displayed in *Finder*.

☞ **Make sure the path bar and the status bar are displayed, by changing the menu options in the same way as the example above**

# 3.3 The Various Components in Finder

*Finder* does not just display the contents of a folder. The *Finder* window contains specific sections that will help you navigate through the folders on your computer. Take a closer look now at these components:

*Navigation pane*:
In this window pane you will see the folders that are most important to you:

The blue bar indicates which folder or view has been selected:

In the *file list*, the files in this folder are displayed as icons:

In the *path bar* you can view the location of a selected folder or file:

In the *status bar* you can see how many files are contained within a folder and how many files are selected:

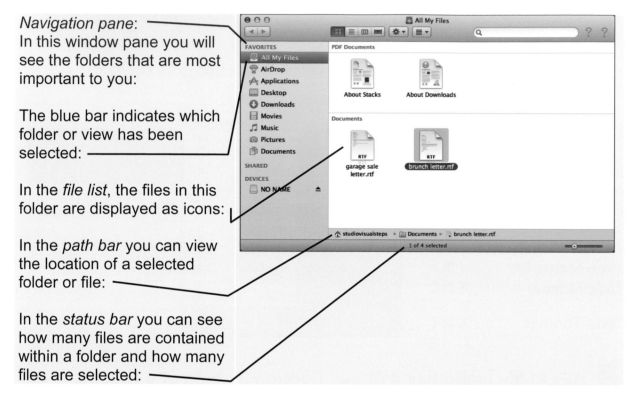

By using the *navigation pane* on the left-hand side, you can quickly open a folder on your computer. When you click a folder in the *navigation pane*, the contents of this folder will be displayed *Finder*.

## 💡 Tip

**Icons for files and folders**
By default, *OS X* will display a miniature preview of the file or folder in the icon that goes with this file or folder.

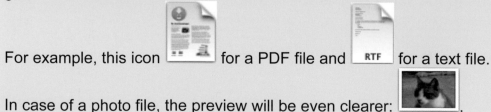

For example, this icon for a PDF file and for a text file.

In case of a photo file, the preview will be even clearer:

# 3.4 Creating a New Folder

You can use folders to arrange your files in an orderly way. Each file on your computer is stored in a folder. A folder may also contain another folder. A folder contained within another folder is called a *subfolder*.

You can create your own new folders. For example, it may be useful to separate your letters from other documents. To see how this is done, you are going to create a new subfolder in the 📄 **Documents** folder. First, you need to open the *Documents* folder:

☞ **If necessary, click**

**📄 Documents**

You will see the contents of the *Documents* folder:

Your *Documents* folder will contain at least three files. These are the letters you have written in the previous chapter and the document called *About Stacks*.

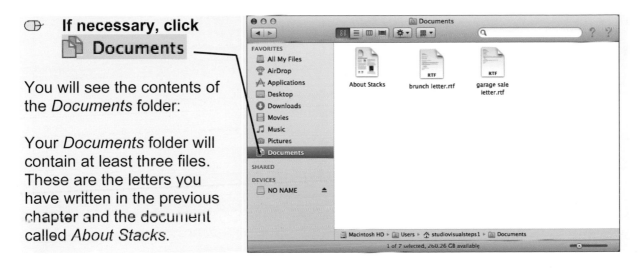

💡 **Tip**

**Path bar**
This is what you currently see in the path bar

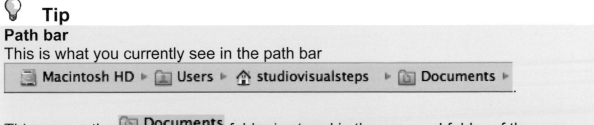

This means the 📄 **Documents** folder is stored in the personal folder of the user called 🏠 **studiovisualsteps**.

The 📇 **Users** folder contains the personal folders of all the users on this computer, and can be found on the hard disk (HD = *hard disk*) of this *Macintosh* computer.

Now you can create a new folder:

⊕ Click **File**

⊕ Click **New Folder**

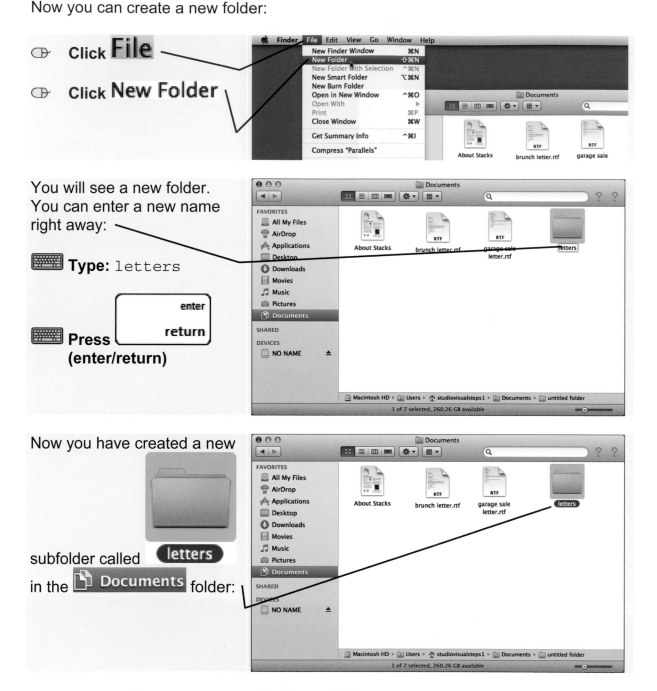

You will see a new folder. You can enter a new name right away:

⌨ **Type:** letters

⌨ **Press** (enter/return)

Now you have created a new subfolder called **letters** in the **Documents** folder:

In the next section, you can use the *letters* folder to save a letter you will write in *TextEdit*. First, you are going to minimize the *Finder* window:

☞ **Minimize the *Finder* window**  ⌛15

# 3.5 Save in a Folder

You are going to write a letter in *TextEdit* and save it in the new letters folder. The same operation can be used with many other programs.

☞ **Open** *TextEdit* ✂¹¹

Type a short sentence:

⌨ **Type:** Letter for saving

☞ **Click File**

☞ **Click Save...**

First, enter a name for the new document:

⌨ **Type:** letter

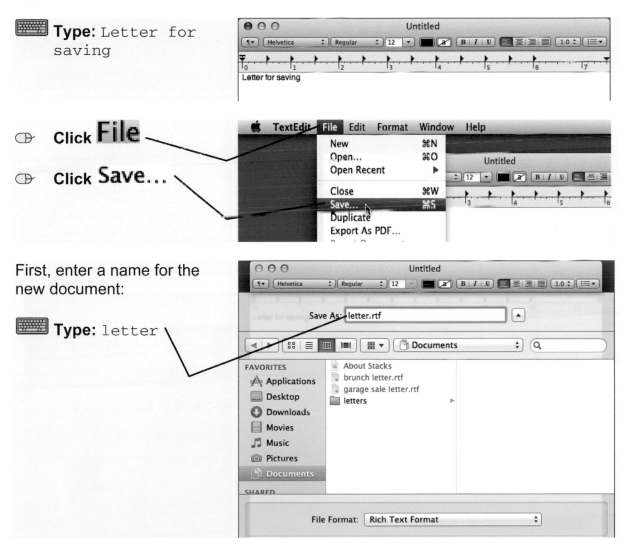

*TextEdit* will immediately assume that you want to save the new document in the *Documents* folder too. But now you are going to select the *letters* subfolder instead:

☞ **Click** 📁 **letters**

You can see that the *letters* folder is still empty:

Now you can save the new document:

☞ **Click** **Save**

Now the file called *letter* has been saved in the *letters* folder.

☞ **Close the *TextEdit* window** ✌13

☞ **Quit *TextEdit*** ✌25

You can open *Finder* once again, to check whether your file has been saved in the *letters* folder. For this, you are going to use the *Dock*:

☞ **Click**

You can quickly open the *letters* folder by *double-clicking*. Here is how to do that:

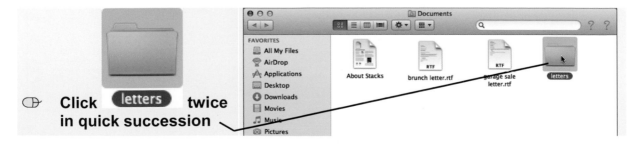

☞ **Click** **letters** **twice in quick succession**

In the title bar you can see that the *letters* folder has been opened:

In the file list you will see the document you saved:

You can go back to the *Documents* folder:

☞  **Click** 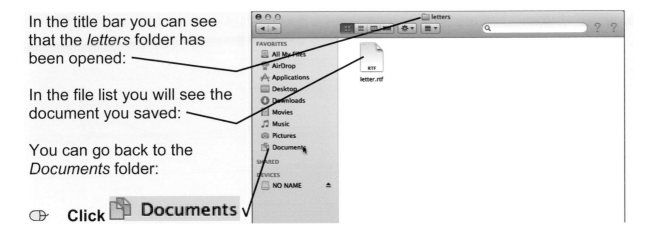 **Documents** √

# 3.6 Copying a File

You can also copy files. For example, if you want to make a second copy of a letter, so that you can change a few things. As an exercise, you are going to copy the *brunch letter* file to the *letters* folder. Before you can copy the letter, you need to select it first:

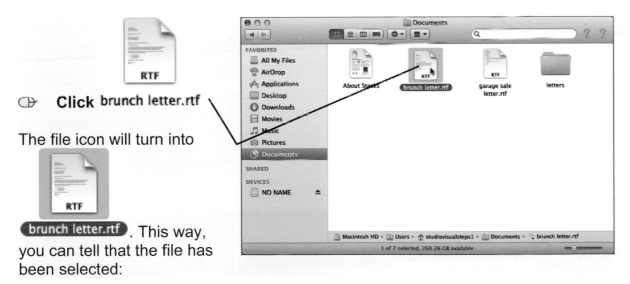

☞  **Click brunch letter.rtf**

The file icon will turn into

**brunch letter.rtf** . This way, you can tell that the file has been selected:

Now you can use the menu bar to copy the file:

☞  **Click Edit**

☞  **Click Copy "brunch letter.rtf"**

You will not see anything happen, but *OS X* will know that you want to copy the file. Now you can paste the copied file into the *letters* folder:

First, open the *letters* folder:

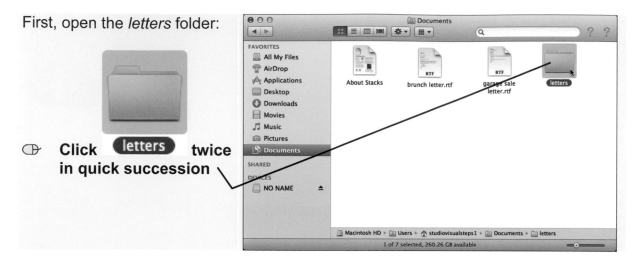

⊕  **Click  letters  twice in quick succession**

### ➥ Please note:

From this point on in the book, the command ⊕ **Click ... twice in quick succession** will be shortened to ⊕ **Double-click...**

### HELP! The name is displayed in a light-blue frame.

Do you see a light-blue frame around the name? Has the pointer turned into Ⅰ? For

example:  **letters** .

⊕  **Click in a different area of the window**

☞  **Try again to double-click**

You will see the contents of the *letters* folder. Now you can paste the copied f‌i
the folder:

⊕ Click **Edit**

⊕ Click **Paste Item**

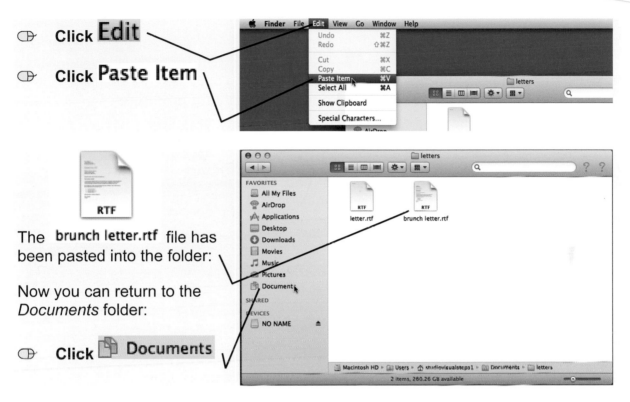

The **brunch letter.rtf** file has been pasted into the folder:

Now you can return to the *Documents* folder:

⊕ Click 🗂 **Documents**

# 3.7 Moving a File

In *Finder*, you can also move a file to a different folder. You can do this by dragging the file to another folder. Go ahead and try it:

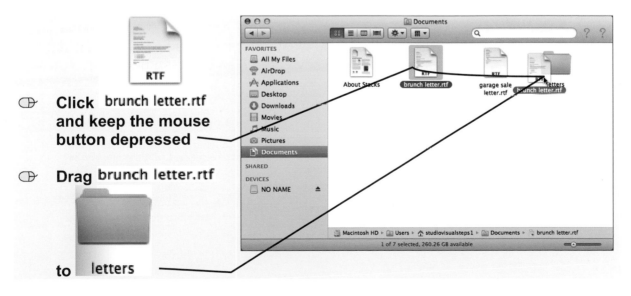

⊕ Click **brunch letter.rtf** **and keep the mouse button depressed**

⊕ **Drag brunch letter.rtf**

**to letters**

This is how you drag a file with a trackpad:

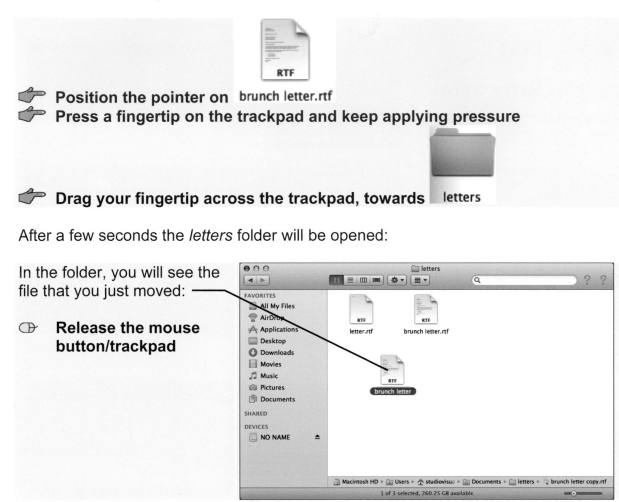

☞ **Position the pointer on** brunch letter.rtf
☞ **Press a fingertip on the trackpad and keep applying pressure**

☞ **Drag your fingertip across the trackpad, towards** letters

After a few seconds the *letters* folder will be opened:

In the folder, you will see the file that you just moved:

◉ **Release the mouse button/trackpad**

You will see the *Copy* window. Previously, you had already copied the same file to the *letters* folder, but you cannot save two files with the exact same name in the same folder. In *OS X* you can choose if you want to replace the first file by the file you are currently moving, or if you want to save both files in the same folder. You are going to save both files:

◉ **Click**

**Keep Both Files**

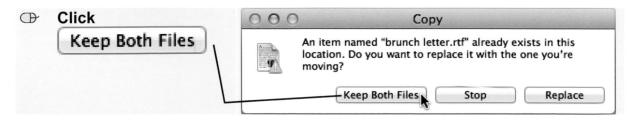

## ➥ Please note:

If the folder to which you are moving or copying a file does not already contain a file with the same name, you will not see the *Copy* window. The file will simply be moved or copied to the folder right away.

You will see that the file you moved has been called **brunch letter copy.rtf** :

Even if the content of both files is exactly the same, they still need to have different file names. That is why the system automatically adds the word *copy* to the second file.

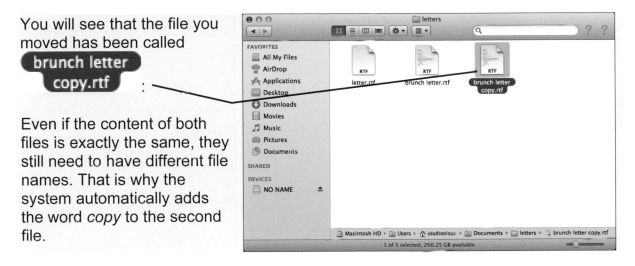

# 3.8 Selecting Multiple Files

You can also select multiple files at once and copy or move them. First, you need to select the files. Just try it:

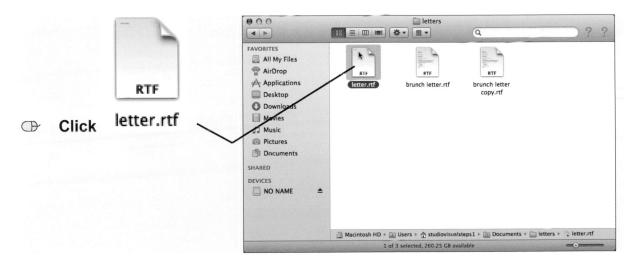

Now the *letter* file has been selected.

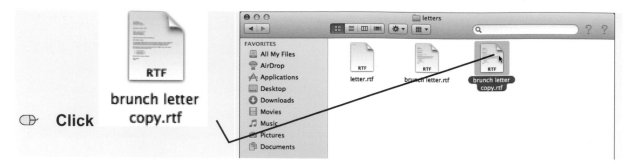

You will see that currently, the file called *brunch letter copy* has been selected, and the *letter* file is no longer selected. This is because you can only select a single file by clicking it. You can select more than one file by using the Command key:

The Command key always has the ⌘ sign on it:

You will find the Command key to the left and to the right of the space bar:

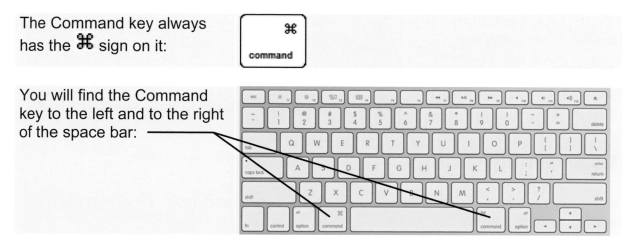

You use the Command key together with the mouse or the trackpad. The file called *brunch letter copy* is still selected:

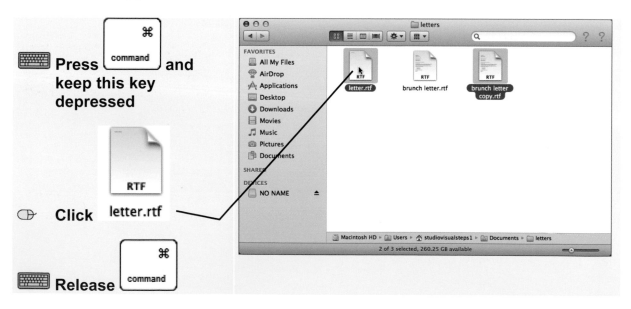

Now both files have been selected. This is how you move the selected files to the *Documents* folder:

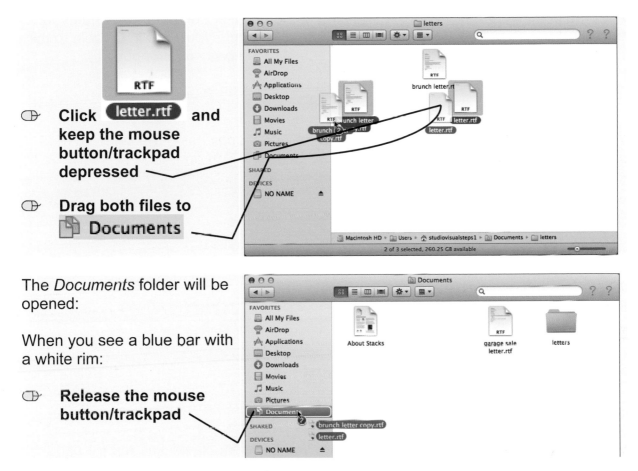

☞ **Click** **letter.rtf** **and keep the mouse button/trackpad depressed**

☞ **Drag both files to** **📄 Documents**

The *Documents* folder will be opened:

When you see a blue bar with a white rim:

☞ **Release the mouse button/trackpad**

Now both files have been moved to the *Documents* folder. You can undo this action:

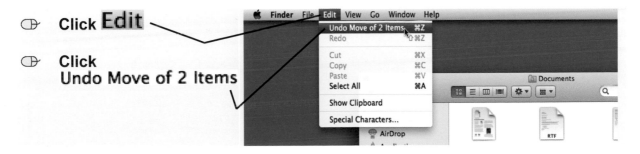

☞ **Click Edit**

☞ **Click Undo Move of 2 Items**

The documents called *letter* and *brunch letter copy*, which you just moved, will now be removed from *Documents* folder and will be stored in the *letters* folder once again.

👉 **Open the *letters* folder** ✂️**26**

# 3.9 Changing the File Name

At some point, you may want to change the name of a file. For instance, when you have written several documents about the same topic and you want to be able to tell them apart. You can practice this now by renaming the *brunch letter copy* file:

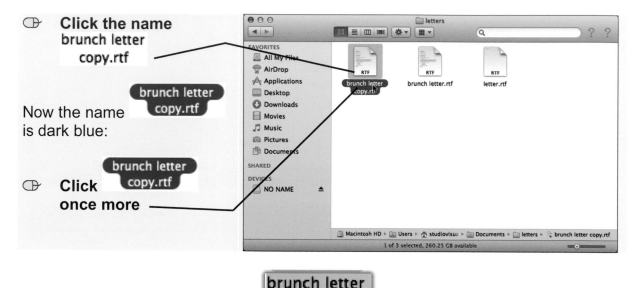

☞ **Click the name**
brunch letter
    copy.rtf

Now the name
is dark blue:

☞ **Click**
**once more**

The file name has been selected:
**brunch letter copy.rtf** .

## HELP! I see a different window.

Do you see the *TextEdit* window now? Then you have double-clicked the file and have inadvertently opened the program. This is easy to remedy, just:

☞ **Close the *TextEdit* window** 𝄐𝄐13

☞ **Quit *TextEdit*** 𝄐𝄐25
☞ **Try again**

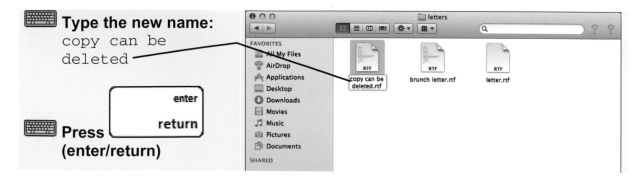

⌨ **Type the new name:**
copy can be
deleted

⌨ **Press** (enter/return)
enter
return

The name has changed:

## HELP! Name already in use.

A folder cannot contain files with exactly the same name. If you try to use an existing name for a file, you will see this window:

Click **OK**

Now you can select the file name once more, and try a different name.

The name "brunch letter" with extension ".rtf" is already taken. Please choose a different name.

OK

## Tip
**Folder**
You can rename a folder in the same way you rename a file.

# 3.10 Deleting a File

It is a good idea to delete files you no longer use. This way, you will keep your folders orderly and well-arranged. In *OS X* you use the *Trash Bin* to delete files. You are going to move the file you just renamed to the *Trash Bin*:

The file called *copy can be deleted* is still selected:

Click **File**

Click **Move to Trash**

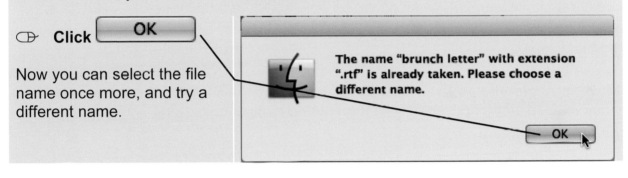

Now you will hear the sound of a wad of paper being tossed into the waste-paper basket. The *copy can be deleted* file has been removed from the *letters* folder. But the files you have moved to the *Trash Bin* have not yet completely disappeared. Once you empty the *Trash Bin,* the file will be permanently deleted. As long as a file is stored in the *Trash Bin*, you can still retrieve it, if you want.

### ➥ Please note:

**Only your own files**
Be careful in deleting files. Only delete the files you have created yourself. If you did not create a file yourself, you may not be able to delete it because it is locked and you do not have permission to modify it.

### 💡 Tip

**Move multiple files to the Trash Bin at once**
You can also move multiple files to the *Trash Bin*, all at once. First, you need to

select these files by clicking them, while you keep the Command key depressed. Afterwards, you can move them to the *Trash Bin*.

### 💡 Tip

**Delete an entire folder**

You can also delete an entire folder . You select a folder by clicking it. After that, you can move the folder to the *Trash Bin*.

### 💡 Tip

**Drag**
Another method is to drag the desired files and folders from *Finder* to the *Trash Bin* in the *Dock*.

# 3.11 The Trash Bin

Now you are going to take a look at the contents of the *Trash Bin*. You can open the *Trash Bin* through the *Dock*:

⊕  **Click**

You will see the *Trash Bin* window, containing the deleted file called *copy can be deleted*. Now you can empty the *Trash Bin*:

⊕  **Click**

⊕  **Click Empty Trash**

Just to be sure, you will be asked to confirm this operation:

⊕  **Click**
    **Empty Trash**

Now the file has been permanently deleted. You cannot retrieve it anymore.

☞  **If necessary, close the *Trash Bin* window** ✂️[13]

💡 **Tip**

**Recover file from Trash Bin**

Have you accidentally moved the wrong file to the *Trash Bin*? Or have you changed your mind and do you want to retrieve the file you deleted? Then you need to do this:

☞ **Click the file you want to recover**

☞ **Click** ⚙️ ▾

☞ **Click Put Back**

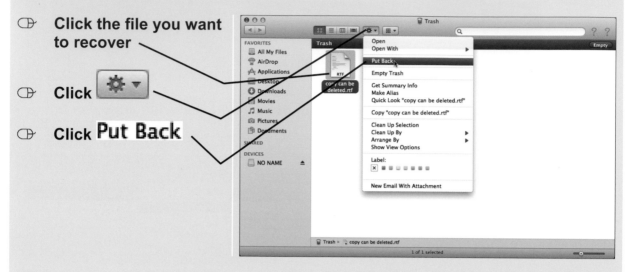

If you select multiple files at once, you can recover all these files in the same way as described above.

💡 **Tip**

**Does the Trash Bin contain any items?**

You can tell if there is anything in the *Trash Bin,* by looking at the *Dock*. The icon in the *Dock* will change:

 full           empty

💡 **Tip**

**When do you need to empty the Trash Bin?**

You do not always need to empty the *Trash Bin*, whenever you delete a file. If you empty the *Trash Bin* every once in a while, this will be sufficient.

# 3.12 Copying to a USB Stick

If you want to copy a file to another computer, or want to make a safety copy (backup copy) and save it on a different medium, you can copy the file to a USB stick. A USB stick is also called a USB memory stick or memory stick. Now you are going to save a copy of the *brunch letter* file on a USB stick.

### 🖐 Please note:

To work through this exercise, you will need to have a USB stick. A USB stick is a small device that can be connected to your computer's USB port. You can also use an external hard disk. This is an external storage device that is connected to your computer through a USB cable. A USB stick or an external hard disk is a medium for storing information, just like on your computer's hard disk. Only, it is much easier to transfer data to other computers by using a mobile storage device.

If you do not own a USB stick or an external hard disk, you can just read through this section. In this example we will be using a USB stick. If you use an external hard disk, the working method will be exactly the same.

First, you need to insert your USB stick into the USB port on your computer.

The iMac has four USB ports on the back of the monitor:

The Mac mini has four USB ports on the back of the case:

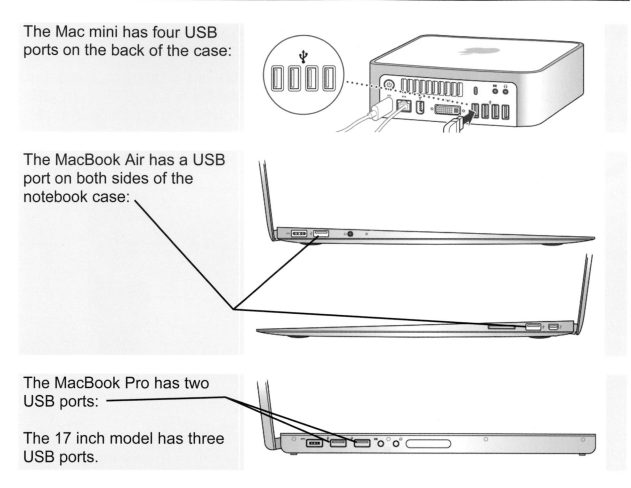

The MacBook Air has a USB port on both sides of the notebook case:

The MacBook Pro has two USB ports:

The 17 inch model has three USB ports.

☞ **Insert the USB stick carefully into a USB port**

It does not seem to go in?

☞ **Turn over the USB stick (half-turn) and try again**

As soon as the USB stick is recognized, it will appear in the *Finder's Navigation pane*, under **DEVICES**:

In this example, the USB stick is called 📀 **USB STICK**:

Your own USB stick will probably have a different name.

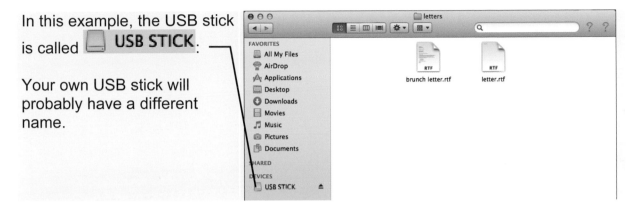

You can copy a file to the USB stick by dragging it to the stick. The *letters* folder is still open:

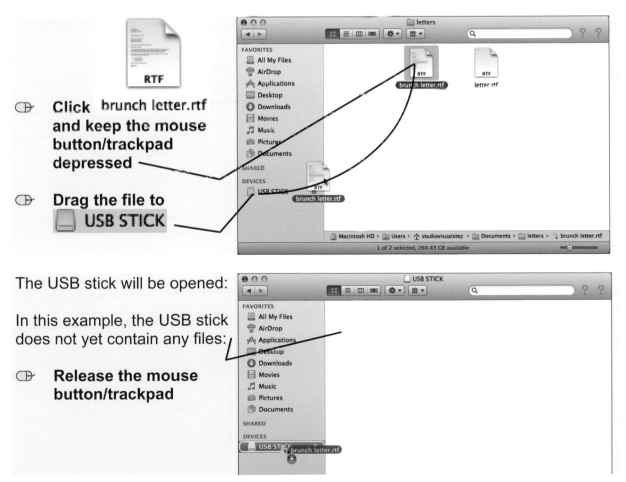

Click **brunch letter.rtf** and keep the mouse button/trackpad depressed

Drag the file to 📀 **USB STICK**

The USB stick will be opened:

In this example, the USB stick does not yet contain any files:

☞ **Release the mouse button/trackpad**

The file has been copied to
the USB stick: ————————

Now you are going to check if
the file is still present in the
*letters* folder:

☞  **Click** 🗐 **Documents**

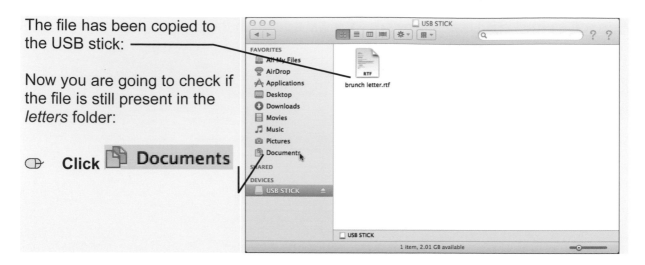

☞ **Open the *letters* folder** ♋²⁶

You will see that the file
called *brunch letters* is still
stored in this folder too: ———

This means the file has been
copied to the USB stick, not
moved.

## 🐾 **Please note:**

If you drag a file (or folder) to another folder on the same hard disk (on your own
computer), the file (or folder) will be **moved** to this folder.

If you drag a file (or folder) to a folder on a different hard disk or USB stick, the file
(or folder) will be **copied** to the folder on the other hard disk or USB stick.

# 3.13 Safely Disconnect the USB Stick

Whenever you want to remove storage devices, such as USB sticks, you always need to check whether the computer has finished storing the information. This is how you can safely disconnect the USB stick:

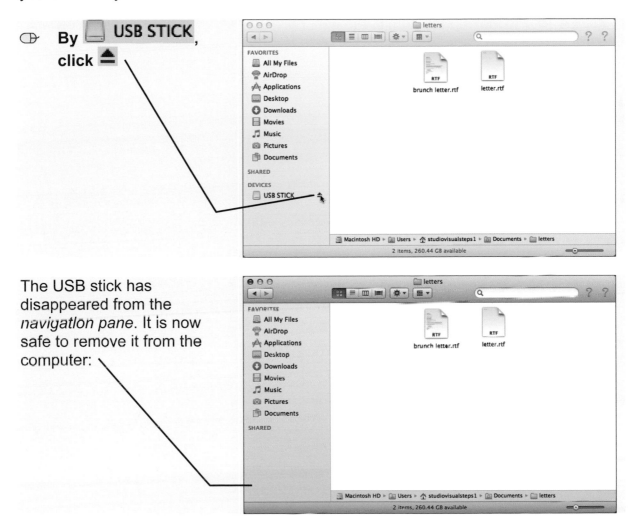

By 🖴 **USB STICK**, click ⏏

The USB stick has disappeared from the *navigation pane*. It is now safe to remove it from the computer:

☞ **Remove the USB stick from the computer**

☞ **Close the *Finder* window** ✌[13]

In this chapter you have learned how to work with folders and files in *Finder*. You have practiced moving, deleting, copying and renaming files as well as dragging files to a USB stick. In the following exercises you can repeat these operations.

## 3.14 Exercises

To be able to quickly apply the things you have learned, you can work through these exercises. Have you forgotten how to do something? Use the numbers next to the footsteps ⚹¹ to look up the item in the appendix *How Do I Do That Again?* You will find the appendix at the end of this book.

## Exercise: Copy a File

☞ Open *Finder*. ⚹²⁷

☞ Open the *Documents* folder. ⚹²⁸

☞ Open the *letters* folder. ⚹²⁶

☞ Copy the file called *brief letter* to the *Documents* folder. ⚹²⁹

## Exercise: Move a File to a New Folder

☞ If necessary, open the *Documents* folder. ⚹²⁸

☞ Create a new folder and call it *practice*. ⚹³⁰

☞ Move the *brunch letter* file to the *practice* folder. ⚹³¹

## Exercise: Rename a File

☞ If necessary, open the *practice* folder. ⚹²⁶

☞ Change the name of the *brunch letter* file and call it *practice letter*. ⚹³²

☞ Close *Finder*. ⚹¹³

## Exercise: The Trash Bin

☞   Open *Finder*. 🐾²⁷

☞   Open the *Documents* folder. 🐾²⁸

☞   Open the *practice* folder. 🐾²⁶

☞   Move the file called *practice letter* to the *Trash Bin*. 🐾³³

☞   Move the *practice* folder to the *Trash Bin*. 🐾³³

☞   Open the *Trash Bin*. 🐾³⁴

☞   Empty the *Trash Bin*. 🐾³⁵

☞   If necessary, close the *Trash Bin* window. 🐾¹³

☞   Close *Finder*. 🐾¹³

## Excrcise: Copy a File to a USB Stick

☞   Open *Finder*. 🐾²⁷

☞   Open the *letters* folder. 🐾²⁶

☞   Insert the USB stick into the computer.

☞   Copy the *brunch letter* file to the USB stick by dragging it. 🐾³⁶

☞   Safely disconnect the USB stick. 🐾³⁷

☞   Remove the USB stick from the computer.

☞   Close *Finder*. 🐾¹³

# 3.15 Background Information

### Dictionary

| | |
|---|---|
| **All my files** | An option in the *Finder* navigation pane, which provides a clear overview of all your files. Only the files you open in a regular way will be displayed, such as documents, pictures and videos; system files will remain hidden. |
| **Contextual menu** | A menu that is displayed when you right-click an item in *OS X*. You will see different menu options, depending on the item you have right-clicked. |
| **Double-click** | Press the mouse twice, in rapid succession (on a Magic Mouse), press the left mouse button (on a regular mouse), or press the (Magic) trackpad. If you double-click a folder's icon in *Finder*, you will open the folder. |
| **File** | The collective name for all the data stored on your computer. A file can be a program, a data file containing several names, a text file written by you, or a photo. A file consists of a name and a file extension. An extension is a series of characters that come after the dot at the end of a file name, for instance: photo.jpg. |
| **File list** | The contents of an open folder are displayed in a file list. |
| **Finder** | Component of *OS X*. The *Finder* provides an orderly view of the files and folders stored on your computer and stored on disks and devices connected to your computer. Also, you can use *Finder* to search for/manage information on disks and devices. |
| **Folder** | You can use a folder to arrange your files. On your computer, each file is stored in a folder. A folder can also contain other folders (subfolders). |
| **Hard disk** | A storage medium where you can store your programs and files. |
| **Navigation pane** | This pane displays the list of folders that can be opened in the folder pane. |

*- Continue on the next page -*

| | |
|---|---|
| **Path bar** | The path bar is displayed beneath the *file list*. In the path bar you can see which folder has been opened in the folder pane, and the exact location of this folder on the computer. |
| **PDF file** | PDF stands for *Portable Document Format*. This file format is often used for information you can download, such as product manuals and brochures. |
| **Right-click** | Another name for a *secondary click*. |
| **Secondary clicking** | Also called *right-clicking*. This is a method of clicking which opens a contextual menu. Remember that for some mouse types, such as the Magic Mouse, the secondary clicking option still needs to be activated in *OS X*, in the *System Preferences*. |
| **Select** | A mouse operation with which you can mark part of a document. |
| **Spotlight** | A search technology that is built-in in the *Macintosh* computers. *Spotlight* builds a database with information on all the files stored on the computer. When you type a keyword in the *Spotlight* search box, the database will be searched for files that match this keyword. A list with the search results will be displayed. |
| **Status bar** | In the status bar you can view the number of files stored in a specific folder, the amount of remaining free disk space and the number of files that have been selected. The status bar will be displayed below the path bar. |
| **Subfolder** | A folder that is stored within another folder. |
| **Trash Bin** | When you delete a file or a folder, it will be moved to the *Trash Bin*. As long a file resides in the *Trash Bin*, you can still recover it. But when you empty the *Trash Bin*, the contents will be lost once and for all. |
| **USB port** | A narrow, rectangular connector on a computer, to which you can connect a USB (Universal Serial Bus) device, such as a USB stick. |
| **USB stick** | A small device on which you can store data. A USB stick is connected to the USB port on your computer. *Finder* will display the USB stick in the navigation pane, under the *Devices* header. |

*Source: Apple Dictionary, www.apple.com*

**Store on your computer**

A computer contains a certain amount of *working memory*. Your work is temporarily saved in this working memory. When you turn your computer off, the contents of this working memory will be erased. That is why you need to save your work regularly.

There are several kinds of storage media: for example, the computer's hard disk or an external hard disk, but USB sticks and writable CD and DVD disks are also called storage media.

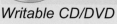

*Hard disk*          *USB memory stick*          *External hard disk*          *Writable CD/DVD*

**Hard disk**

When you are using your computer, you will mostly save your work on the computer's hard disk. This is a tightly sealed, built-in box in your computer.

*Hard disk*          *Mac Mini computer case*

Within this box, a small disk is revolving. This is a magnetic disk, which enables it to record information.

You can decide what to store on your hard disk. For instance, you can save text, photos, or computer programs on this disk.

Each item that is stored on a hard disk is called a *file*. This may be a text, but it can also be a program or a digital photo.

As you have learned in this chapter, you can copy, move, rename and delete files on this hard disk.

# 3.16 Tips

## ♀ Tip

**Cover Flow**

Apart from the icons, the list and the panes, *Finder* contains another special feature for viewing the contents of the computer. This graphical user interface is called the *Cover Flow*. With *Cover Flow* you can flip through your files and folders in 3D (three-dimensional view). This is how you can change the view of the *Finder* to *Cover Flow*:

☞ **Click**

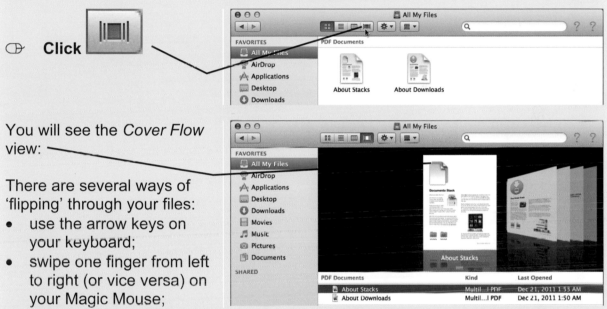

You will see the *Cover Flow* view:

There are several ways of 'flipping' through your files:

- use the arrow keys on your keyboard;
- swipe one finger from left to right (or vice versa) on your Magic Mouse;
- swipe <u>two</u> fingers from left to right (or vice versa) across your trackpad.

**Please note:** if you use the touch operations on the Magic Mouse or the trackpad, the pointer needs to be positioned on the *Cover Flow* and not on the file list.

## ♀ Tip

**Quick copy with the contextual menu**

Instead of using the menu bar, you can also use the *contextual menu* for copy operations.

This is a menu that appears whenever you click an item while keeping the Control

key ⎡ **control** ⎤ depressed. This menu contains all relevant commands, which you can also find by using the menu bar.

*- Continue on the next page -*

This is how you copy a file using the contextual menu:

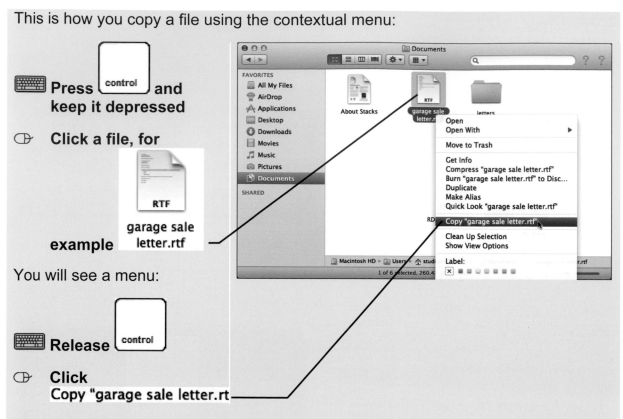

**Press** `control` **and keep it depressed**

⊕ **Click a file, for**

**example** garage sale letter.rtf

You will see a menu:

**Release** `control`

⊕ **Click**
Copy "garage sale letter.rt

Now the letter has been copied. You can also paste a file using the contextual menu:

☞ **Open the *letters* folder** ✂²⁶

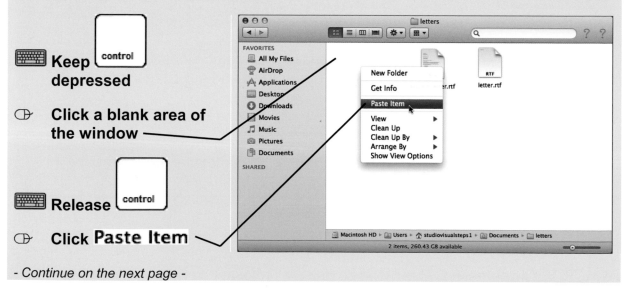

**Keep** `control` **depressed**

⊕ **Click a blank area of the window**

**Release** `control`

⊕ **Click Paste Item**

*- Continue on the next page -*

Now the letter has been copied:

You can also use the contextual menus by *secondary* clicking. This is also called *right-clicking*. For some mouse types, such as the Magic Mouse, the setting in *OS X* needs to be adjusted. In the tip below you can read how to do this.

## 💡 Tip

**Secondary clicking**

You can also use the contextual menus by right-clicking (secondary clicking) with your mouse or trackpad. In order to do this, you may need to modify a setting in *OS X*. In the *Dock* you will find the *System Preferences* program:

Click

You will see the *System Preferences* window:

If you are using a mouse:

Click **Mouse**

If you are using a trackpad:

Click **Trackpad**

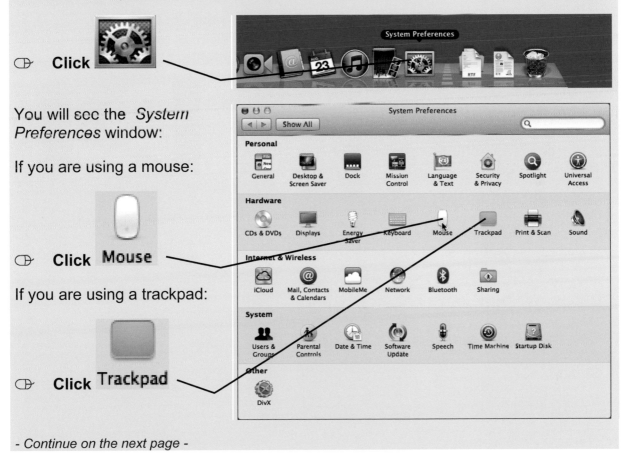

*- Continue on the next page -*

This is how you change the mouse settings:

⊕ **Check the box ☑ next to Secondary click**

☞ **Close the *Mouse* window** 🐾13

By default, the secondary clicking option is already enabled for the trackpad.

If you want to modify one of the other settings:

⊕ **If necessary, check the box ☑ next to the desired option**

☞ **Close the *Trackpad* window** 🐾13

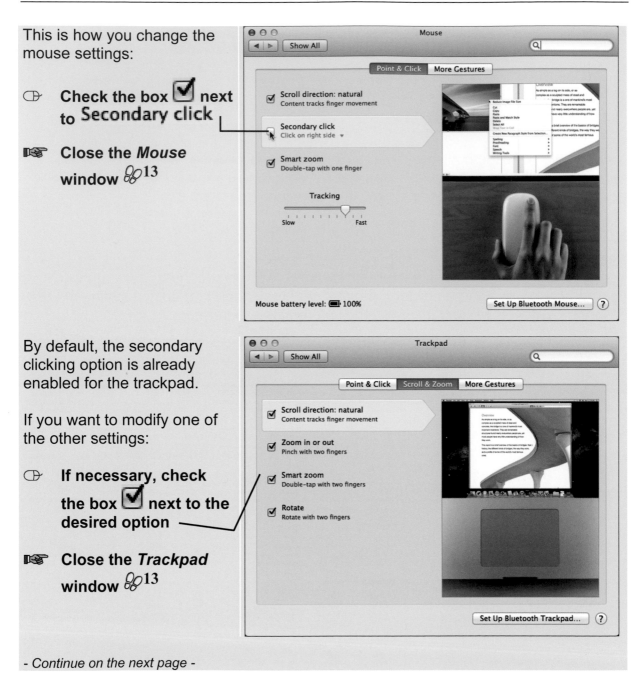

*- Continue on the next page -*

This is how you can use the secondary clicking option with the contextual menus:

With the Magic Mouse:

☞ **Press the top right-hand corner of the mouse**

With a regular mouse:

☞ **Press the right mouse button**

With the (Magic) trackpad:

☞ **Simultaneously press two fingers on the trackpad**

It does not matter on which part of the trackpad you press.

# 🔦 Tip

**Search box in Finder**

With the *Finder* search box you can quickly find a document or any other type of file:

☞ **Click the search box**

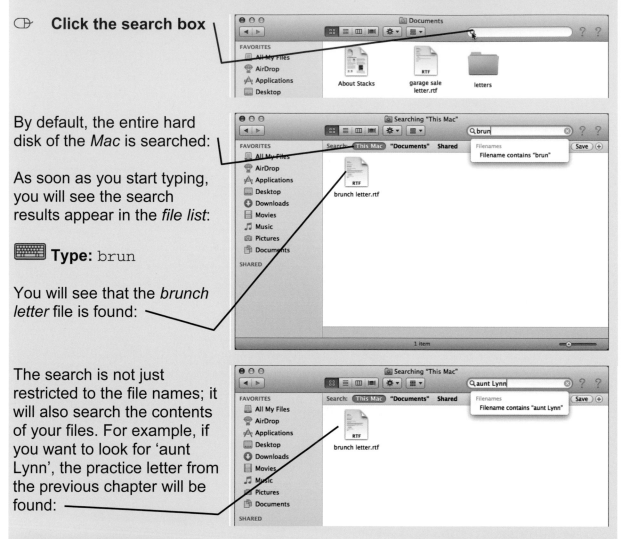

By default, the entire hard disk of the *Mac* is searched:

As soon as you start typing, you will see the search results appear in the *file list*:

⌨ **Type:** brun

You will see that the *brunch letter* file is found:

The search is not just restricted to the file names; it will also search the contents of your files. For example, if you want to look for 'aunt Lynn', the practice letter from the previous chapter will be found:

You do not need to know the exact file name to be able to retrieve a document. *Finder* uses the *Spotlight* search technology of *OS X*. In the next tip you can read how to use *Spotlight* right away.

### 💡 Tip
**Search with Spotlight**
*Spotlight* is the powerful search technology in *OS X*. You do not need to open *Finder* to use *Spotlight*. You can conduct a *Spotlight* search right from your desktop:

☞ **In the top right corner of the screen, click** 🔍

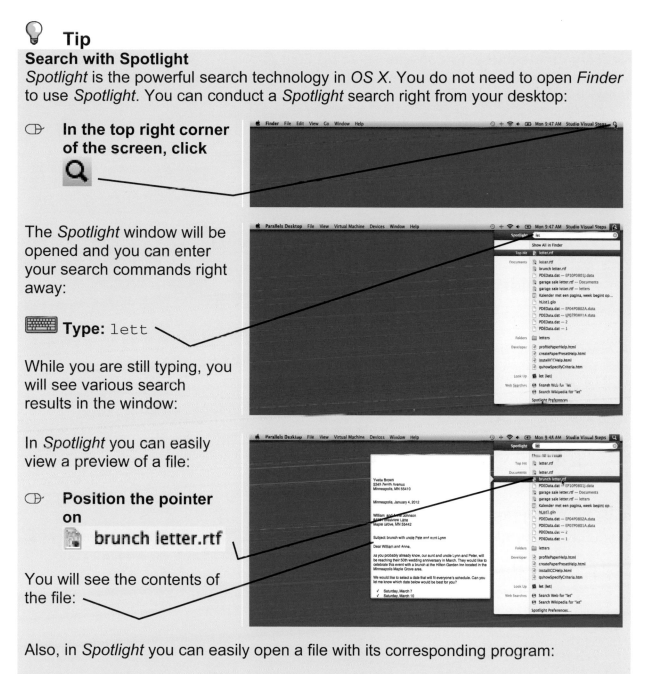

The *Spotlight* window will be opened and you can enter your search commands right away:

⌨ **Type:** `lett`

While you are still typing, you will see various search results in the window:

In *Spotlight* you can easily view a preview of a file:

☞ **Position the pointer on** 📄 **brunch letter.rtf**

You will see the contents of the file:

Also, in *Spotlight* you can easily open a file with its corresponding program:

☞ **Click** 📄 **brunch letter.rtf**
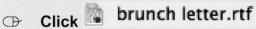

The letter will be opened in *TextEdit*.

## 💡 Tip

**Quickly create a new folder with selected files**
With the *New Folder with Selection* option in *OS X*, you can quickly create a new folder in, containing a number of selected files.

☞ **Select a couple of files** ⌘102

In this example we have selected three files:

👆 Click **File**

👆 Click **New Folder with Sele**

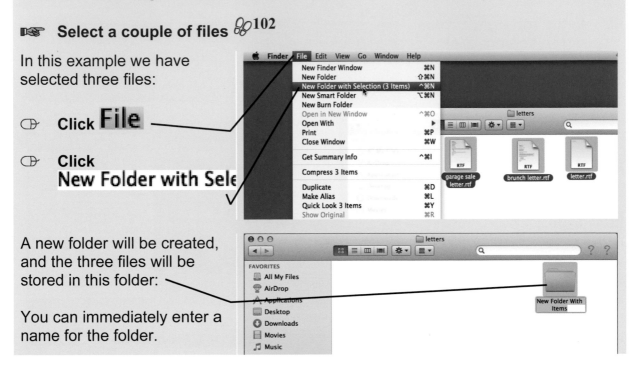

A new folder will be created, and the three files will be stored in this folder:

You can immediately enter a name for the folder.

## 💡 Tip

**Sort files in Finder**
If you have stored a lot of files in a folder, you may lose the overall picture and things may seem somewhat confusing. The useful sorting option in *Finder* will help you regain a clear overview. You can sort your files in different ways. For instance, alphabetically, by file name, creation date, size, or corresponding software program. This is how you can view the various sorting options in *OS X*:

👆 Click ▦▾

You will see a menu with all the sorting options:

To select a sorting method, click the desired method.

You can set a different sorting method for each individual folder.

# 4. Surfing with Safari

The internet is a large network of computers that is connected to many smaller networks located all over the world. On all these computers data is stored, on a very wide range of topics. You can use your own computer to view the information on these computers. To do this, you need to use a program called an *internet browser* or a *browser*. *Browsing* is much the same as browsing through a newspaper or a magazine, but instead of your hands, you use a mouse, touchpad or short-cut keys to flip through the pages of information. *Safari* is the internet browser used by *Apple*.

The information on the Internet is stored in websites. Usually, a website consists of multiple web pages. You can jump (or navigate) from one web page to the other or to another website, by clicking a link (also called hyperlink) on the page. This is called *surfing*.

In this chapter you will learn how to open a web page, and how to zoom in, zoom out and scroll. If you are using a (Magic) trackpad, you can use various touch gestures for these actions. We will also discuss how to open a link on a web page and how to save web pages on the *bookmarks toolbar*. And finally you will learn how to set the homepage and explore the *Top Sites* function.

In this chapter you will learn how to:

- open *Safari*;
- open a web page;
- zoom in and zoom out;
- scroll;
- open a link on a web page;
- open a link in a new tab;
- switch between open tabs;
- close a tab;
- go to the previous or next page;
- add a bookmark or a folder to the bookmarks bar;
- use *Top Sites*;
- change the settings for the homepage;
- search;
- quit *Safari*.

# 4.1 Opening Safari

Here is how to open *Safari*, the program that lets you surf the Internet:

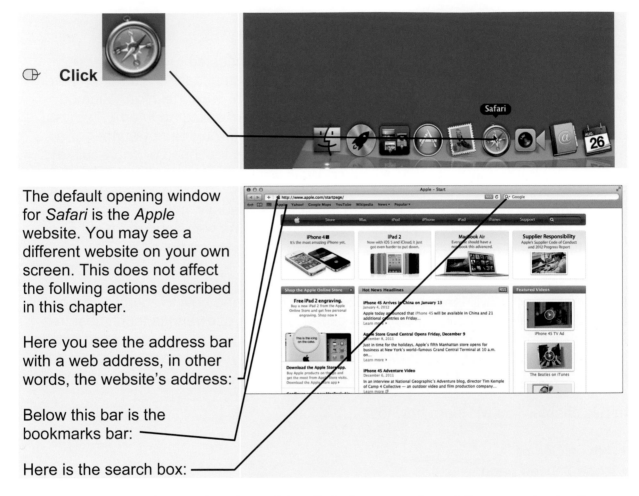

👆 **Click**

The default opening window for *Safari* is the *Apple* website. You may see a different website on your own screen. This does not affect the follwing actions described in this chapter.

Here you see the address bar with a web address, in other words, the website's address:

Below this bar is the bookmarks bar:

Here is the search box:

You are going to change the view of the *Safari* program by adding an extra toolbar:

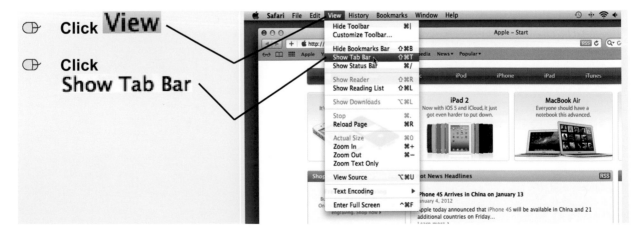

👆 **Click View**

👆 **Click Show Tab Bar**

**HELP! I see Hide Tab Bar**.

If you see the option **Hide Tab Bar** in the menu, the tab bar has already been added to the view.

You will see the

**Apple – Start**

tab:

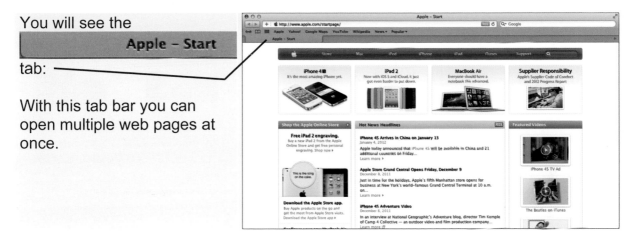

With this tab bar you can open multiple web pages at once.

## 4.2 Opening a Web Page

You can open a web page by entering the web address in the address bar:

☞ **Click the address bar three times**

Now the web address has been selected:

## Tip
**Short-cut key combination**
By using the key combination Command and L you can quickly select the web address in the address bar:

**Press** ⌘ command **and** L **simultaneously**

Now you can type the web address:

**Type:**
www.visualsteps.
com

**Press**
(enter/return)

enter

return

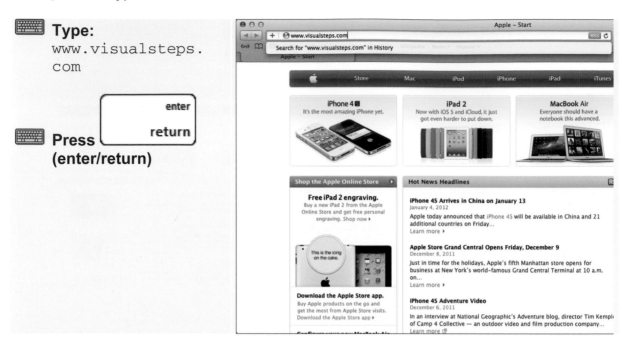

## ➡ **Please note:**

If you copy a web address from a newspaper or a magazine, it is important to type the dots and slashes (/) in the right places. Otherwise, the web page will not be found by the browser.

Does the web address start with http://www...? Then you do not need to type the prefix http://.

Now you will see the Visual Steps website:

The page may look a bit different now, but this will not affect the following tasks you are going to do.

## 4.3 Zooming In

If you think the letters and images on a website are a bit small, you can zoom in and enlarge them. First, we will show you how to do this with the Magic Mouse and the (Magic) trackpad.

If you are using a Magic Mouse, you can quickly zoom in by tapping the Magic Mouse with one finger:

**Position the pointer next to Welcome**

**Tap the Magic Mouse twice, in rapid succession**

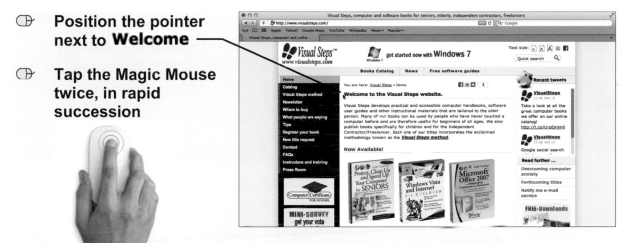

**Please note:** tapping is not the same as clicking!

If you are using a (Magic) trackpad, you can zoom in by tapping with two fingers:

**Position the pointer next to Welcome**

**Tap the (Magic) trackpad twice in succession with two fingers**

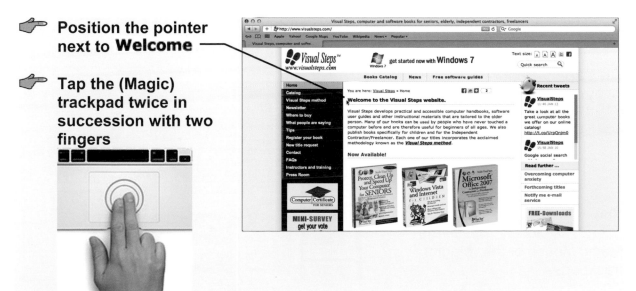

If you cannot zoom in while following these instructions, you can also use a different method for zooming in with the trackpad. In the *Tips* at the end of this chapter you can read how to do this.

### HELP! A different web page is opened.

If another web page is opened, you have been clicking instead of tapping.

In the top left of the window:

☞ **Click** ◀

☞ **Try it again**

You will see that the web page is displayed in a much larger size:

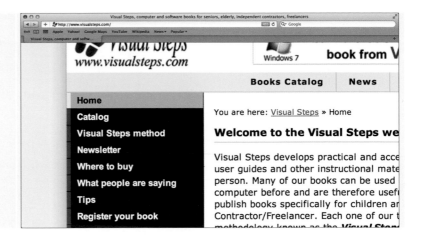

If you do not use a Magic Mouse or a (Magic) trackpad, you can use the key combination Command and + to gradually zoom in:

☞ **Position the pointer next to Welcome**

⌨ **Simultaneously press**

⌘ command **and** + =

You will zoom in on the page, but not as closely as with the Magic Mouse or the (Magic) trackpad.

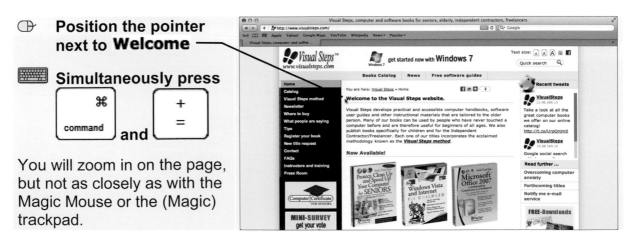

☞ **Zoom in on the dark blue menu on the left three more times** ✍[38]

Now the letters and images
have become much larger:

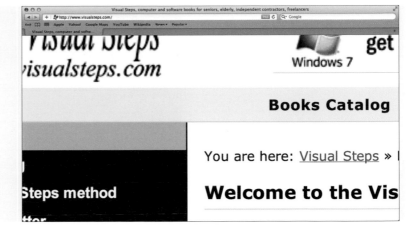

## 4.4 Scrolling

Scrolling is useful when you cannot see the entire web page at once on your screen.
Most of the time you will want to move up and down through the page, but sometimes
you may need to scroll from side to side. This is how you do it with a Magic Mouse:

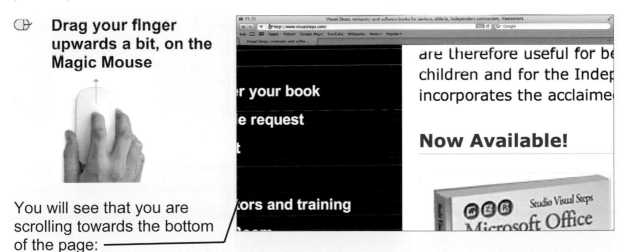

⊕ **Drag your finger
upwards a bit, on the
Magic Mouse**

You will see that you are
scrolling towards the bottom
of the page:

This is how you scroll upwards:

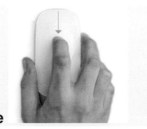

⊕ **Drag your finger downwards a bit, on the Magic Mouse**

If you are using a (Magic) trackpad you need to scroll with two fingers:

👉 **Drag two fingers upwards a bit, on the trackpad**

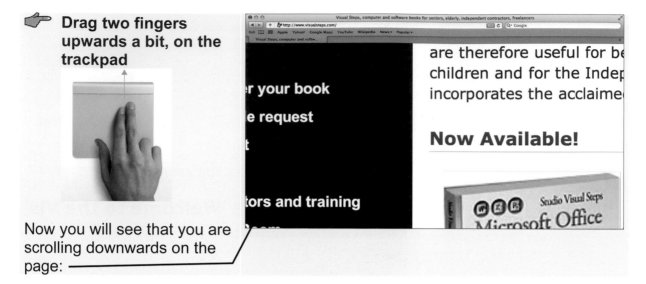

Now you will see that you are scrolling downwards on the page:

This is how you scroll in upward direction:

👉 **Drag two fingers a downwards a bit, on the (Magic) trackpad**

💡 **Tip**

**Scrolling sideways**
If the web page is wider than the *Safari* window, you can also scroll from side to side. You do this by moving your finger(s) from right to left or from left to right across the surface of your Magic Mouse or (Magic) trackpad.

If you are using a regular mouse with a scroll wheel, you can scroll downwards by spinning the scroll wheel. The scroll wheel is located between the left and right mouse buttons.

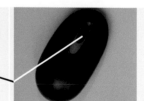

This is how you scroll downwards:

👉 **Spin the wheel towards yourself**

Scrolling upwards is just the other way round:

⏍    **Spin the wheel away from yourself**

You can also scroll by using the scroll bars to the right and at the bottom of the window. These scroll bars are only displayed when you start spinning the scroll wheel or start scrolling by dragging your fingers on the (Magic) Mouse or the (Magic) trackpad.

Here you see the scroll bars: ──

This is how you scroll sideways:

⏍    **Position the pointer on the scroll bar** ────

⏍    **Press the mouse button/trackpad and keep it depressed**

⏍    **Drag the scroll bar to the right**

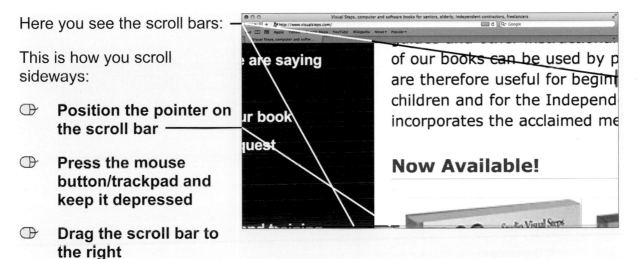

## 4.5 Zooming Out

If you want to view the web page from a distance again, you can zoom out. The letters and images will then become smaller. This is how you zoom out with the Magic Mouse:

⏍    **Tap the Magic Mouse twice, in rapid succession**

**Please note:** tapping is not clicking!

This is how you zoom out with the (Magic) trackpad:

☞ **Tap the (Magic) trackpad twice, with two fingers, in rapid succession**

If you cannot zoom out by rapidly tapping twice, you can use a different method for zooming out with the trackpad. In the *Tips* at the end of this chapter you can read how to do this.

If you do not use a Magic Mouse or a (Magic) trackpad, you can use the key combination Command and – to gradually zoom out:

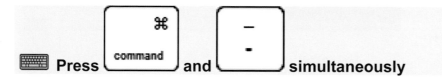

⌨ **Press** ⌘ **command and** – **simultaneously**

☞ **Repeat the same action until the web page is displayed in the desired size**

Now you will see the Visual Steps website again in its orignal size:

# 4.6 Opening a Link on a Web Page

You can jump from one web page to another by clicking a link (also called hyperlink) on the page. A link refers to a different web page. Just try it:

☞ **Position the pointer on Where to buy**

The pointer turn into a hand 🖑 and the menu item changes color:

By this you can tell that the pointer is pointing at a link.

☞ **Click Where to buy**

You will see the web page with information on where to find the Visual Steps books:

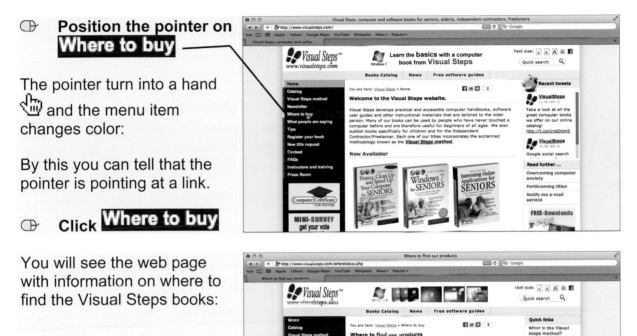

# 4.7 Working with Tabs

A link can also be opened in a new tab. You can do this by using the Command key:

**Press ⌘ command and keep it depressed**

☞ **Click Visual Steps method**

**Release ⌘ command**

The link will be opened in a new tab. This is how you go to this tab:

👆 **Click the**

    The Visual Steps Metho

**tab**

You will see the page with information about the Visual Steps Method. This is how you return to the first tab:

👆 **Click the**

    Where to find our pr

**tab**

Now you will again see the first tab. You can close the second tab:

👆 **On the second tab,**

**click** ▒

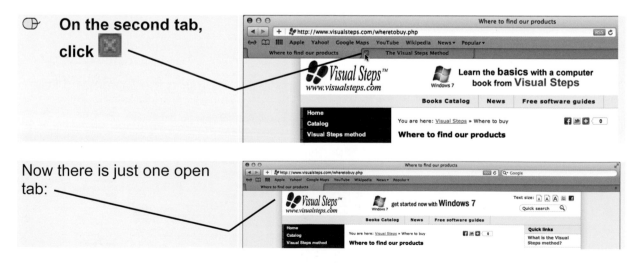

Now there is just one open tab:

In *section 4.12 Top Sites* you can read how to open a tab without having to click a link.

## 4.8 Go to Previous or Next Page

After you have opened a link, you can quickly return to the page you previously visited. Just try it:

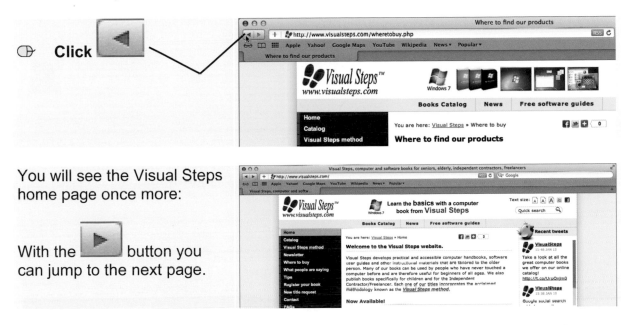

☞ **Click** [◀]

You will see the Visual Steps home page once more:

With the [▶] button you can jump to the next page.

In the *Tips* at the end of this chapter you will find an additional tip for flipping through the web pages you just visited

## 4.9 The Bookmarks Bar

In *Safari* you can add a button to the bookmarks bar for the websites you regularly visit. In this way, you can quickly access these websites whenever you want. Just take a look at the buttons that are already in place on the bookmarks bar:

You will see buttons for the *Apple*, *Yahoo!*, *Google Maps*, *YouTube*, and *Wikipedia* websites:
These buttons are called bookmarks.

☞ **Click Wikipedia**

You will see the *Wikipedia* homepage:

*Wikipedia* is an online encyclopedia, maintained and edited by Internet users.

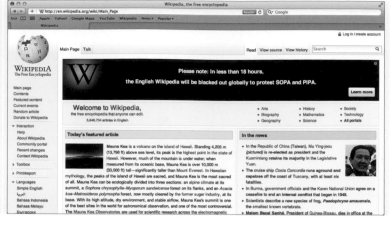

With the **News ▼** and **Popular ▼** buttons you can open a menu that contains multiple websites. Just take a look at the contents of the *News* menu:

👆 **Click News ▼**

You will see a menu with various popular news websites:

👆 **Click 🌐 CNN**

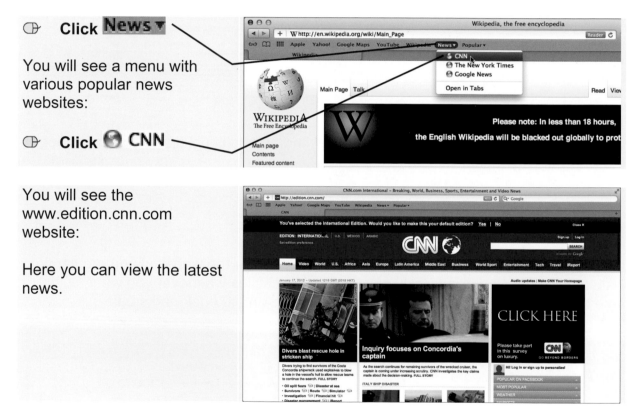

You will see the www.edition.cnn.com website:

Here you can view the latest news.

# 4.10 Adding a Bookmark to the Bookmarks Bar

You can also add a new button to the bookmarks bar yourself. You can practice doing this by adding a bookmark for the Visual Steps website:

☞ **Return to the Visual Steps website** ℰℰ³⁹

⊕ **Click** **+**

You will see a window where you can select the location for adding this bookmark. You are going to select the bookmarks bar:

⊕ **Click** ▼

⊕ **Click**
**▢ Bookmarks Bar**

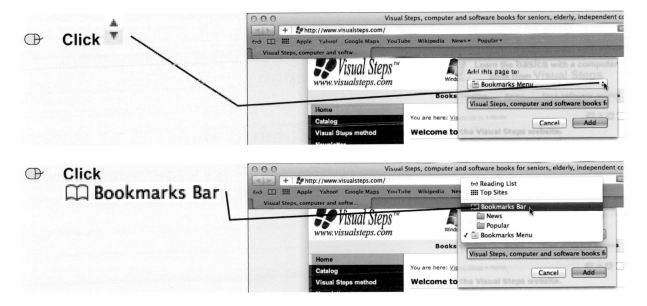

If the names of the bookmarks on the bookmarks bar are very long, you will not be able to fit a lot of bookmarks on the bar. You can shorten the names by using the Backspace key:

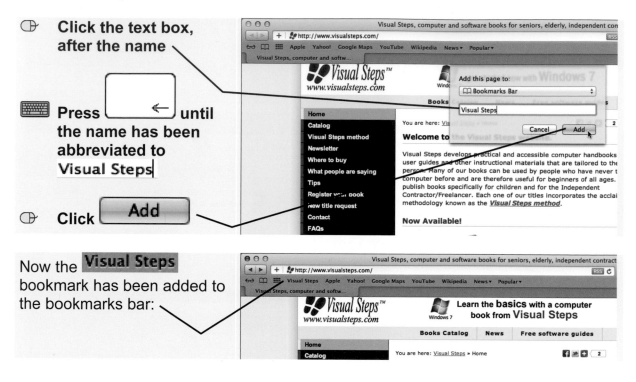

**Click the text box, after the name**

**Press** ⟵ **until the name has been abbreviated to Visual Steps**

**Click Add**

Now the **Visual Steps** bookmark has been added to the bookmarks bar:

## 4.11 Adding a Folder to the Bookmarks Bar

You can also add an entire folder to the bookmarks bar. The bookmarks in this folder will be displayed on the bar as a menu, just like the **News ▼** and **Popular ▼** folders. This is how you create a new folder:

**Click** 📖

Now the bookmarks library will be opened. This is a window in which you can create, view and arrange your bookmarks. Among other items, the bookmarks library contains the browser history, folders with bookmarks and links to the Address Book.

⊕  **If necessary, click**
   📖 **Bookmarks Bar**

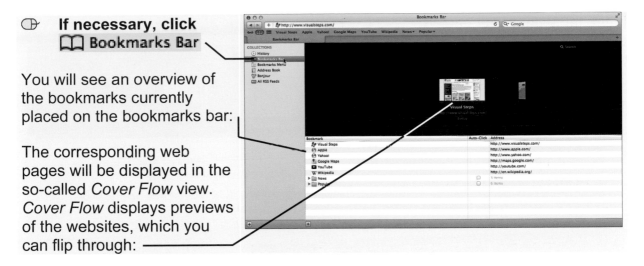

You will see an overview of
the bookmarks currently
placed on the bookmarks bar:

The corresponding web
pages will be displayed in the
so-called *Cover Flow* view.
*Cover Flow* displays previews
of the websites, which you
can flip through: ────────

In the *Tips* at the end of *Chapter 3 Working with Folders and Files in Finder* you can
read more about the *Cover Flow* view.

⊕  **Click** ➕ ──────

A new folder will be added. You can enter a name for the folder right away·

⌨  **Type:** Example ──

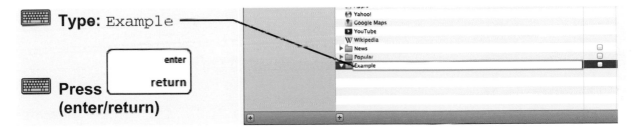

⌨  **Press**
   **(enter/return)**

The folder is ready for use. Now you are going to add the bookmark for the Visual
Steps website to this folder:

⊕  **Click** 👣 **Visual Steps**
   **and keep the mouse**
   **button/trackpad**
   **depressed** ──────

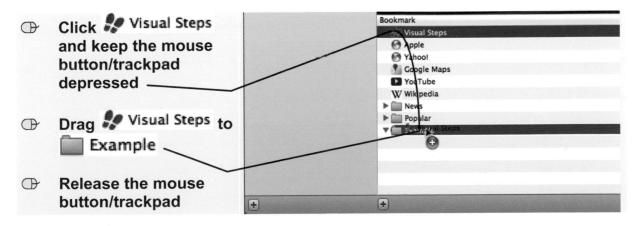

⊕  **Drag** 👣 **Visual Steps to**
   📁 **Example** ──

⊕  **Release the mouse**
   **button/trackpad**

In the bookmarks bar you will see that the Example ▾ folder has been added:

The Example folder contains the Visual Steps website:

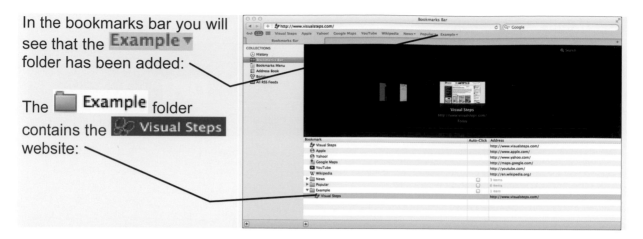

Now you can close the bookmarks library and return to the website:

👆 **Click** 📖

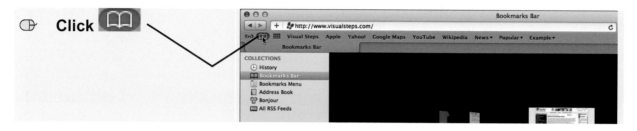

You will see the Visual Steps homepage once again.

💡 **Tip**

**Remove a bookmark or a folder from the bookmarks bar**
You can quickly remove the buttons you do not often use from the bookmarks bar:

👆 **Click** 📖
👆 **If necessary, click** 📖 **Bookmarks Bar**
👆 **Click the bookmark or folder you want to remove**

⌨ **Press** ⬑ **(Backspace)**

Now the bookmark or folder has been removed from the bookmarks bar.

If the bookmark you want to remove has been placed in a folder:

👆 **Double-click the folder**
👆 **Click the bookmark you want to remove**

⌨ **Press** ⬑ **(Backspace)**

# 4.12 Top Sites

*Safari* keeps track of your favorite websites, by monitoring your surfing behavior. These websites will be added to the *Top Sites* page. If you want to take a quick look at one of your favorite websites while reading something on another website, you can open *Top Sites* in a new tab. The default setting is to open *Top Sites* when you add a new tab:

**Click**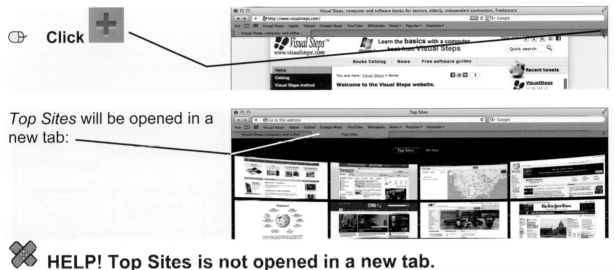

*Top Sites* will be opened in a new tab:

**HELP! Top Sites is not opened in a new tab.**
If *Top Sites* does not open automatically when you add a new tab, you can also use the Command key, like this:

**Press** command **and keep it depressed**

**Click**

In the *Tips* at the end of this chapter you can read how to change the settings for adding new tabs.

You are going to close the new tab, and then you are going to open *Top Sites* in the first tab:

**On the second tab,**
**click**

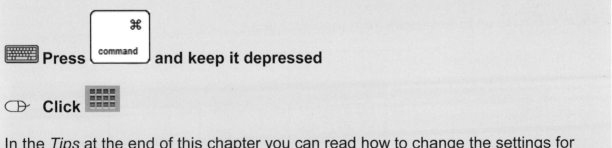

This is how you open *Top Sites* in the current tab:

**Click**

The *Top Sites* page will be opened. The page on your screen will look different than the one shown here in the screen shot. More than likely you will see some of your own frequently visited websites.

If you have not done a lot of surfing yet, *Safari* will add popular websites on its own, such as CNN and eBay:

When you start surfing a bit more, these websites will be replaced by the other websites you visit.

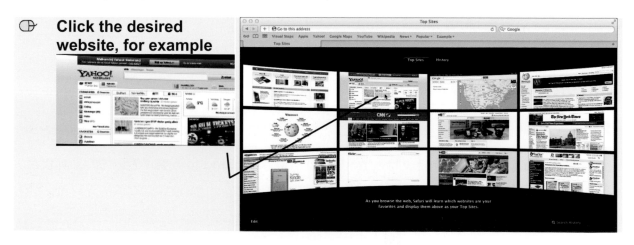

This is how you open a website from the *Top Sites*:

**Click the desired website, for example**

In this example you will see the www.yahoo.com website:

It has a search engine and links to many other topics. It is updated frequently. What you see on your screen will look different than what you see here in the example.

This will not affect the following actions.

# 4.13 Set a Homepage

The homepage is the website you first see when you open *Safari*. By default, you will see the *Apple* website. But you can also change the settings and set your own favorite website as your homepage.

☞ **Open the news.cnet.com website** ⚟ **40**

Now you will see the latest news on the CNET news site:

On your own screen, this page will look different than the example shown here.

On the menu bar, you can set this website as a homepage:

⊕ **Click Safari**

⊕ **Click Preferences...**

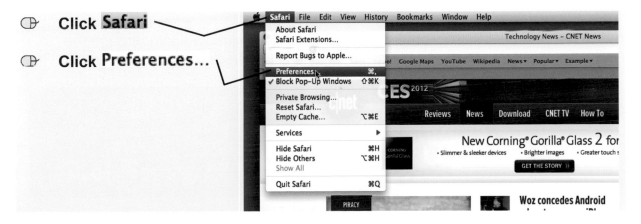

Here you see the web
address of the current
homepage:

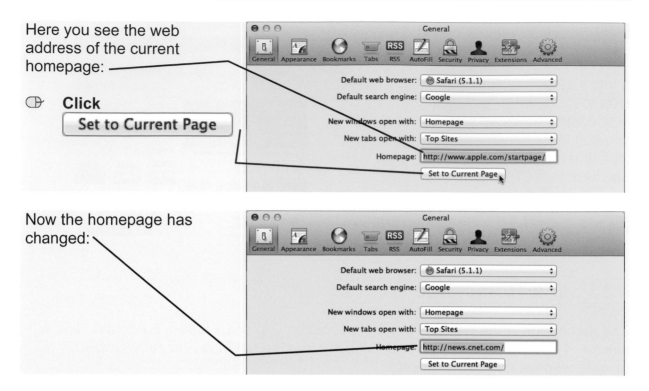

- **Click**

  **Set to Current Page**

Now the homepage has
changed:

You can close the open windows:

☞ **Close the** *General* **window** ✍13

Now you are going to open a different website, just to check if *Safari* is going to open
with the correct homepage:

☞ **Open the www.visualsteps.com website** ✍40

You will see the Visual Steps website again. Now you can close *Safari*:

☞ **Close the** *Safari* **window** ✍13

At present, *Safari* is still active. If you open the *Safari* window again through the
*Dock*, the new homepage will be displayed. You can check to verify this now:

- **Click**

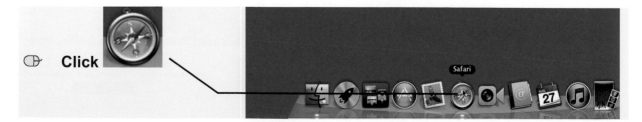

Here you will see the CNET website once again:

# 4.14 Searching

The *Safari* program contains a useful search box to help you quickly find information on all sorts of subjects. This is how you use it:

☞ **Click the search box**

Now you can type a keyword:

⌨ **For example, type:**
`magic mouse`

You will immediately see several suggestions for relevant keywords:

You can select a keyword by clicking it. For now, this is not necessary.

To use your own keyword:

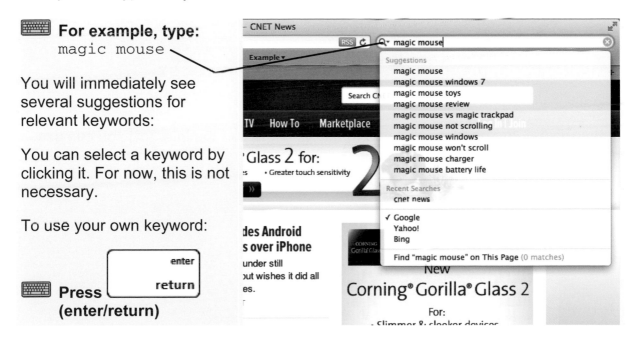

⌨ **Press (enter/return)**

Here you see the search
results:

To view a search result, just
click the link. For now, this is
not necessary.

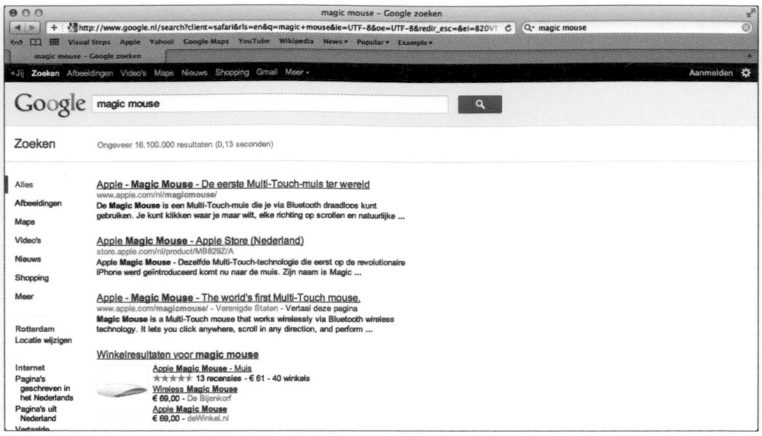

## 4.15 Quitting Safari

In *OS X*, to close an application completely, you need to explicitly tell it to quit. It is
not enough to simply close a window. This may take some getting used to, if you are
a previous *Windows* user. This is how you quit *Safari*:

☞  Click **Safari**

☞  Click **Quit Safari**

Now the *Safari* program is no longer running.

In this chapter you have learned how to use *Safari* to surf the Internet. You can use
the following exercises to practice these skills once more.

## 4.16 Exercises

To be able to quickly apply the things you have learned, you can work through these exercises. Have you forgotten how to do something? Use the numbers next to the footsteps 🐾¹ to look up the item in the appendix *How Do I Do That Again?* You will find the appendix at the end of this book.

## Exercise: View a Web Page

In this exercise you are going to view a web page in *Safari*.

☞ Open *Safari*. 🐾⁴¹

☞ Open the website at www.nytimes.com 🐾⁴⁰

☞ Zoom in on the web page. 🐾⁴²

☞ Scroll downwards, to the end of the web page. 🐾⁴³

☞ Scroll upwards, to the beginning of the web page. 🐾⁴⁴

☞ Zoom out again. 🐾⁴⁵

## Exercise: Links and Tabs

In this exercise you are going to repeat the operations with links and tabs.

☞ If necessary, open the www.nytimes.com website 🐾⁴⁰

☞ Open a link to an interesting news item. 🐾⁴⁶

☞ Return to the previous page. 🐾³⁹

☞ Open a link in a new tab. 🐾⁴⁷

☞ Display the new tab. 🐾⁴⁸

☞    Return to the first tab. 🐾⁴⁸

☞    Close the second tab. 🐾⁴⁹

## Exercise: Add a Bookmark

In this exercise you are going to add a bookmark to the bookmarks bar.

☞    Add the current www.nytimes.com web page to the bookmarks bar.
     Shorten the name of the page to *ny.com* 🐾⁵⁰

☞    Add a new folder called *Practice* to the bookmarks bar. 🐾⁵¹

☞    Move the bookmark for *ny.com* to the *Practice* folder. 🐾⁵²

☞    Move the bookmark for *ny.com* to the *News* folder. 🐾⁵²

☞    Delete the *Practice* folder. 🐾⁵³

☞    Close the bookmarks page. 🐾⁵⁴

## Exercise: Top Sites

In this exercise you are going to take another look at your *Top Sites*.

☞    Open *Top Sites*. 🐾⁵⁵

☞    Open one of the websites. 🐾⁵⁶

☞    Return to the previous page. 🐾³⁹

☞    Close the *Safari* window. 🐾¹³

☞    Open *Safari*. 🐾⁴¹

☞    Quit *Safari*. 🐾⁵⁷

# 4.17 Background Information

**Dictionary**

| | |
|---|---|
| **Bing** | Search engine manufactured by *Microsoft*. |
| **Bookmark** | A web address that is stored in a list, so you can easily retrieve a web page at a later stage. |
| **Bookmarks bar** | A toolbar that contains links to your favorite websites. |
| **Bookmarks library** | A window in which you can create, view and arrange bookmarks. |
| **Browser** | A computer program that can display web pages, for example, *Safari*. |
| **Google** | A company that develops a large number of computer applications, such as the *Google* search engine, *Google Maps* and *Google Earth*. |
| **Google Maps** | A website created by the manufacturers of the well-known *Google* search engine, where you can view maps and satellite photos, search for locations and plan trips. |
| **Homepage** | The starting or landing page of a website. The web page that is opened when you open *Safari* is also called a homepage. |
| **Hyperlink** | Also called a link. |
| **Internet** | A worldwide network of millions of computers that are connected on the basis of a general set of communication protocols. Most people are familiar with its Internet section, called the World Wide Web (usually called the Web). |
| **Link** | A link is a navigational tool on a web page that automatically leads the user to the information when clicked. A link may be displayed in a text or an image, such as a picture, a button or an icon. Also called a hyperlink. |
| **Reading list** | A feature which lets you collect web pages in a separate pane, so you can refer to them later. |

*- Continue on the next page -*

| | |
|---|---|
| **Safari** | A browser application made by *Apple*. |
| **Safari Reader** | A function in *Safari* with which you can display an article without any advertising banners, which makes it more pleasant to read. |
| **Scroll** | Moving a web page upwards, downwards, or from side to side. |
| **Scroll bar, scroll block** | A horizontal or vertical bar that appears whenever the content on a web page is greater than the size of the browser window. You can drag the scroll bar up or down, or from side to side to display the parts of the web page not in view. |
| **Surf** | Displaying one web page after the other by clicking links (hyperlinks). |
| **Top Sites** | A function in *Safari*. *Top Sites* remembers which websites you visit the most. You can open the websites on the *Top Sites* page, with a single mouse click. |
| **Web address** | Each web page has its own unique address. This address is called the Uniform Resource Locator (URL). For example, the URL for the Visual Steps homepage is **http://www.visualsteps.com** |
| **Web page** | A web page is a source of information on the World Wide Web, and can be viewed by a browser application. |
| **Website** | A website is a collection of web pages linked together. |
| **Wikipedia** | An online encyclopedia that is maintained and edited by Internet users. |
| **WWW** | (World Wide Web) A large network of computers connected to many other smaller networks located all over the world. This huge network contains an infinite number of web pages. |
| **Yahoo!** | A search engine. |
| **YouTube** | A website where the visitors can upload videos. These videos can be viewed by other visitors. |
| **Zoom in** | View an item more closely; the letters and images will become larger. |
| **Zoom out** | View an item from a distance; the letters and images will become smaller. |

*Source: Apple website, Wikipedia*

## 4.18 Tips

### 💡 Tip

**Add a bookmark to a folder on the bookmarks bar**
You can directly add a new bookmark to a folder on the bookmarks bar:

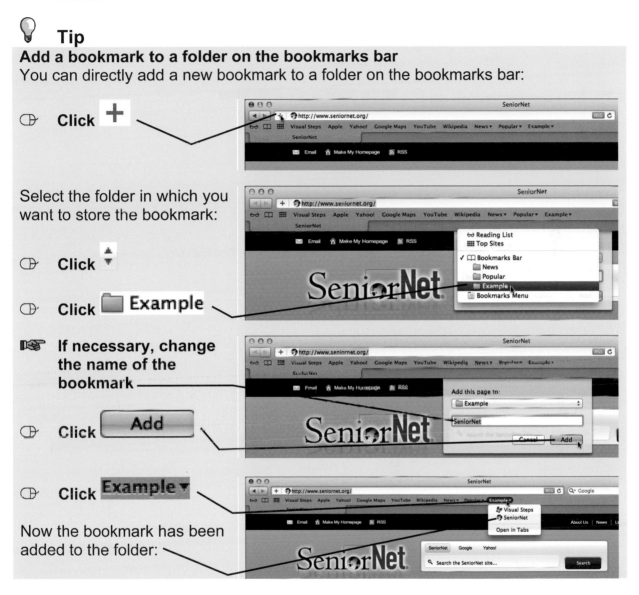

Click **+**

Select the folder in which you want to store the bookmark:

Click ⬍

Click 📁 **Example**

☞ **If necessary, change the name of the bookmark**

Click **Add**

Click **Example ▾**

Now the bookmark has been added to the folder:

### 💡 Tip

**Quickly scroll through a long page**
If you want to quickly scroll through a lengthy page, you can use a swiping movement for this. For instance, this is how you quickly scroll downwards with the Magic Mouse:

☞ **Quickly swipe upwards with one finger, over the Magic Mouse**
With a (Magic) trackpad:

☞ **Quickly swipe upwards with two fingers, over the (Magic) trackpad**
To quickly scroll downwards, make the same movement, but in the opposite direction.

### ☼ Tip
**Zoom in and zoom out with touch gestures**
If you are using a (Magic) trackpad on a MacBook Pro, you can zoom in and zoom out on websites by using touch gestures. This is how you zoom in with the (Magic) trackpad:

☞ **Move your thumb and index finger away from each other on the (Magic) trackpad**

To zoom out again, you move your thumb and index finger towards each other (pinch).

### ☼ Tip
**Quickly revert to original size**
After you have zoomed in, you can quickly revert to the website's actual size, like this:

☞ Click **View**

☞ Click **Actual Size**

The same thing can be done with the short-cut key combination Command and 0 (zero):

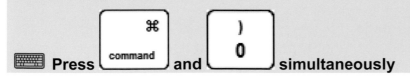
⌨ Press ⌘ command and ) 0 simultaneously

## 💡 Tip

**Directly add a new bookmark to Top Sites**
When you create a new bookmark, you can also add this bookmark to *Top Sites*, instead of to the bookmarks bar.

In the address bar:

☞ Click **+**

Now you can select where to add the bookmark:

☞ Click ⊼

☞ Click ⦂⦂⦂⦂ **Top Sites**

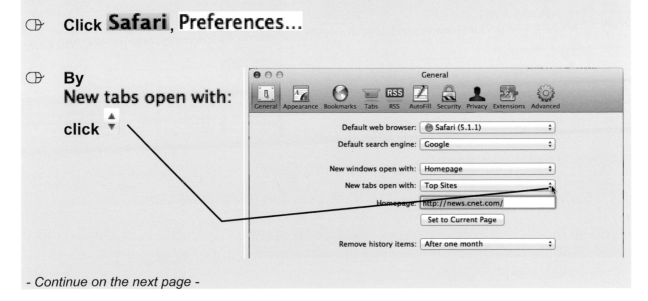

The bookmark has been added to *Top Sites*.

## 💡 Tip

**Settings for a new tab**
By default, *Top Sites* will be displayed when you open a new tab. If you do not want this, you can change the settings and select a different event for opening a new tab.

☞ Click **Safari**, **Preferences...**

☞ By
**New tabs open with:**

click ⊼

*- Continue on the next page -*

You will see a menu with various options:

You can also open a new tab with:
- the homepage you have set;
- a blank page;
- the same page, already open;
- the bookmarks page.

## 💡 Tip

**Flip through pages with touch gestures**
If you are using a Magic Mouse or a (Magic) trackpad, you can also use touch gestures to quickly flip through the pages you have visited, one after the other.

This is how you go back to the previous page with the Magic Mouse:

👉 **Swipe one finger from left to right over the Magic Mouse**

You will see that the current page is pushed to the right:

With the (Magic) trackpad:

👉 **Swipe two fingers from left to right over the (Magic) trackpad**

If you have zoomed in on the page, these touch gestures will result in displaying the left side of the page first. By repeating the same movement once again, you will return to the previous page.

## 💡 Tip

**Mark a web page as a permanent Top Site**

The pages that are displayed in *Top Sites* are constantly changing, as a result of your surfing behavior on the Internet. You can mark a web page as a permanent *Top Site*, which means it will always be displayed when you open *Top Sites*. This is how you do that:

🖰 **Click** ▦

You will see the *Top Sites* page:

🖰 **Click** Edit

In all *Top Sites* pages you will see the ⊗📌 buttons appear:

With the ⊗ button you can remove a web page from the *Top Sites*. With the thumbtack button 📌 you can "pin" a page as a *Top Site*:

🖰 **By the desired website, click** 📌

The thumbtack button has changed into 📌:

🖰 **Click** Done

Now the website will always be visible as a *Top Site*, even if you do not visit this site for a while.

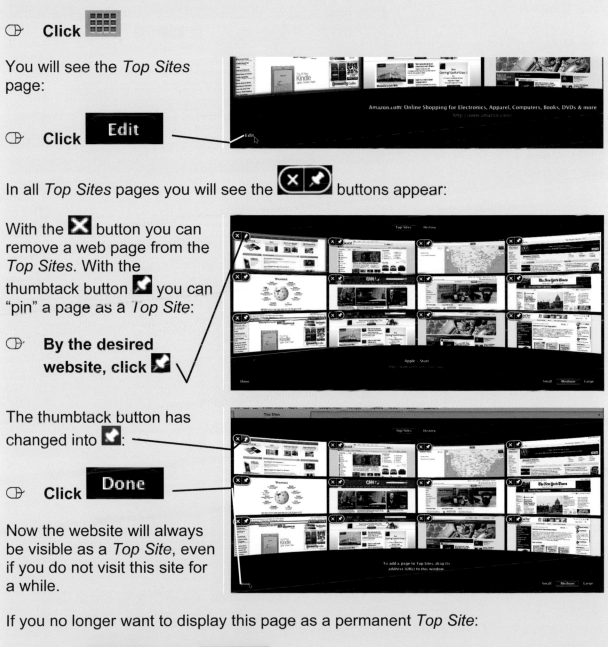

If you no longer want to display this page as a permanent *Top Site*:

🖰 **Click** Edit , 📌 , Done

## 💡 Tip

**Reading list**

Instead of bookmarks, you can also use the *Reading List*. If you come across an interesting web page while surfing, and would like to visit this page at a later stage, you can add this page to the *Reading List*. Here is how to do that:

⊕ **Click** 👓

The *Reading List* is opened on the left side of the window:

⊕ **Click** **Add Page**

A link to the web page has been added to the *Reading List*:

This is how you close the *Reading List*:

⊕ **Click** 👓

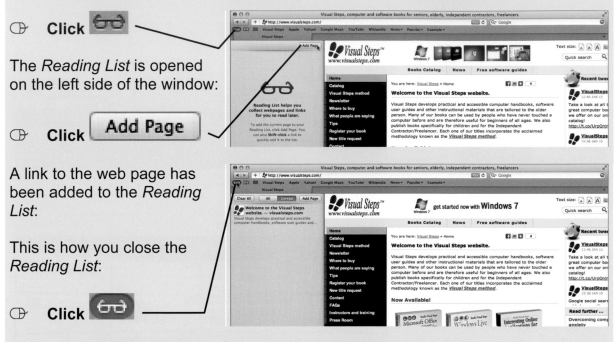

This is how you open a page you have stored in the *Reading List*:

⊕ **Click** 👓
⊕ **Click the desired page**

If the *Reading List* becomes too long, you can also delete links:

⊕ **Position the pointer on the link you want to delete**

⊕ **Click** ⊗

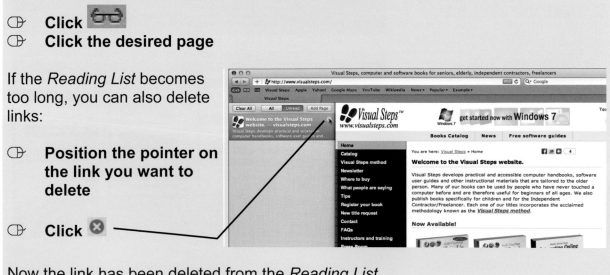

Now the link has been deleted from the *Reading List*.

## Tip

**Select a different search engine**

By default, *Safari* uses the well-known *Google* search engine. But you can also use the *Yahoo!* and *Bing* search engines:

Click

The ✓ Google search engine has been marked. If you click **Yahoo!** or **Bing**, this search engine will be selected:

## Tip

**Safari Reader**

*Safari Reader* removes all advertisements and other distracting elements from the online articles you want to read. This option will only be visible when a web page contains articles.

In this example, you will see all sorts of animated advertising banners above and next to the article:

*Safari* has identified an article on this web page. You can tell this by the **Reader** button in the address bar:

Click **Reader**

The article will be opened in a separate window, without the advertisements:

Now you can quietly read the article without being distracted.

*- Continue on the next page -*

⊕ **Move the pointer across the bottom of the window**

You will see a toolbar:

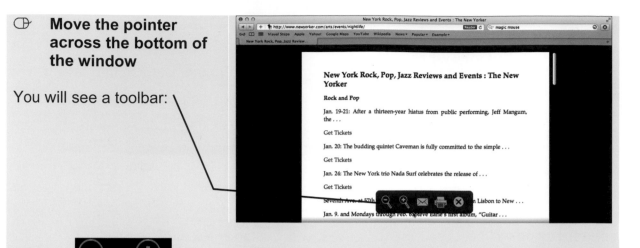

With the [buttons] buttons you can zoom in and out. If you want to render the letters a little larger by zooming in, *Safari* will remember this. Next time you open an article in *Safari Reader*, the size of the text will automatically be adjusted.

With the [X] button you can close *Safari Reader* again.

# 5. Sending E-mails with Mail

One of the most useful and frequently used applications on the Internet is the electronic mail function: *e-mail*. You simply type your message on the computer and send it to someone else, all through the Internet.

*Mac OS X* contains a simple e-mail program called *Mail* that allows you to quickly and easily send and receive e-mail messages. In this chapter you will learn how to set up your e-mail account in *Mail*. We will show you how to configure an e-mail account from Internet providers such as AOL or Verizon as well as from web-based e-mail services such as *Windows Live Hotmail* or *Gmail*. *Hotmail* accounts, for example, are e-mail addresses that end with hotmail.com or live.com. If you use multiple e-mail accounts, you can set them all up in the *Mail* e-mail program.

In this chapter we will explain the basics of how to send and receive an e-mail message. You will also learn how to add the e-mail address from a sender to your *Address Book* so that the next time you send this person a message you will no longer need to type the e-mail address.

The fun thing about e-mail is that you can send all sorts of things along with your e-mail message. For example, a text file or a picture you just made. The items you send with your e-mail message are called *attachments*. In this chapter you will also learn how to add an attachment to an e-mail and how to view and save an attachment that you have received.

In this chapter you will learn how to:

- set up your e-mail account;
- open *Mail*;
- write, send, receive and read an e-mail;
- add an e-mail address to the *Address Book*;
- send, view and save an attachment;
- delete an e-mail message;
- stop *Mail*.

## ➥ Please note:

To work through this chapter, you will need to have your own e-mail address, including a user name and a password. Your Internet provider has probably supplied this information. You may have also saved the data yourself, while creating a *Windows Live Hotmail* account.

# 5.1 Setting Up an E-mail Account

Before you can start sending e-mails, you need to set up an e-mail account. In this section you will learn how to do that with an account from your Internet Service Provider (ISP), such as AOL or Verizon. You will need to have the data provided by the ISP at hand. This includes your user name and password.
You can also add a web-based e-mail account (also called webmail) to *Mail*, for example a *Windows Live Hotmail* account. *Hotmail* is a popular e-mail service that can be accessed via an internet browser, such as *Safari*. You can send and retrieve your e-mail messages from any location in the world, as long as you are connected to the Internet.

If you have both an e-mail account from an ISP as well as a webmail account, it still can be useful to set up your webmail account in *Mail*. In that way, you can retrieve your e-mail messages in the e-mail program installed on your computer without having to go online first. In the *Tips* at the end of this chapter you can read how to add a webmail account to *Mail*.

### ➥ Please note:

If you have an e-mail account already set up, just continue reading until *section 5.2 Sending an E-mail*. You can continue with the steps again from that point on.

Now you are going to set up an account with an Internet Service Provider (ISP). First, you open the *System Preferences* in *OS X*.

☞ **Click**

Open the *Mail* settings:

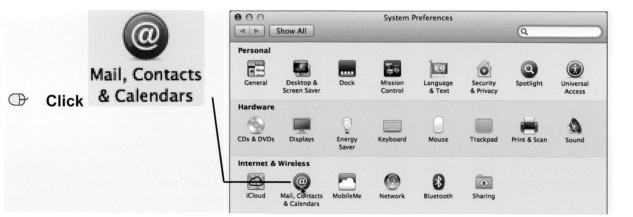

☞ **Click** **Mail, Contacts & Calendars**

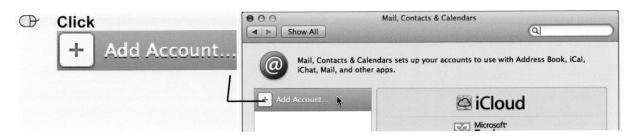

⊕ **Click**

You can choose from various pre-set templates for providers of e-mail accounts. These templates only require that you enter your user name and password. In this example, we will set up an e-mail address with an Internet Service Provider. In most cases, you will then need to select the **Other** option:

At the bottom of the window:

⊕ **Click Other**

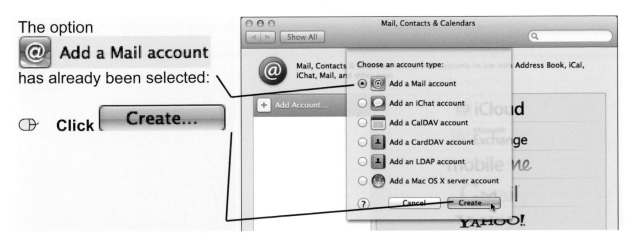

You will see a window where you can select the type of account you want to add:

The option

**Add a Mail account**

has already been selected:

⊕ **Click Create...**

In the next window you are going to enter some basic information about your e-mail account:

⌨ **If necessary, type your name**

⌨ **By Email Address:, type your e-mail address**

⌨ **By Password:, type the password**

After you have entered all the data:

☞ **Click Create...**

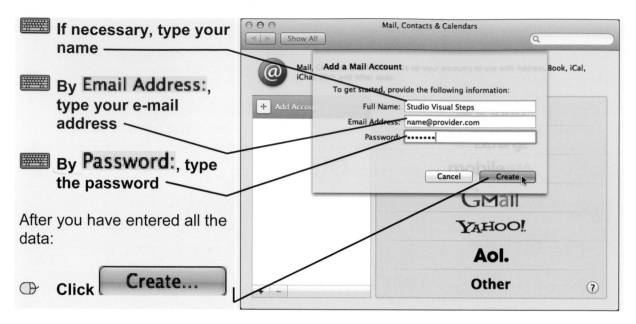

The settings for your e-mail account may be found automatically. If that does not happen:

☞ **Click Continue**

Now the *Mail* program is opened and you will see a window in which you need to enter your e-mail address and password once more:

If necessary, type your name

By Email Address:, type your e-mail address

By Password:, type the password

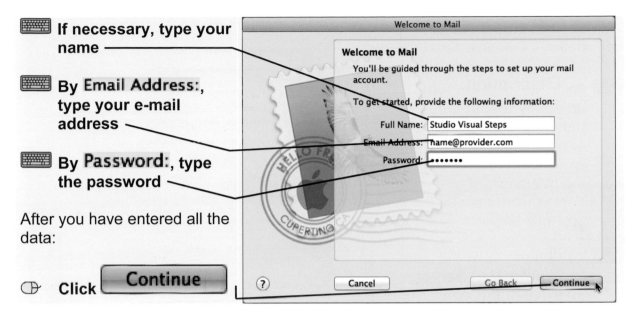

After you have entered all the data:

Click **Continue**

Now you can choose whether to set up your e-mail account as an *IMAP* or *POP* account:

- IMAP stands for *Internet Message Access Protocol*. This means that you will manage your messages on the mail server. This server is a central storage medium owned by your Internet provider. The messages you have read will be saved on the mail server, until you delete them.
  IMAP is useful if you want to view, send and manage your e-mails on multiple computers or devices, such as an iPad or tablet. Your e-mail folders (mailboxes) will look the same on each device. If you create new folders for storing your e-mail messages, these folders will appear on each computer.
  If you want to use IMAP, you will need to set up your e-mail account as an IMAP account. This will need to be done for each computer you use. You cannot use IMAP if you want to add a *Hotmail* account.
- POP stands for *Post Office Protocol*, which is the traditional way of managing e-mail messages. As soon as you retrieve your messages, most e-mail programs will delete the messages from the server and only store the messages on your own computer.
  However, the default setting for POP accounts in *Mail* is to save a copy of the message on the server, even after you have retrieved the message. This means that you can also retrieve this message on a different computer or device. In the *Tips* at the end of this chapter you can read how to modify these settings.

In this example we will set up a POP account. The procedure for setting up an IMAP account is very similar:

The 🌐 **POP** account type has already been selected:

⌨ By Description:, type an easily identifiable name for your e-mail account

Your Internet provider will have sent you the data for the incoming mail server:

⌨ **Type the Incoming Mail Server: address in the box**

⊕ **Click** Continue

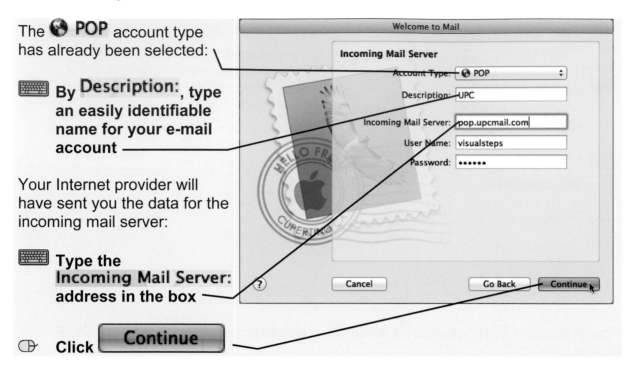

Now the connection with the mail server will be checked. You may see a window with a warning message:

⊕ **Click** Continue

Now you still need to enter the mail server's address for outgoing messages. Your Internet provider has supplied you with this data as well:

By **Outgoing Mail Server**:

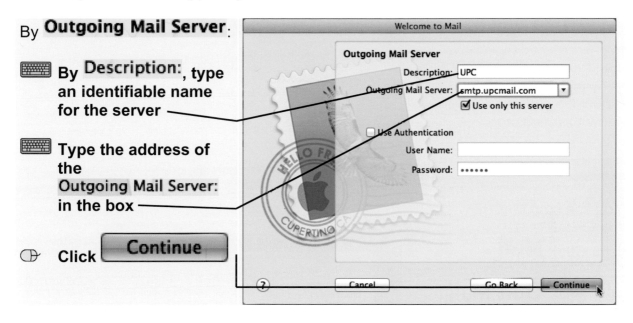

By **Description:**, type an identifiable name for the server

Type the address of the **Outgoing Mail Server:** in the box

Click **Continue**

The connection with the mail server for outgoing mail will also be verified. Afterwards you may see the window below, with the option of securing your outgoing mail through SSL, a security protocol for Internet traffic. This will not be necessary:

**If necessary, click Continue**

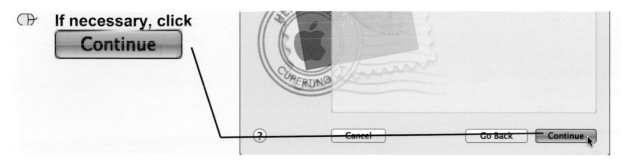

You will see the account summary where you can check the data you have entered. If everything is okay, you can create the e-mail account:

At the bottom of the window:

Click **Create...**

The e-mail account will be added.

This is what the *Mail* window looks like:

You may see some new messages arrive at once, otherwise your screen will show this message:

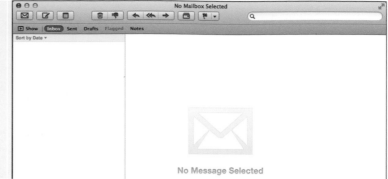

You can stop *Mail*:

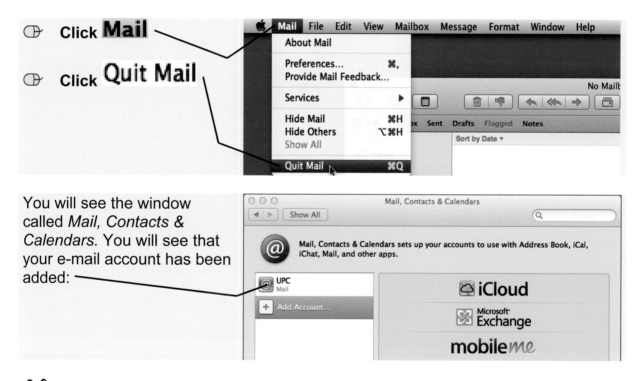

☞ Click **Mail**

☞ Click **Quit Mail**

You will see the window called *Mail, Contacts & Calendars.* You will see that your e-mail account has been added:

# 🩹 HELP! It does not work.

Many providers such as AOL and Verizon have posted instructions on their websites for setting up an e-mail account in *Mac OS X*. Look for "e-mail settings Mac" or "e-mail settings Apple mail" on your provider's website and follow the instructions that are given.

You can close the *Mail, Contacts & Calendars* window:

☞ Close the *Mail, Contacts & Calendars* window 𝒶𝒷 13

# 5.2 Sending an E-mail

Just for practice, you are going to write and send yourself an e-mail. First, you open the *Mail* program:

**Click**

The program will check for new messages right away. In this example there are no new messages found, but in your own e-mail program, it is possible that a few new messages have arrived. Now you will start a new, blank mail:

**Click**

The new message window is opened. First, you are going to add the recipient. In this example you are going to send the e-mail to your own address:

By **To:**, type your own e-mail address

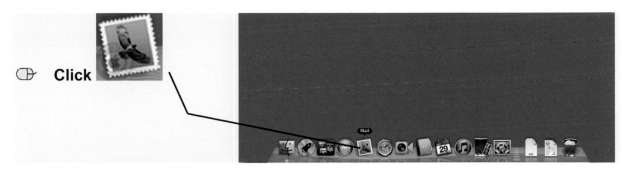

Each e-mail message has a subject:

☞ **Click the box next to**
**Subject:**

⌨ **Type:** Test

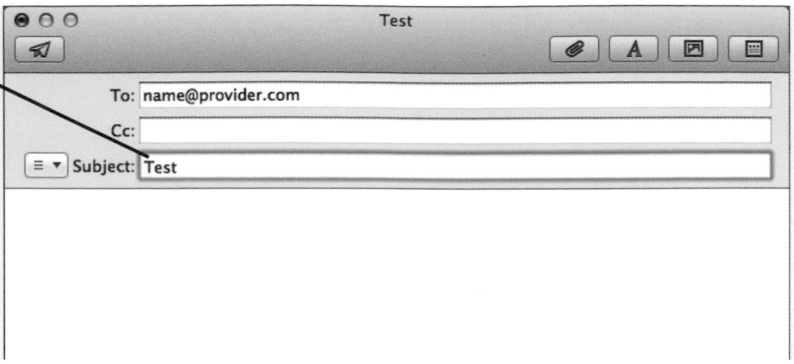

💡 **Tip**

**Select a sender**
If you have set up multiple e-mail accounts in *Mail*, you will see an extra line in the message header.
With the small arrows in the box next to **From:** you can select the e-mail address you want to use as a sender for this particular message:

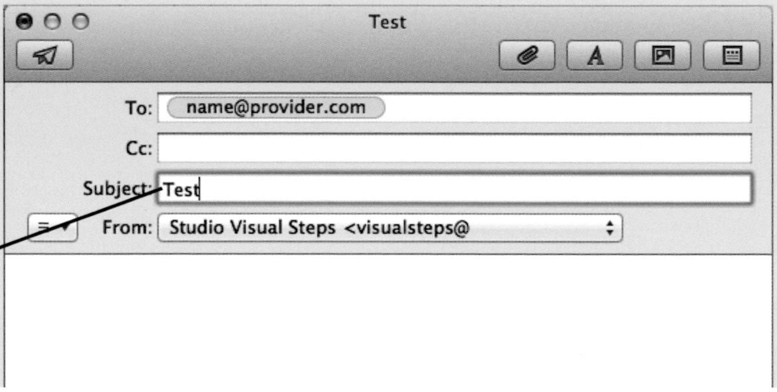

If there is a reply to your message, the answer will be sent to that e-mail address.

Now you can type your message:

☞ **Click the blank space where you want to type your message**

⌨ **Type:**
This is a test.

Continue on a new line:

⌨ **Press** enter / return

*Mac OS X* contains a dictionary which will help you while you are typing. Just see what happens when you deliberately make a spelling mistake:

**Type:** Type a speling mistike

You can correct the misspelled word very easily:

A dotted red line appears under the misspelled word **mistike**:

⊕ **Right-click the word**

⊕ **Click the correct suggested word in the list that appears**

## Tip

**Disable Autocorrection**

In the *Tips* at the end of this chapter you can read how to disable the autocorrection function during typing. **Please note:** if you do disable the autocorrection function, this will become the setting for all the other programs that allow you to type text.

Now you can send your test e-mail:

⊕ **Click** 

Your e-mail message has been sent. If the sound on your *Mac* is on, you will hear a sound signal.

## 5.3 Receiving an E-mail

Your message will be received shortly after you have sent it. You will hear a second sound signal. If you do not receive a message right away, you can retrieve your new messages in the following way:

Your e-mail message will be received and you will hear a second sound signal. This is how you go to the *Inbox* where you can find the messages you have received:

☞  Click **Inbox (1)**

## HELP! I have not received anything.

Just wait for a few minutes and click ⬚ once more.

The number on the **Inbox (1)** button displays the number of new messages. In this example there is only one new message, but you may have received multiple new messages on your own computer:

An unread message is marked by a blue dot ● next to the e-mail message:

☞  **If necessary, click the received message**

You will see the contents of the message:

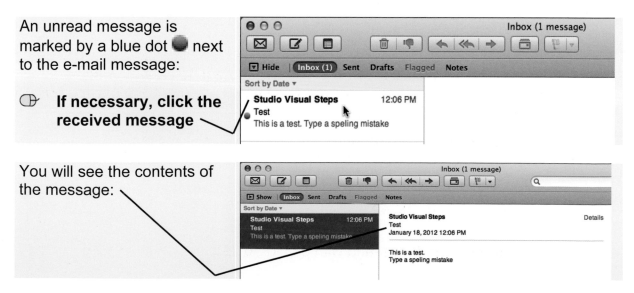

## Tip

**How many new messages are there?**
After you close the *Mail* window, the program will still be active. In the *Dock* you can

see the number of new messages you have received: .

By default, the program will check for new e-mail messages every five minutes, even when you have the program window closed (so long as you have not quit *Mail*).

You will see the main window again in *Mail*. In this window you will find a toolbar with several buttons:

.

These are the functions of the buttons:

    Retrieve new messages for all accounts.

    Write a new message.

    Open a new note.

    Move the message to the *Trash Bin*.

    Mark the selected message as unwanted junk.

    Reply to the selected message. A return e-mail message will be created with the recipient's e-mail address already entered. The original message will be sent with it.

    If there are multiple recipients, all recipients of the selected message will receive a reply. A return e-mail message will be created. Each recipient's e-mail address is already entered. The original message will be sent with it.

    Forward the selected message. The original e-mail message will be converted into a new e-mail message, which you can send to someone else.

    Show related messages.

    Mark the selected message with a colored flag.

## ➥ Please note:

In *OS X* there is no descriptive caption below the buttons, but if you move your pointer over any of the buttons, a small pop-up message will be displayed with information. You can also add text to the icons. In the *Tips* at the end of this chapter you can read more about this feature.

## 💡 Tip

### Open message in separate window

Sometimes, the message is easier to read if you open it in a separate window. This is how you do that:

☞ **Double-click the message**

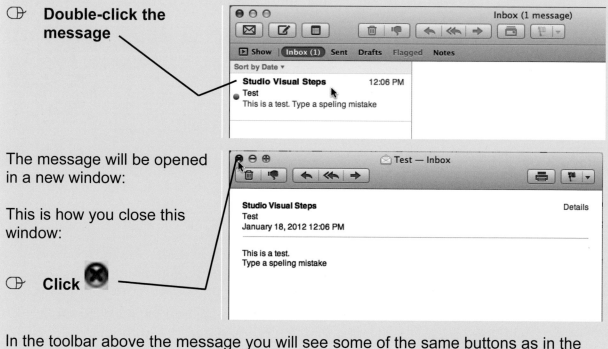

The message will be opened in a new window:

This is how you close this window:

☞ **Click** ✖

In the toolbar above the message you will see some of the same buttons as in the main window of the *Mail* program. But you have not seen the [🖶] button before. With this button you can print a message.

## 5.4 Adding a Sender to the Address Book

If you add the sender of an e-mail message you received to your *Address Book*, you will not need to type the address of this person every time you want to send a new e-mail. You can simply select the address from your *Address Book*. The e-mail you just sent to yourself is still selected. This is how you add your own address to the *Address Book*:

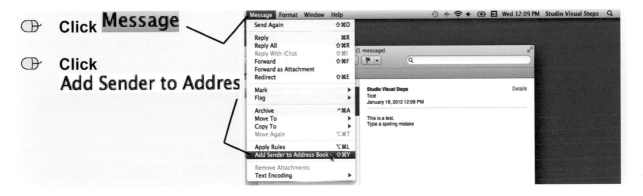

☞ Click **Message**

☞ Click **Add Sender to Addres**

The e-mail address will be added to the address book. In the next section you will use the e-mail address from the *Address Book* to send a new e-mail.

## 5.5 Sending an E-mail with an Attachment

The nice thing about e-mail is that you can send all sorts of items along with your e-mail message. For example, you can send a photo, drawing or a document. An item that is sent along with an e-mail message is called an *attachment*. Now you are going to open a new message and add an attachment:

☞ Open a new e-mail message 🦶58

You can add the e-mail address in the *Address Panel*. This is how you open the *Address Panel*:

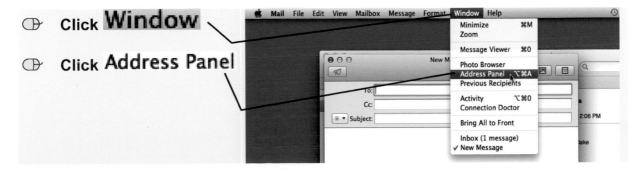

☞ Click **Window**

☞ Click **Address Panel**

## 💡 Tip

**Open the Address Panel with a key combination**
It is quicker to open the *Address Panel* with the short-cut key combination
Command, Alt and A:

The *Address Panel* will be opened. You will see your own address if you have added this in the previous section. Select your own e-mail address:

👆 **Click your e-mail address**

👆 **Click** To:

The e-mail address will be entered in the new message:

You will only see the name of the recipient:

Now you can close the address panel:

👆 **Click** ✖

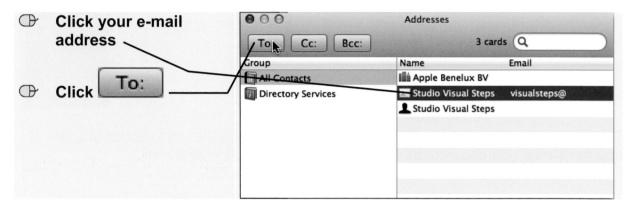

Add a subject:

☞ **Add this subject:** Test with attachment ✀**59**

Type a short message:

### ☞ **Add the following text** ✂60

```
Here is the letter about the brunch.

Kind regards,
(Your name)
```

To add an attachment to your e-mail, you can use the button with the paperclip icon:

⊕ **Click**

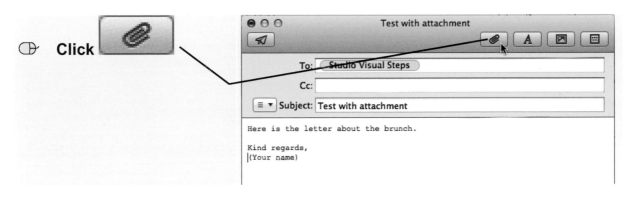

By default, the *Documents* folder will be opened. You are going to add a letter you have written in one of the previous chapters:

⊕ **If necessary, click**

⊕ **Click brunch letter.rtf**

⊕ **Click Choose File**

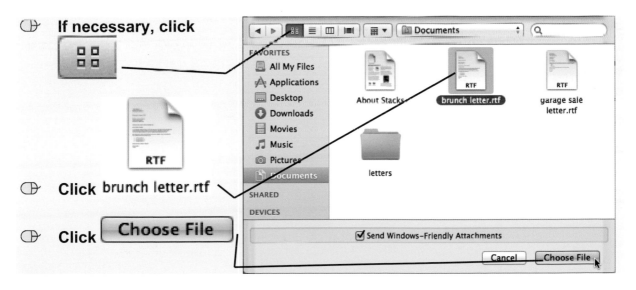

### 🩹 **HELP! I do not have this file.**

If you have not saved the file called *brunch letter.rtf*, you can also select a different document, for instance *garage sale letter*. This will not make any difference for this exercise.

You will see that the attachment is inserted at the spot where the cursor is:

| | Test with attachment |
|---|---|
| To: | Studio Visual Steps |
| Cc: | |
| Subject: | Test with attachment |

Here is the letter about the brunch.

Kind regards,

(Your name) brunch letter.rtf (2 KB)

It is better to insert a blank line first. This looks a bit tidier:

**Click between your name and the attachment**

enter

**return**

**Press twice**

Now the attachment is placed a little lower in the message:

| | Test with attachment |
|---|---|
| To: | Studio Visual Steps |
| Cc: | |
| Subject: | Test with attachment |

Here is the letter about the brunch.

Kind regards,
(Your name)

brunch letter.rtf (2 KB)

You can send the e-mail:

☞ **Send the e-mail** ✂︎⁶¹

# 5.6 Opening and Saving an Attachment

You may receive the e-mail right away. If this is not the case:

☞ **Retrieve your new messages** &⁶²

The e-mail with the attachment is received:

The paperclip ✐ indicates
that the e-mail contains an
attachment:

⊕ **Click the message**

You will see the contents of
the message and the
attachment:

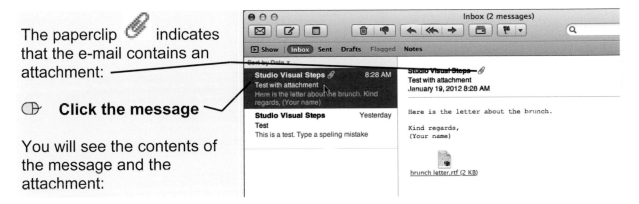

This is how you can quickly view the message:

⊕ **Click Details**

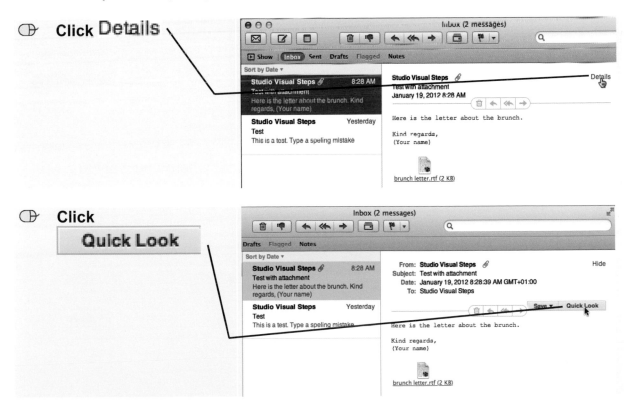

⊕ **Click**

**Quick Look**

You will see the contents of the attachment:

You can close this window:

⊕   **Click**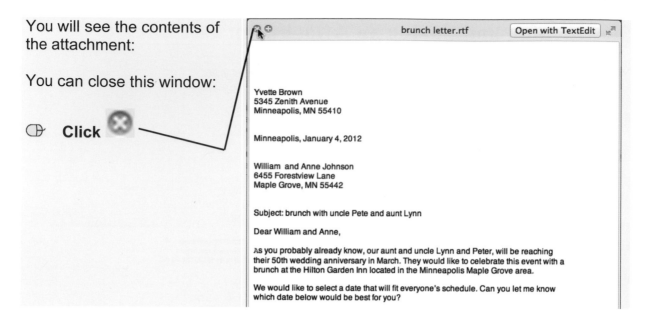

If you want to save the attachment:

⊕   **By** Save ▼ , click ▼

⊕   **Click** 📄 brunch letter.rtf

Now you can rename the attachment and select the folder where you want to save the file:

⌨   **Type:**
attachment.rtf

⊕   **Click** 📁 Downloads

In the list displayed, select the *Documents* folder to save the attachment:

⊕ **Click**
**📄 Documents**

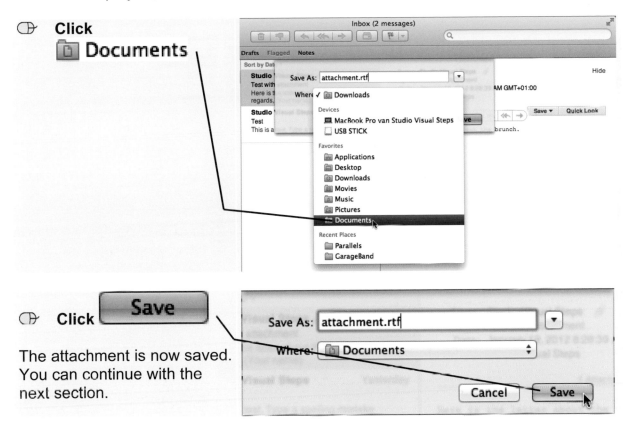

⊕ **Click** **Save**

The attachment is now saved.
You can continue with the
next section.

## 5.7 Deleting an E-mail

If you want to keep your *Inbox* tidy, you can delete all the old messages you no
longer need. You can try that now:

⊕ **If necessary, click the**
**message with the**
**attachment again**

⊕ **Click** 🗑

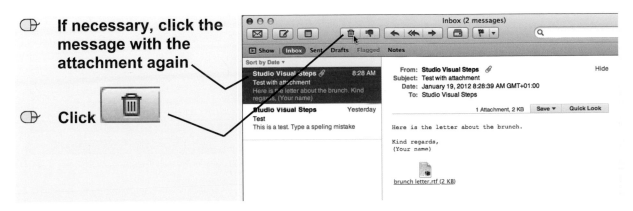

The message has been moved to the *Trash* mailbox:

In this example there is still one message left in the *Inbox*: ———

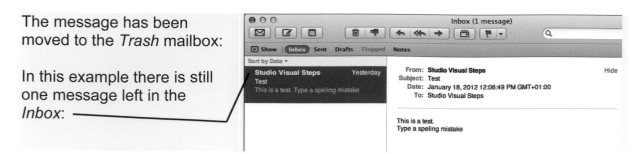

You can view the contents of the *Trash* mailbox like this:

👉 Click **▶ Show**

You will see an extra column in the *Mail* window, displaying various mailboxes:

You will see the *Inbox, Sent* and *Trash* mailboxes: ↘

👉 Click 🗑 **Trash**

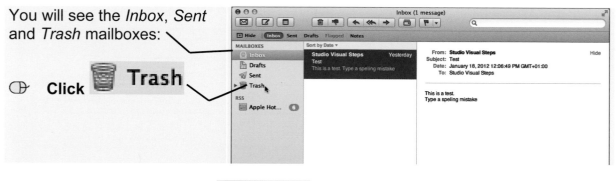

**HELP! I do not see** 🗑 **Trash**.

If you do not see the *Trash* mailbox, you may have to open the program, once more.

👉 **Stop** *Mail* 👣⁷⁴

👉 **In the** *Dock*, **click** 🏞

The deleted message has been moved to the *Trash* mailbox:

## 💡 Tip

**Empty Trash mailbox automatically**
By default, the messages in the *Trash* mailbox will be removed automatically after one month. In the *Tips* at the end of this chapter you can read how to change this setting.

This is how you permanently delete all the messages in the *Trash* mailbox:

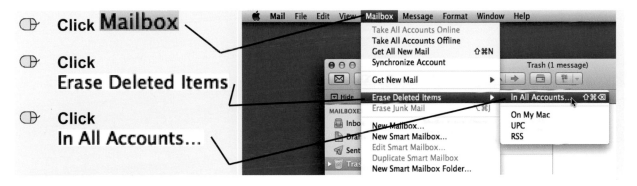

☞  Click **Mailbox**

☞  Click
    **Erase Deleted Items**

☞  Click
    **In All Accounts...**

You will see a warning message. If you really want to delete all the messages in the *Trash* mailbox for good:

☞  Click  **Erase**

> **Are you sure you want to erase deleted items in the Trash mailbox?**
>
> Erasing deleted items such as messages, notes, and mailboxes permanently deletes them. This action cannot be undone.
>
> Cancel    Erase

Now the *Trash* mailbox is empty.

## 5.8 Stop Mail

Now you can close the *Mail* window:

**☞ Close the *Mail* window** ✻¹³

*Mail* will still remain active. You can tell this by the luminous globe below the

icon. Every five minutes, the program will continue to check for new messages.

If you want to stop *Mail* altogether:

You have learned how to send and receive e-mail messages. In the following exercises you can practice these actions once more.

# 5.9 Exercises

To be able to quickly apply the things you have learned, you can work through these exercises. Have you forgotten how to do something? Use the numbers next to the footsteps ℗¹ to look up the item in the appendix *How Do I Do That Again?* You will find the appendix at the end of this book.

## Exercise: Send an E-mail with an Attachment

In this exercise you are going to send an e-mail message and attach the document called *letter* to the message. In *Chapter 3 Working with Folders and Files in Finder* you created this document and stored it in the *letters* folder. If you have not done this, you can select a different text file as an attachment.

☞ Open *Mail.* ℗⁶³

☞ Open a new e-mail message. ℗⁵⁸

☞ Add your own e-mail address with the *Address Panel.* ℗⁶⁴

☞ Close the *Address Panel.* ℗¹³

☞ Enter the following subject for this message: E-mail with attachment. ℗⁵⁹

☞ Enter this text: ℗⁶⁰
Hereby I send you the text file.
Kind regards,
(Your name)

☞ Add the text file called *letter* from the *letters* folder, as an attachment. ℗⁶⁵

☞ Insert two blank lines between your name and the attachment. ℗⁶⁶

☞ Send the e-mail message. ℗⁶¹

## Exercise: Receive and View an E-mail with an Attachment

☞  Check for new messages. $\wp\wp^{62}$

☞  If necessary, open the *Inbox*. $\wp\wp^{67}$

☞  Open the message with the attachment. $\wp\wp^{68}$

☞  View the attachment. $\wp\wp^{69}$

☞  Close the window with the attachment. $\wp\wp^{13}$

☞  Save the attachment in the *Documents* folder with the name:
    letter as an attachment $\wp\wp^{70}$

## Exercise: Delete an E-mail

☞  Move the e-mail message to the *Trash* mailbox. $\wp\wp^{71}$

☞  View the contents of the *Trash* mailbox. $\wp\wp^{72}$

☞  Delete all the messages in the *Trash* mailbox. $\wp\wp^{73}$

## Exercise: Stop Mail

☞  Close the *Mail* window. $\wp\wp^{13}$

☞  Quit *Mail*. $\wp\wp^{74}$

# 5.10 Background Information

**Dictionary**

| | |
|---|---|
| **Account** | A combination of a user name and a password, that provides access to a particular private service. A subscription with an Internet Service Provider (ISP) is also called an account. |
| **Address Book** | An *OS X* program that lets you save, view and change the data of your contacts. |
| **Address Panel** | A window in *Mail* where you can select an e-mail address for the e-mail message you want to send. |
| **AOL** | Short for *America Online*, a well-known American Internet provider. |
| **Attachment** | Documents, images and other files that are sent with an e-mail message. You can recognize a message that contains an attachment by the paperclip icon. |
| **E-mail** | Short for *electronic mail*. These are messages sent through the Internet. |
| **E-mail account** | The server name, user name, password and the e-mail address that are used by *Mail* to connect to an e-mail service. |
| **Gmail** | Free e-mail service provided by the manufacturers of the well-known *Google* search engine. |
| **Hotmail** | Free e-mail service, part of *Windows Live Essentials*. |
| **IMAP** | IMAP stands for *Internet Message Access Protocol*. This means that you manage your e-mail messages on the mail server. The messages you have read will remain stored on the mail server, until you delete them. IMAP is useful when you manage your e-mail messages on multiple computers. Your mailbox will look the same on each computer or device. If you create new folders to organize your messages, these same folders will be visible on each computer. If you want to use IMAP, you will need to set up your e-mail account as an IMAP account on each individual computer or device. IMAP cannot be used with *Hotmail* accounts. |

*- Continue on the next page -*

| | |
|---|---|
| **Inbox** | A mailbox in *Mail* in which you can view received messages. |
| **Internet Service Provider** | A company that provides access to the Internet, usually for a fee. The usual way of connecting to an Internet Service Provider (also just called provider or ISP) is through a broadband connection, such as a fixed cable connection or DSL. Many Internet providers offer additional services, such as e-mail accounts, spam filters and space to host a website. |
| **Mail** | A program in *OS X* that lets you send and receive e-mail messages. |
| **Mailbox** | A folder in *Mail*. *Mail* contains default mailboxes called *Inbox*, *Sent* and *Trash*. |
| **POP** | POP stands for *Post Office Protocol*, which is the traditional method for managing e-mail messages. When you retrieve your e-mail, the messages are usually immediately deleted from the server. But the default setting for POP accounts in *Mail* is for saving a copy on the server after the message has been retrieved, for one week. This means you have enough time to retrieve this message on your computer or on a different device. |
| **Provider** | See Internet Service Provider. |
| **Sent** | A mailbox in *Mail* where the messages you sent are stored. |
| **Synchronize** | Literally: make the same. You can synchronize the contents of your *Mail* folders with the contents on the mail server of your provider. You can also do this for multiples devices at once, for example, on your iPad or iPhone. |
| **System preferences** | In the *System Preferences* window you can view and change your computer's settings. The sections in the window are divided into categories, such as the Dock, Sound, Mouse and General. |
| **Trash** | A mailbox in *Mail*, where the deleted messages are stored. A message is only permanently deleted after you have deleted it from the *Trash* mailbox. By default, the messages in the *Trash* mailbox from *Mail* are deleted after one month. |
| **Yahoo!** | A search engine that also offers free e-mail services. |

*Source: Apple Dictionary, Wikipedia*

# 5.11 Tips

## 💡 Tip

**Set up a Hotmail account in Mail**
If you have a *Windows Live Hotmail* account, you can also set up this account in *Mail*:

☞ **Click File**

☞ **Click Add Account...**

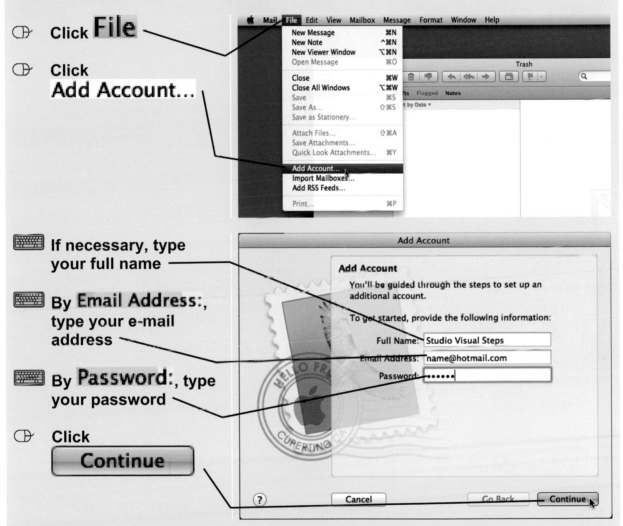

⌨ **If necessary, type your full name**

⌨ **By Email Address:, type your e-mail address**

⌨ **By Password:, type your password**

☞ **Click Continue**

**Please note:** if you have an e-mail address that ends with *hotmail.com*, the settings of your e-mail account will automatically be found. The account will be added. In this case, you can skip the rest of this tip.

*- Continue on the next page -*

⌨ By Description:, type
an identifiable name
for your e-mail
account

⌨ By
Incoming Mail Server:,
type: pop3.live.com

⌨ By User Name:, type
your full e-mail
address

⊕ Click

**Continue**

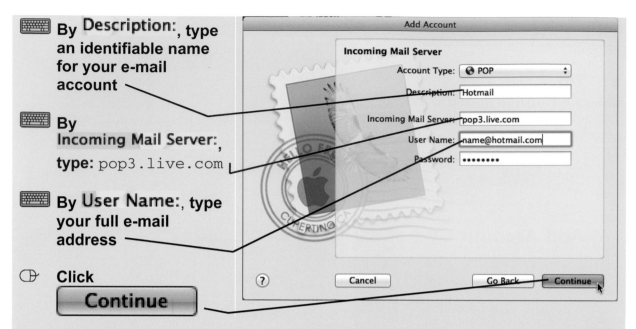

The connection to the mail server will be verified: Now you still need to enter the mail server's address for outgoing mail:

By **Outgoing Mail Server**.

⌨ By Description:, type
an identifiable name
for the server

⌨ By
Outgoing Mail Server:,
type: smtp.live.com

⊕ Click

**Continue**

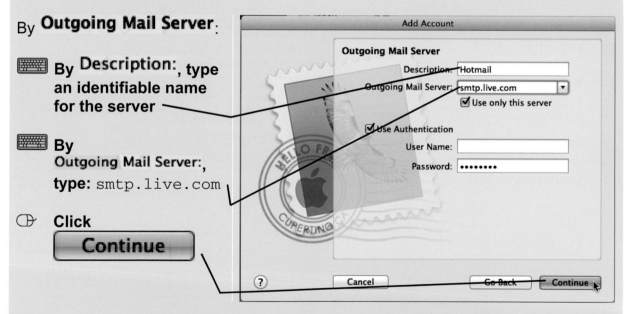

Now the connection with the outgoing mail server will also be verified.
Afterwards you will see your account summary, where you can check the data you have entered.

*- Continue on the next page -*

If all the information is correct, you can create the e-mail account:

☞ **Click**

   **Create**

The e-mail account will be created.

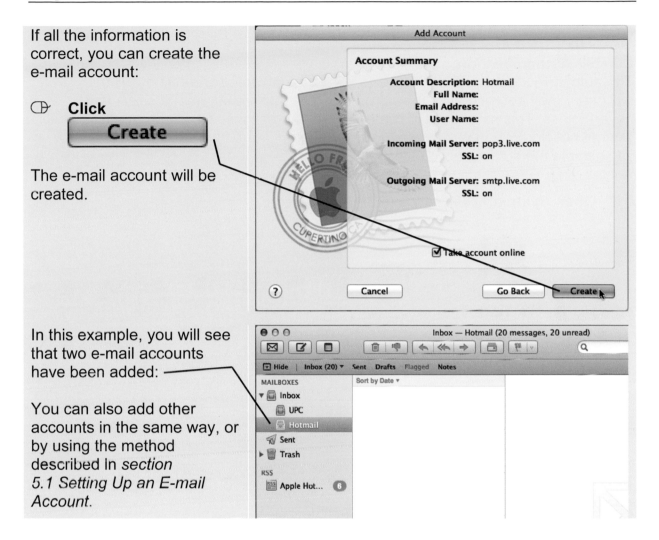

In this example, you will see that two e-mail accounts have been added: ——

You can also add other accounts in the same way, or by using the method described In *section 5.1 Setting Up an E-mail Account*.

## ♀ Tip
**Disable Autocorrection**
The autocorrection function in *OS X* may lead to unwanted corrections. The dictionary may not recognize the words you type, but will suggest a correction nevertheless. This may result in some strange corrections, which you might accept without noticing, when you type a full stop, a comma or a blank space. This is how you disable the autocorrection function:

☞ **Open** *System Preferences* ⚹⁷⁵

**Language & Text**

⊕ **Click**

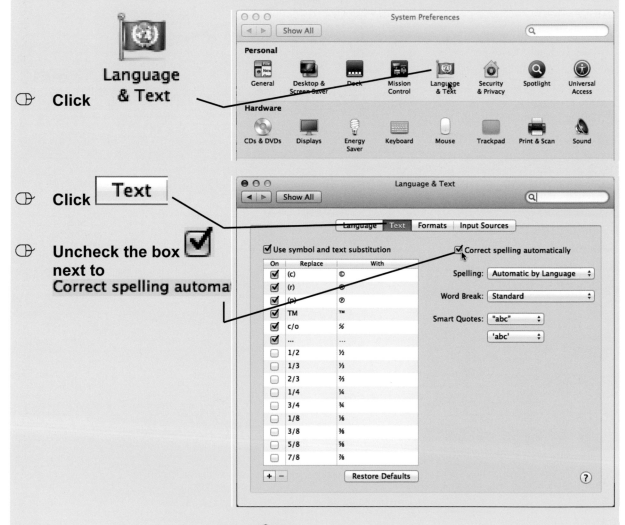

⊕ **Click** Text

⊕ **Uncheck the box** ☑
**next to**
**Correct spelling automati**

☞ **Close** *System Preferences* ⚹¹³

Now the text will no longer be corrected while you are typing.

## 🔆 Tip
### Search the text of the e-mail messages
If you search with *Spotlight*, the program will also search the text of the e-mail messages in your mailboxes:

In this example we have searched for the word "spelling mistake":

Two messages have been found:

These are the two e-mail messages you have sent and received.

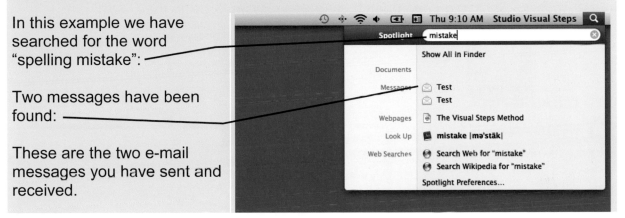

## 🔆 Tip
### Add text to the Mail buttons
Do you have trouble remembering the functions of the buttons on the *Mail* toolbar? By using the Control key, you can easily add text to these buttons:

⌨️ **Press** `control` **and keep the key depressed**

🖱️ **Click a blank area on the toolbar**

🖱️ **Click** **Icon and Text**

Now a descriptive text will appear below the buttons:

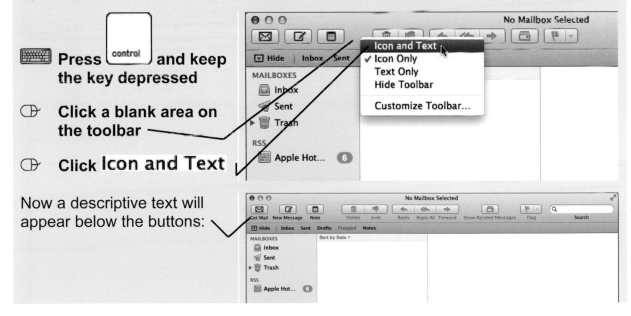

## Tip

**Use the Address Book**
In this chapter you have added an e-mail address to the *Address Book*. Apart from
e-mail addresses, you can also store home address information and phone numbers
in the *Address Book*. You can open the *Address Book* through the *Dock*:

⊕  **Click**

The *Address Book* is opened.
It looks like this:

You will see your own name
and e-mail address:

You can add extra
information:

⊕  **Click** Edit

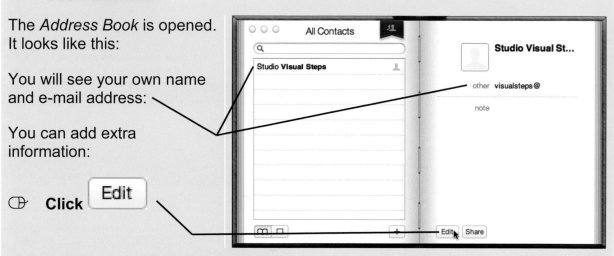

For instance, you can add a phone number:

⊕  **By** work **, click**
**Phone**

⌨  **Type the phone**
**number**

In the same way you can
enter other data. After you
have finished entering data:

⊕  **Click** Done

Use the ⊞ button to add new contacts.

## 💡 Tip

### Save e-mail messages on the server or not?

For POP e-mail accounts, you can set your own preferences for saving a copy of the incoming messages on the mail server. If a copy is saved, you can also retrieve the message on your desktop computer or iPad, after you have received the message on your laptop, for example. This is how you can change the *Mail* settings:

☞ **Click Mail**

☞ **Click Preferences...**

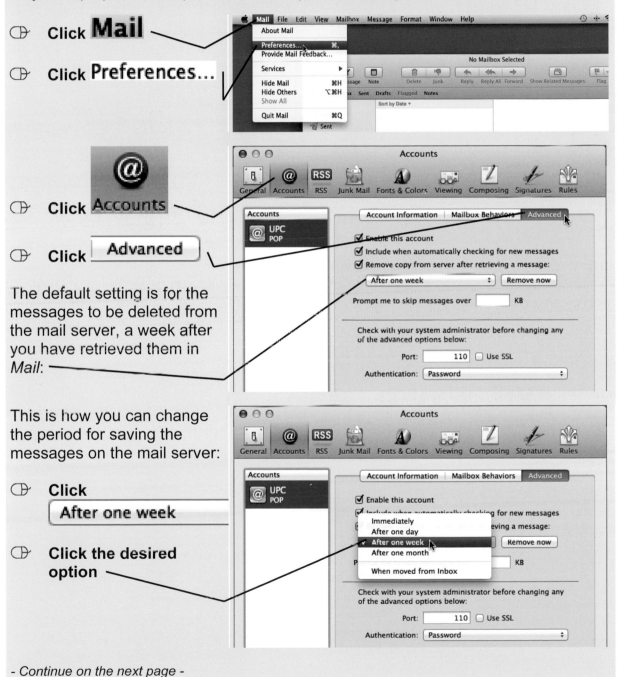

☞ **Click Accounts**

☞ **Click Advanced**

The default setting is for the messages to be deleted from the mail server, a week after you have retrieved them in *Mail*:

This is how you can change the period for saving the messages on the mail server:

☞ **Click**
**After one week**

☞ **Click the desired option**

*- Continue on the next page -*

If you do not want to automatically delete the messages from the mail server:

☞ **Uncheck the box** ☑️
   **next to**
   **Remove copy from** s

☞ **Click** ⦿

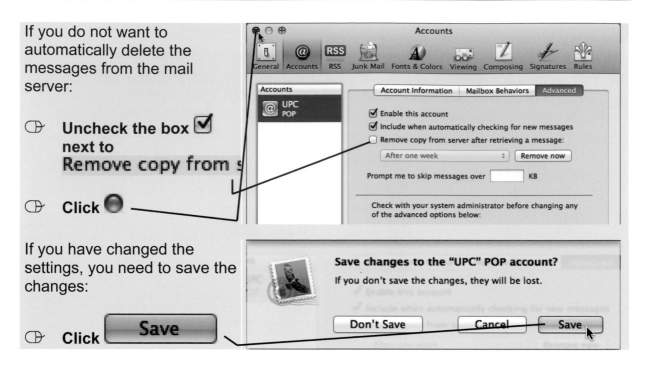

If you have changed the settings, you need to save the changes:

☞ **Click** **Save**

## 💡 Tip

**Automatically empty the Trash mailbox or not?**

By default, the messages in the *Trash* mailbox are automatically deleted after one month. You can change this period of time, or choose not to empty the *Trash* mailbox automatically:

☞ Click **Mail**, **Preferences...**, **@Accounts**

☞ **Click**
   **Mailbox Behaviors**

The messages you delete will be moved to the *Trash* mailbox:

Here you can select the options for permanently deleting the messages in the *Trash* mailbox: never, after a day, a week, a month or after you have stopped the *Mail* program:

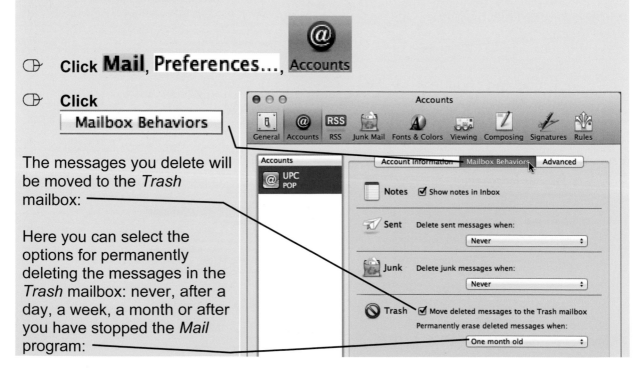

## 💡 Tip

### Conversations

*Mail* will automatically group the messages from a thread with a particular contact, on a particular subject. This makes your mailbox easy to manage. A group of messages is called a *conversation*.

In this example, the conversation consists of 2▶ messages:

⊕ **Click the message**

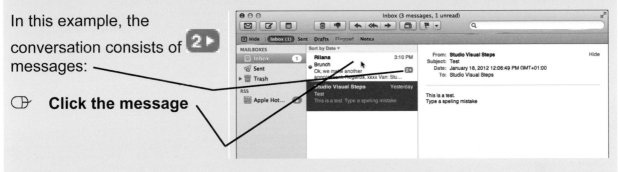

In a conversation, only the received messages will be counted. The messages sent by you will not be counted. In this example, the contact has sent three e-mail messages on the same subject.

The messages are displayed one below the other. The most recent message is at the top:

The messages are numbered. The last message has number **2**:

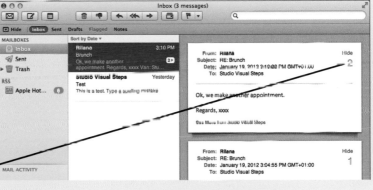

A huge advantage of these conversations is, that *Mail* will hide repeated occurrences of the same text in messages, such as e-mail signatures. As a result, you will only see the parts of the conversation that are important to you.

If you would like to see the entire message after all:

⊕ **Click**
**See More** from Studi

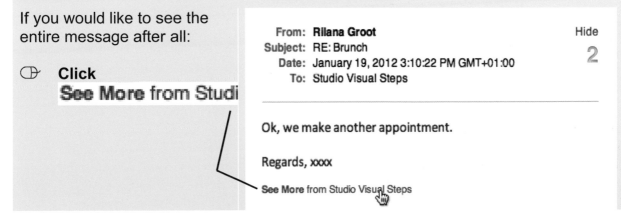

| | |
|---|---|
| From: **Rilana Groot** | Hide |
| Subject: RE: Brunch | **2** |
| Date: January 19, 2012 3:10:22 PM GMT+01:00 | |
| To: Studio Visual Steps | |

Ok, we make another appointment.

Regards, xxxx

See More from Studio Visual Steps

# Notes

Write your notes down here.

# 6. Photos, Videos and Music

Your *Mac* has a multitude of built-in programs for handling all of your photo, video and music needs. This chapter covers the basic functionality of *iPhoto, iTunes, QuickTime Player* and *DVD Player*.

The *iPhoto* program lets you transfer (import) photos from your digital camera, iPhone, iPad or iPod touch to your *Mac*. In *iPhoto* you can organize the imported photos by events or by persons.

*iPhoto* also has various options for editing photos. You will learn how remove red eye and how to use the Enhance tool. We will also explain how to crop or straighten a photo and we will introduce you to some of the other options available such as applying effects to your photos.

The *iTunes* program is a very extensive music player for your *Mac*. You can use it to import a CD, play music and purchase new music.

With the *QuickTime Player* program you can play a video file. And you can use the *DVD Player* program to play a DVD. We will show you how to navigate the menu on a DVD and how to play the DVD.

In this chapter you will learn how to:

- import, organize and edit photos with *iPhoto*;
- import a CD and play music with *iTunes*;
- play a video file with *QuickTime Player*;
- play a DVD with *DVD Player*.

### ➥ Please note:

If you want to follow the steps shown in the examples in *section 6.1 Importing Photos with iPhoto* and *6.2 Safely Disconnect the Camera*, you will need to have a digital camera, iPhone, iPad or iPod touch with a few photos stored on the device. If you do not own these items, you can just read through the sections and continue later with the steps in *section 6.3 Organizing Photos by Event*.

### ➥ Please note:

If you are using a MacBook Air or a Mac mini, you will not have a CD/DVD player. In this case, you can just read through the sections about playing a CD or DVD.

**⤷ Please note:**

To work with the section of this chapter that handles *iTunes* and *DVD Player* you will need to have a music CD and a movie or TV series DVD. If you do not have these items, you can just read through the section.

## 6.1 Importing Photos with iPhoto

When you *import* a file, this means you will be transferring it from some other device to your *Mac*. If you want to import the photos from your digital camera, iPhone, iPad or iPod touch, you will need to connect the device to your *Mac* first. For connecting the device you can use a USB cable, for example:

☞ **Connect the digital camera with the cable included in the camera packaging. Insert the other end of the cable into the USB port on your *Mac*. Now turn the camera on.**

With your iPhone, iPad or iPod touch you can use the white Dock Connector-to-USB-cable included in the package:

☞ **Connect the wide end of the white Dock Connector-to-USB-cable to your iPhone, iPad or iPod touch**

☞ **Connect the opposite end to one of the USB ports on your *Mac***

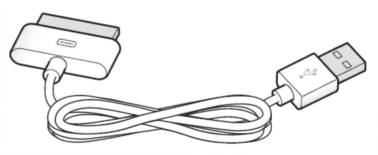

*Source: iPad 2 User Guide*

**💡 Tip**

**USB ports**
You can refer to *section 3.12 Copying to a USB Stick* for more information about the location of the USB ports on your *Mac*.

If you are using an iMac and your digital camera is equipped with an SD memory card, you can insert the SD card directly into the SD card reader.

The SD card reader is located on the right-hand side of the monitor, below the CD/DVD player: ————————————

☞ **Carefully insert the SD card into the slot, with the printed side pointing towards you**

The *iPhoto* program may open right away, as soon as you connect your digital camera, or another device. If this does not happen, you can open *iPhoto* in one of two ways. The first method is through the *Dock*:

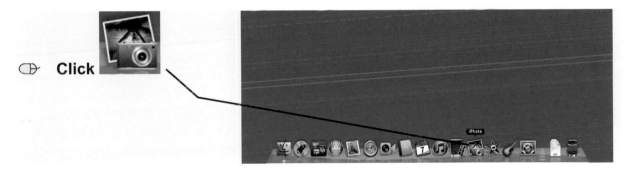

⌗ **Click**

If *iPhoto* does not appear in your *Dock*, you can open the program through *Finder*:

☞ **Open *Finder*** ✋²⁷

**Click**

**Applications**

**Double-click**

**iPhoto**

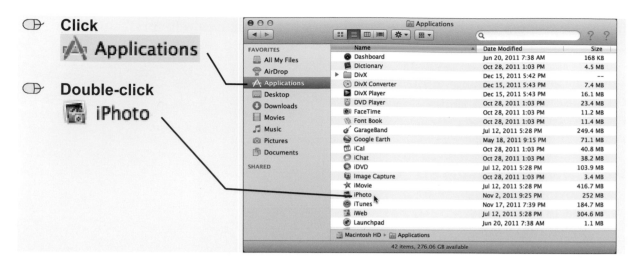

If you use *iPhoto* for the very first time, you will be asked if you want the program to start up automatically when you connect a digital camera (or other device):

**Click** **Yes**

You can always change this preference later on. In the *Tip* about the *Photo Booth* program at the end of this chapter, you can read how to do this.

Subsequently, you will be asked if you want to view the photos on a memory card. Older versions of *iPhoto* may not contain this feature. If your camera is able to store GPS coordinates along with the pictures you take, *iPhoto* can search for the location where the pictures have been taken.

➥ **Please note:**

Not all cameras are equipped with this function, so this setting may not have any effect on your own device. But the iPhone, for example, does have the ability to search for locations.

**Click** **Yes**

In *section 6.4 Viewing Photos on the Map* you can read more about this feature.

Now you will see the *iPhoto* window:

You should be able to recognize some of the photos you have recently taken.

Under **DEVICES** you will see the name of the device whose photos are displayed, in this example [Untitled]: —

If you are using a different device, you may see [iPhone], for example.

## HELP! There are other open programs.

When you connect your camera to your computer, some other program may be opened, for instance, an application that came with your camera. If that is the case, you can simply close that program:

☞ **If necessary, stop the program** ∂∂103

Before you start importing photos, you can enter a name for the event depicted in the photos. In this example we have found some vacation photos on the digital camera:

☞ **Click the text box**

⌨ **Type a name for the event, for instance:**
Barcelona Holiday

Now you can import the photos :

👆 **Click**

**Import 11 Photos**

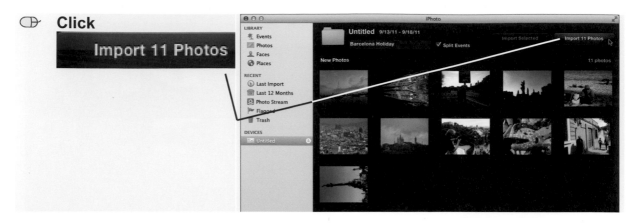

💡 **Tip**

**Importing selected photos**
If you do not want to import all the photos, you can select a number of them with the Command key:

⌨️ **Keep depressed** ⌘ command

👆 **Click the desired photos**

⌨️ **Release** ⌘ command

👆 **Click**

**Import Selected**

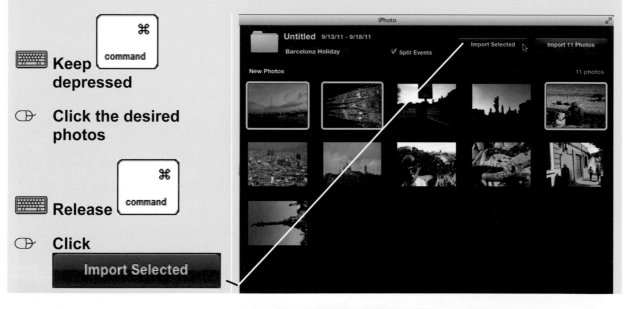

You will see the imported photos pass by, one by one:

Here you can see the progress of the import action:

*iPhoto* will ask if the imported photos should be deleted from the camera. If you keep the photos stored on the camera, you can import them to a another computer:

⊕ **Click** **Keep Photos**

**Delete Photos on Your Camera?**
11 photos were successfully imported into iPhoto.

**Delete Photos**    **Keep Photos**

💡 **Tip**

**Hide imported photos**
If you do decide to keep the photos on the camera, you can hide these photos the next time you connect the camera, by checking the box ✅ next to the option called *Hide imported photos*.

## 6.2 Safely Disconnect the Camera

After you have finished importing the photos, you can deactivate and safely disconnect your digital camera (or other device) from your *Mac*. You do that like this:

⊕ **By the name of your camera, for example,** **Untitled**, **or** **iPhone**, **click** ⏏

Or:

⊕ **Right-click the camera**

⊕ **Click** **Eject**

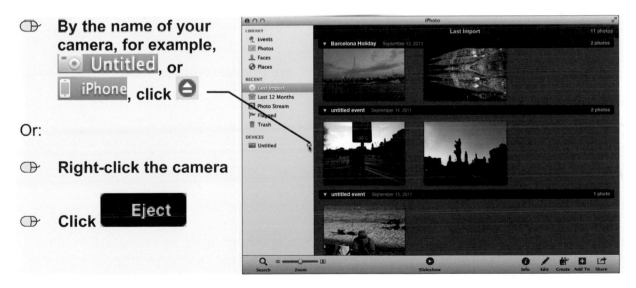

The camera has disappeared from the *iPhoto* window:

Now you can safely disconnect the camera from the computer.

☞ **Disconnect the digital camera from the USB port on your *Mac***

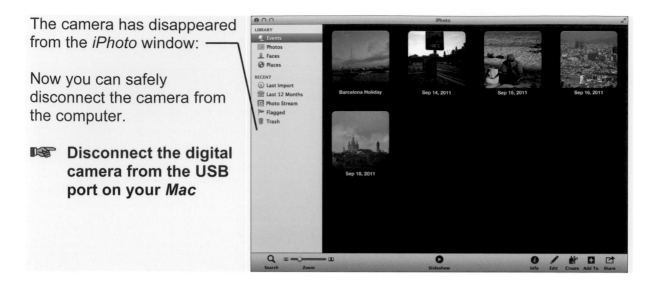

## 6.3 Organizing Photos by Event

The photos have been imported and sorted according to the event:

⊂▷ **If necessary, click**

**Photos**

In this example, only the first two photos have been grouped under the event called *Barcelona Holiday*:

The pictures that have been taken on other dates have been arranged under **untitled event**:

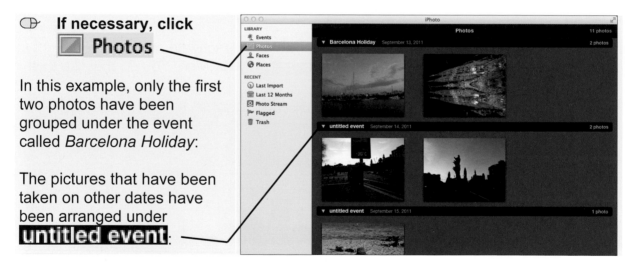

Further on in this chapter you will read how to merge multiple events.

From this point on, you can follow the examples in this chapter by using the practice files that go with this book. This way, you will see the exact same examples from the book on your own screen too. You can download these practice files from the website accompanying this book and import them into *iPhoto*. In *Appendix C Downloading the Practice Files* you can read how to do this.

☞ **Carry out the tasks as instructed in *Appendix C Downloading the Practice Files***

After you have imported the practice files into *iPhoto*, you can take a look at the events that go with these photos:

⊕   Click 🌴 **Events**

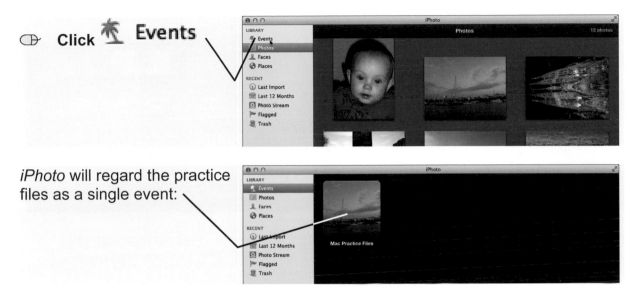

*iPhoto* will regard the practice files as a single event:

Now you are going to split up the event by using the menu:

⊕   **Click the**
     **Mac Practice Files**
     **event**

⊕   Click **Events**

⊕   **Click**
     **Autosplit Selected Eve**

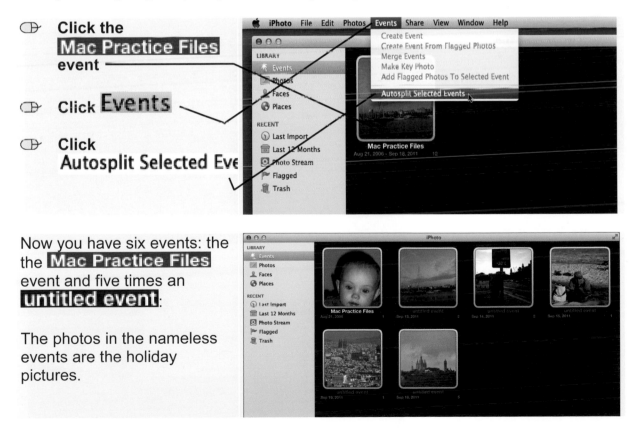

Now you have six events: the the **Mac Practice Files** event and five times an **untitled event**:

The photos in the nameless events are the holiday pictures.

As far as *iPhoto* is concerned, an event exists for a single day (default setting), that is why the holiday photos are split up into multiple events. You can enter a more appropriate name for the first nameless event:

⊙ **Click**
**untitled event**

⌨ **Type:** Barcelona
Holiday

⌨ **Press**   enter   return

Now you can merge all the vacation photos into one event. You do this with the Command key:

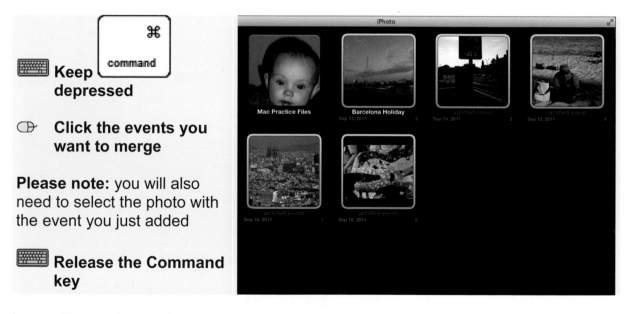

⌨ **Keep**   ⌘ command
**depressed**

⊙ **Click the events you want to merge**

**Please note:** you will also need to select the photo with the event you just added

⌨ **Release the Command key**

You will need to use the menu to merge the events:

⊙ **Click Events**

⊙ **Click Merge Events**

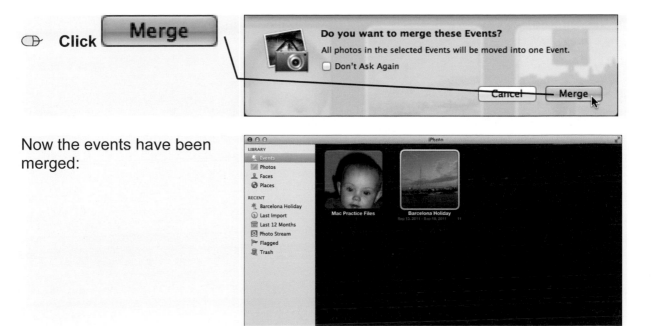

Now the events have been merged:

💡 **Tip**

**View the photos in an event**
If you move your pointer on an event, you will see the various photos that are part of this event.

## 6.4 Viewing Photos on the Map

If the photo you have imported includes GPS coordinates, *OS X* can show you a map of the location where the picture was taken. This function does not exist in older versions of the *iPhoto* program.

☞ **Click 🌐 Places**

In this example, photos with GPS coordinates have been imported:

On this map you see a

number of red pins 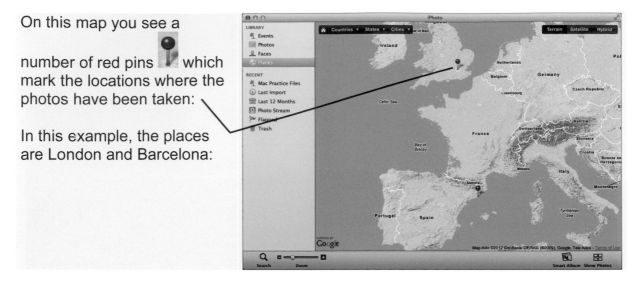 which mark the locations where the photos have been taken:

In this example, the places are London and Barcelona:

The practice files do not contain photos with GPS coordinates. You will see a window with an explanation. For each event, you can add your own location to your photos:

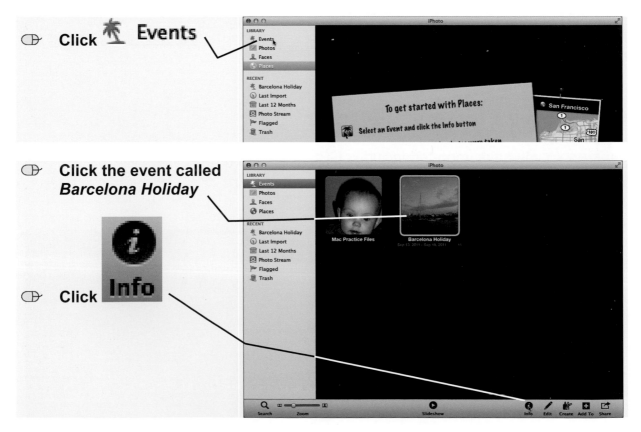

Click 🌴 **Events**

**Click the event called** *Barcelona Holiday*

**Click** **Info**

Now a window pane will be opened, in which you can add extra information about the event:

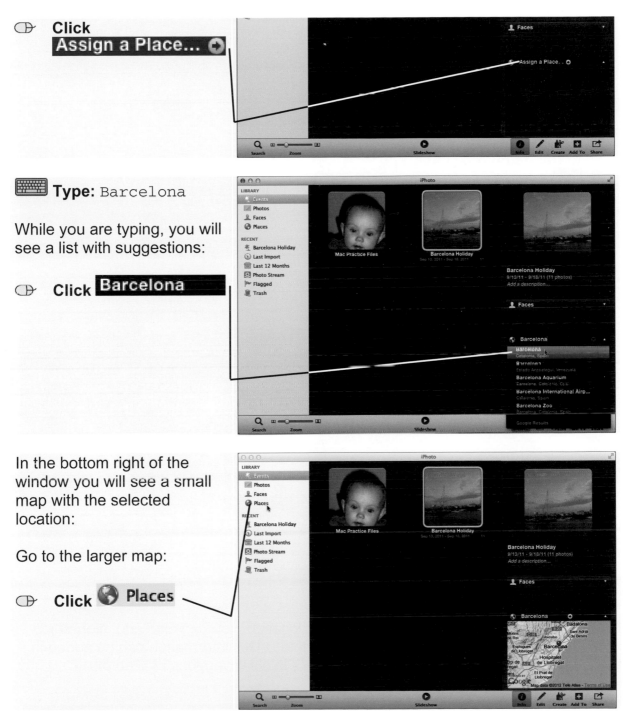

Click
**Assign a Place... ➡**

**Type:** Barcelona

While you are typing, you will see a list with suggestions:

Click **Barcelona**

In the bottom right of the window you will see a small map with the selected location:

Go to the larger map:

Click 🌐 **Places**

Now you will see a map with a red pin, indicating the location of the photos:

**Position the pointer on**

**the red pin**

Now the city name

is displayed:

**In the name box, click**

You will see the photos that have been taken at this location:

Now you can close the *Info* pane again:

**Click**

## 6.5 Faces

Not only can you enter information about the location, you can also add information about the people who are featured in your photos. This information can be added in the Faces Library (this function is not available in older versions of *iPhoto)*:

**Click** *Faces*

In this example *iPhoto* has discovered a number of photos featuring people's faces. By accident, a photo on an advertising poster is also regarded as a face.
You can give the photo featuring a baby a name:

Click

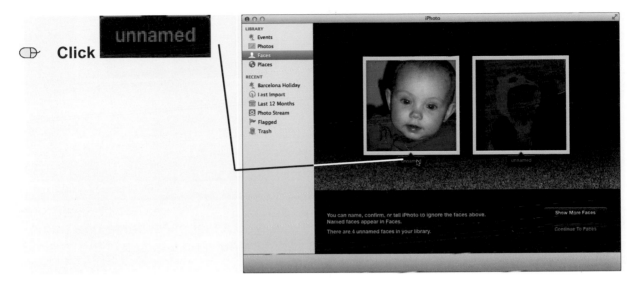

Enter the baby's name:

**Type:** Kay

**Press**

**Click**

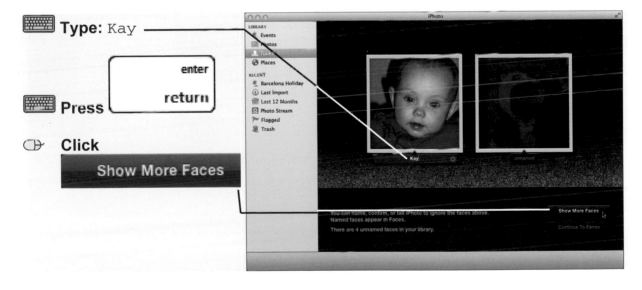

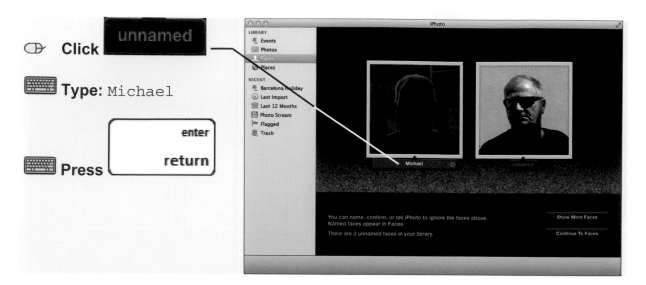

*iPhoto* remembers the names you type. When you type an identical name or a name similar to a previously entered name, you will see a menu. You can select the desired name from the menu:

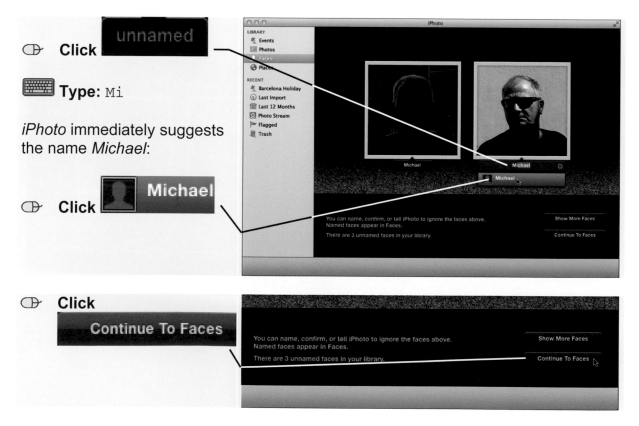

You will see the Faces library with all the people depicted in your pictures:

Just as with the events, the photos on the *Clipboard* are stacked one on top of the other. This is how you can quickly view all of the photos of Michael:

☞ **Double-click the photo**

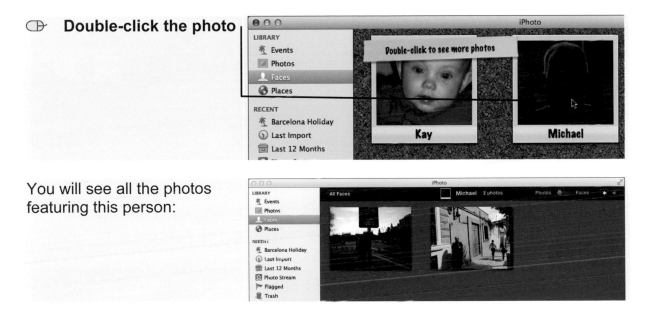

You will see all the photos featuring this person:

# 6.6 Photo Editing

*iPhoto* offers a number of options for editing and enhancing photos. For example, you can:
- rotate photos;
- correct photos automatically;
- correct red eye;
- straighten photos;
- crop photos;
- render photos with warmer and cooler glows;
- use special effects.

You can try out these options by using the practice files.

## 6.7 Correcting Red Eye

If you take a picture of a person while using flash photography, the person's eyes may exhibit a reddish glow in the photo. *iPhoto* contains a useful option for autocorrecting this 'red eye' problem:

☞ **Click** 🔲 **Photos**

☞ **Double-click**

The photo will be opened in the editing window. Now you will clearly see that the baby has red eyes:

☞ **Click Edit**

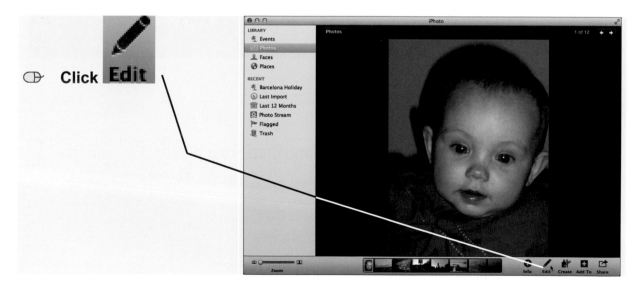

☞ **Click**

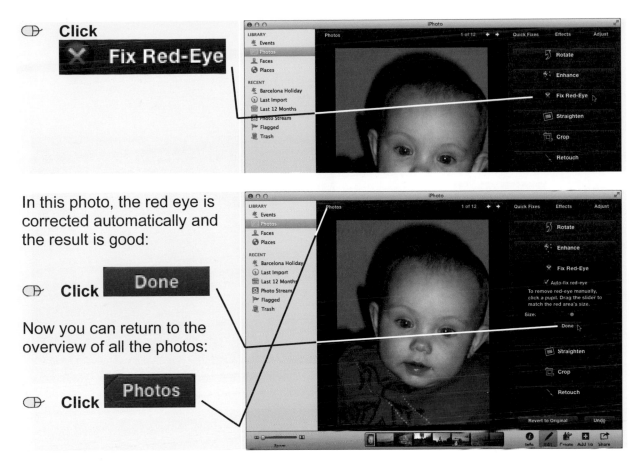

In this photo, the red eye is corrected automatically and the result is good:

☞ **Click** Done

Now you can return to the overview of all the photos:

☞ **Click** Photos

In the *Tips* at the end of this chapter you will find another tip that will show you how to manually correct a red eye problem.


# 6.8 Rotating a Photo

Another common problem that happens to pictures taken with a digital camera is that they are not displayed in the correct orientation and need to be rotated. This is easily done in *iPhoto*. You can practice rotating a photo with the photo of the Sagrada Familia in Barcelona:

☞ **Double-click**

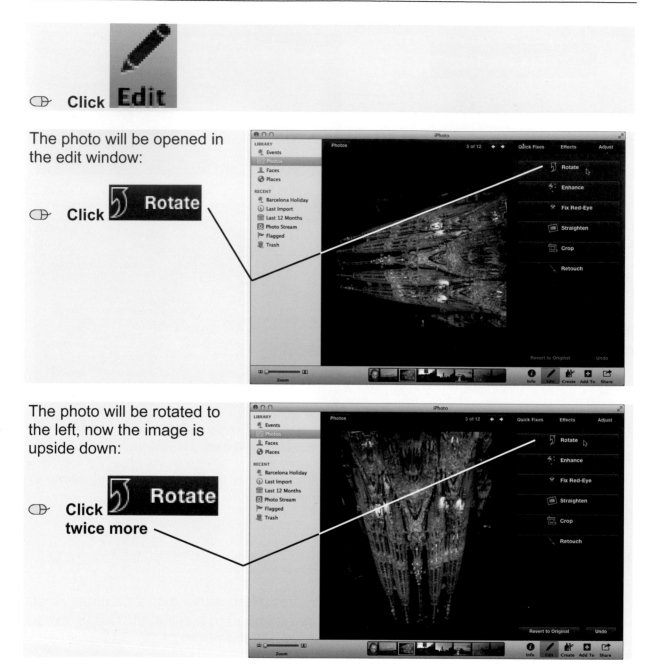

Click **Edit**

The photo will be opened in the edit window:

Click **Rotate**

The photo will be rotated to the left, now the image is upside down:

Click **twice more**

Now the photo is displayed in the correct position:

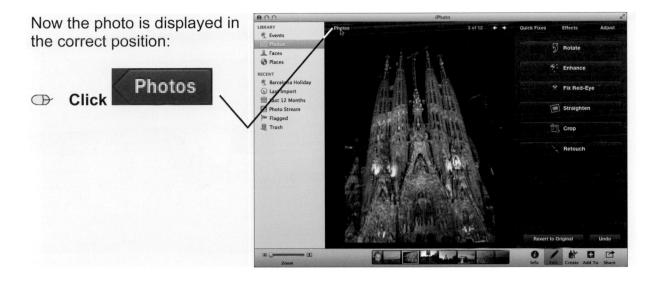

☞ **Click** Photos

## 6.9 Automatic Enhancement of Photos

Sometimes, your pictures turn out to be too dark or too light. The Enhance function gives you the option of applying a quick, automatic fix to an unsatisfactory photo:

👉 **Open the photo**  **in the edit window** 👣⁷⁷

The photo is very dark. It probably should have been taken with the camera's flash mode turned on.

To enhance the photo automatically:

☞ **Click** Enhance

At once, you will see the result:

The photo has become much brighter:

Automatic enhancement does not always produce the desired result right away. You may need to enhance the photo in other ways.

## 6.10 Cropping a Photo

Sometimes, you may see items you that you do not want to display in a picture you have taken. If you crop part of the image, you can determine which part of the photo you want to keep. If you crop the photo shown here for example, you can remove the advertisement board:

You want to crop the photo, but still retain the same dimensions (height/width ratio) of the original photo:

☞ **Check the box ✅ by**
**Constrain:   2560 x 1920**

You will immediately see a white frame in the photo:

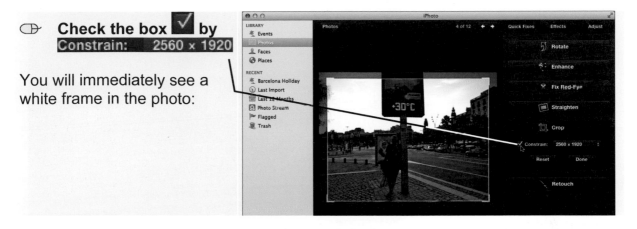

By dragging the borders of the frame, you can determine which part of the photo will be cropped:

☞ **Position the pointer on the top left corner of the frame**

☞ **Keep the mouse button/trackpad depressed**

☞ **Drag the corner to the bottom right**

As soon as the advertisement board appears outside the frame:

☞ **Release the mouse button/trackpad**

Now you can still move the whole frame:

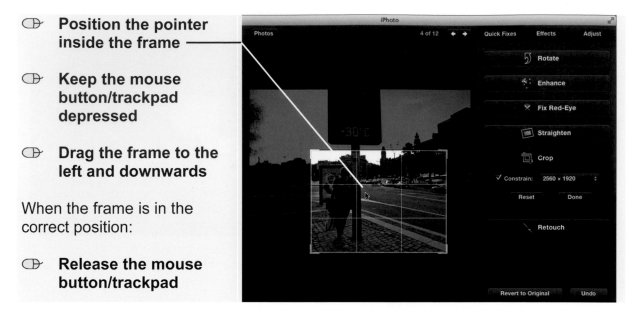

☞ **Position the pointer inside the frame** ——

☞ **Keep the mouse button/trackpad depressed**

☞ **Drag the frame to the left and downwards**

When the frame is in the correct position:

☞ **Release the mouse button/trackpad**

Now you can finish the cropping process:

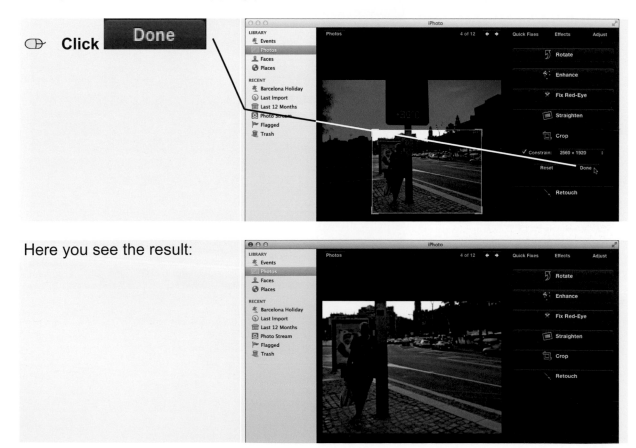

☞ **Click** **Done**

Here you see the result:

## 6.11 Revert to Original Photo

If you are not satisfied with the result of an edit, you can restore the original photo:

☞ **Click**

> **Revert to Original**

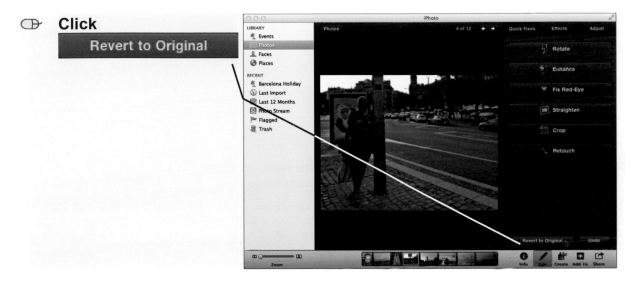

You will see the original, dark, un-cropped photo once more.

## 💡 Tip

**Undo changes**

In *iPhoto*, changes in a photo will automatically be saved while you are working. You will not find a 'Save' command. At any time you can undo one or more edits in a photo.

While you are editing a photo, you can use the **Undo** button to undo the last edit. By clicking this button several times you can undo multiple edits.

If you are editing the photo for the second time, you will see the **Revert to Previous** button. Use this button to return to the situation as it was before the current editing session.

When you start editing a different photo, or stop and restart *iPhoto*, you will no longer be able to use the **Undo** button just to undo the last edit. You can only restore the original photo with the **Revert to Original** button.

If you do not see the **Revert to Original** button, then click **Revert to Previous** several times, until this button changes its name to **Revert to Original**.

## 6.12 Straightening a Photo

It may happen that the camera was not completely held upright while the picture was taken. In *iPhoto* you can easily correct crooked photos and straighten them again.

☞ **Return to the *Photos* overview** 🐾78

☞ **Open the** [photo] **photo in the edit window** 🐾77

You will see that the horizon on the photo is crooked. You can straighten it like this:

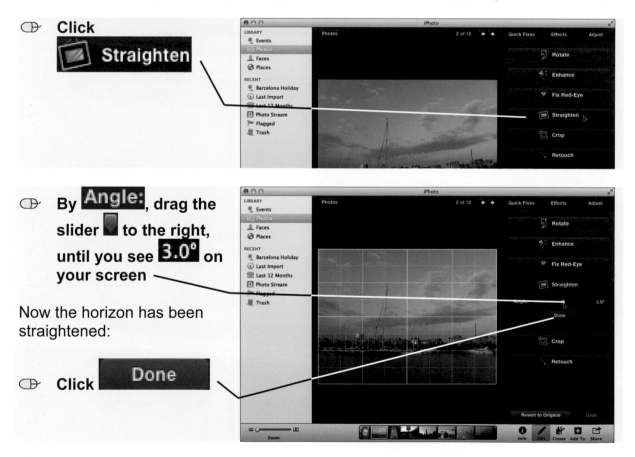

☜ **Click** [ Straighten ]

☜ **By** Angle:**, drag the slider to the right, until you see 3.0° on your screen**

Now the horizon has been straightened:

☜ **Click** [ Done ]

In the next section you will learn about color enhancement and how to apply some special effects.

# 6.13 Using Effects

The photo of the harbor was taken at sunset. This is why the buildings have an orange glow. You can correct this by adjusting the color temperature.

👉 **Click the** **Effects** **tab**

You will see various effects for adjusting the appearance of a photo. The photo contains too many red/orange hues (warm) and needs to become a bit bluer (cooler):

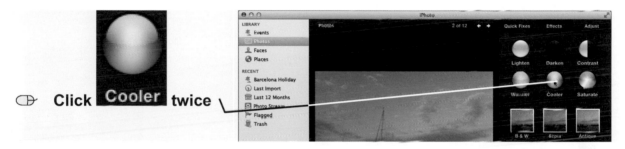

👉 **Click Cooler twice**

You will see the water become bluer and the houses will become less orange:

Of course, you can radically change the photo and turn it into an old-fashioned photo with sepia tones if you want:

☞ **Click** Sepia

The photo will take on a yellow/brownish hue.

If you want to make the photo look older, you can fade the colors a bit:

☞ **Click** Fade **twice**

You will see the result:

☞ **Return to the *Photos* overview** ✐⁷⁸

You have been introduced to some of the options available for editing photos in *iPhoto*. You can use the skills you have acquired to start editing your own photos.

Now you can stop *iPhoto*:

☞ **Stop *iPhoto*** ✐⁷⁹

# 6.14 Opening iTunes

*iTunes* is a user-friendly program for building up, managing and playing your music collection. Furthermore, you can import music from a CD, edit the information of your music files and create playlists. With *iTunes* you can also burn MP3 CDs and DVDs. In this section and in the following sections you will be transferring music (importing) from a CD to the *Mac*. This means you will have a few music files stored on your computer and you will be able to listen to this music right from your computer.

☞ **Click**

If you are using *iTunes* for the first time, you will need to agree to the terms of the licensing agreement:

☞ **If necessary, click** **Agree**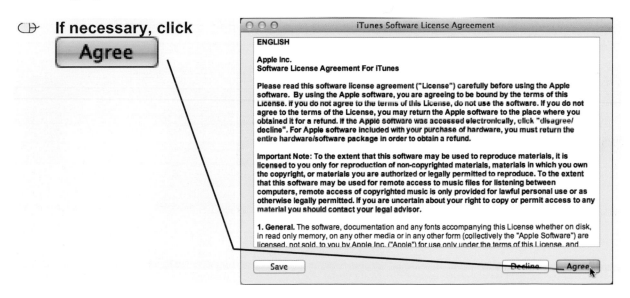

You will see the *iTunes* window:

The *iTunes* library is still empty:

# 6.15 Import a CD

In *iTunes* you can copy the tracks from a music CD and convert them to files that can be used by the computer. In *iTunes* this is called importing a CD. In other music programs it is called 'ripping' a CD.

On the iMac, the CD/DVD player is located on the right-hand side of the screen: ———

☞ **Carefully insert the CD in the slot, with the printed side towards you**

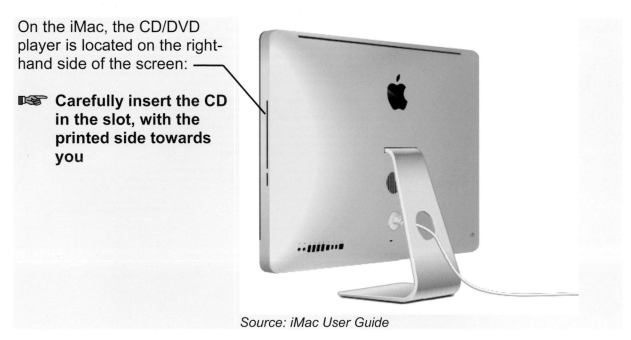

*Source: iMac User Guide*

On the MacBook Pro, the
CD/DVD player is located on
the right-hand side of the
keyboard: ────────

☞ **Carefully insert the CD
in the slot, with the
printed side up**

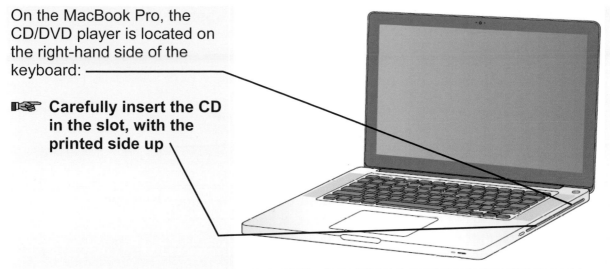

*Source: MacBook Pro User Guide*

🦢 **Please note:**

The Mac mini and the MacBook Air are not equipped with a built-in CD/DVD player.
You can just read through the following sections if you like.

If your computer is connected to the Internet, *iTunes* will search for information about
the CD. The titles of the songs on the CD (also called tracks), will automatically be
downloaded.

Here you see all the titles of
the tracks on the CD:

To the left you will see
**DEVICES** with the title of the
CD below it: ────────

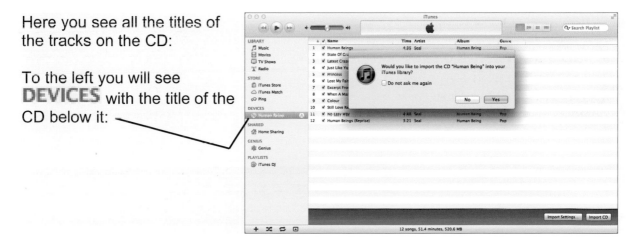

A small popup window appears and *iTunes* asks if you want to import the CD.

☞  **Click** [ **Yes** ]

You will see the progress of the importing process in the *iTunes* window:

Next to the track that is currently being imported, you will see the 🌊 symbol in the list: ────────

In the *Players* information pane you can see which track is being imported and the status of this operation: ────

By default, all tracks have been checked and will be imported: ────────

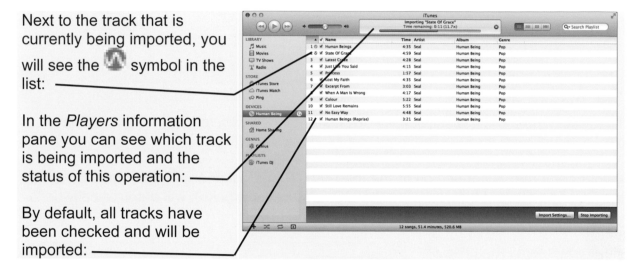

The tracks are imported one by one.

📌 **Please note:**
Importing all the tracks may take a while.

Once the CD has been imported, you will hear a sound signal.

Now all tracks in the list have been marked with the ✅ symbol: ────────

This indicates that the process of importing has successfully completed.

Now you can remove the CD/DVD from the CD/DVD drive. This is how you do that:

By 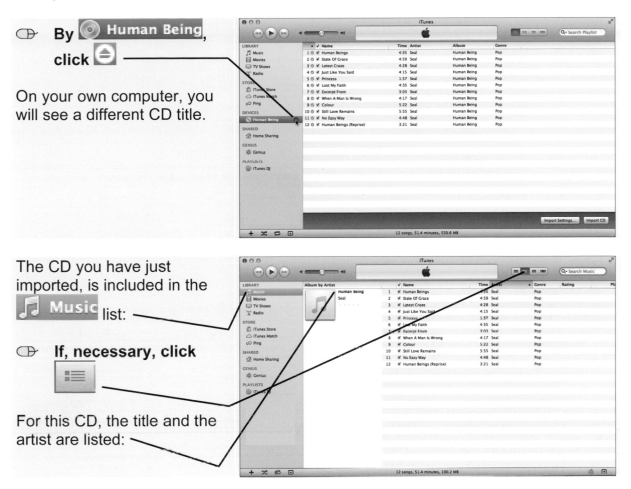 click

On your own computer, you will see a different CD title.

The CD you have just imported, is included in the Music list:

If, necessary, click

For this CD, the title and the artist are listed:

## 6.16 Playing Music

In *iTunes* you can also play music. You are going to play the music you have just imported in the previous step.

You are going to play the first track of the imported CD:

**Double-click the first song**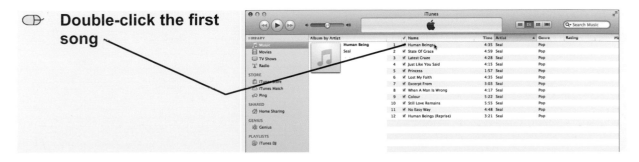

The song that is played is indicated by the 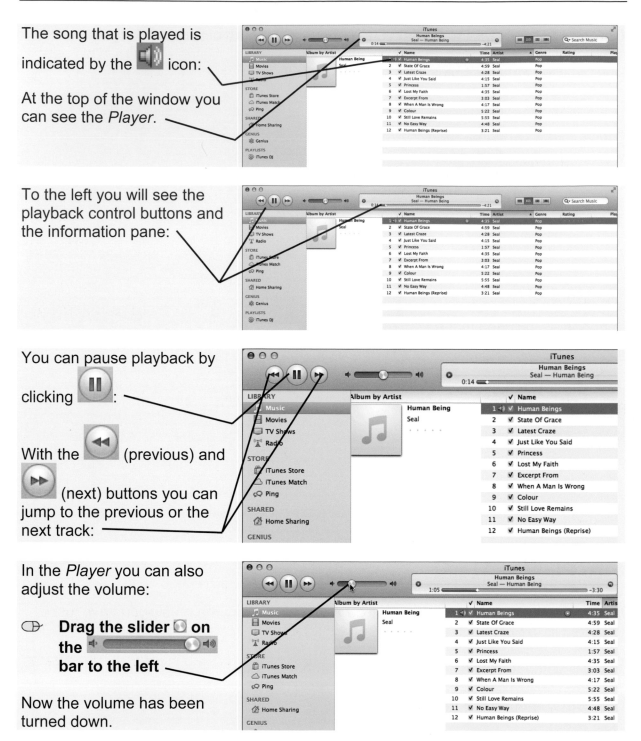 icon:

At the top of the window you can see the *Player*.

To the left you will see the playback control buttons and the information pane:

You can pause playback by clicking :

With the (previous) and (next) buttons you can jump to the previous or the next track:

In the *Player* you can also adjust the volume:

☞ **Drag the slider on the bar to the left**

Now the volume has been turned down.

One of the *iTunes* functions that you are probably already familiar with (from your regular CD player), is the option that allows the random playing of tracks. This option is also called *shuffle*. This is how you use the *shuffle* option in *iTunes*:

In the bottom left of the window:

☞ **Click**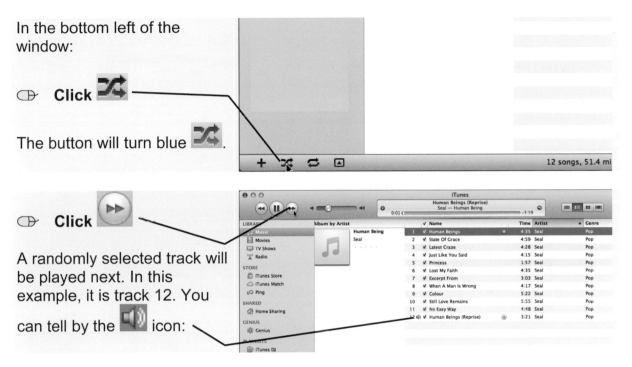

The button will turn blue .

☞ **Click**

A randomly selected track will be played next. In this example, it is track 12. You can tell by the icon:

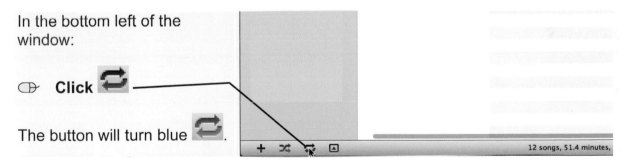

There is another button that lets you repeat the same track over and over again:

In the bottom left of the window:

☞ **Click**

The button will turn blue .

When the CD has finished, it will be played again. You can also repeat a single track:

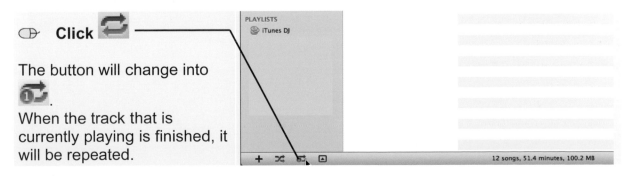

☞ **Click**

The button will change into .

When the track that is currently playing is finished, it will be repeated.

While you are playing music with *iTunes*, you can use your computer for other activities. Here is how to turn the *iTunes* window into a *mini player*:

☞ **Click Window**

☞ **Click Switch to Mini Player**

At the top left you will see a mini player on your desktop. This is how you can enlarge the player:

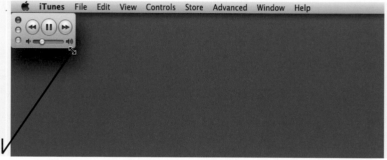

☞ **Click the corner at the bottom right, and drag the pointer to the right**

Now the mini player looks like this:

To return to the full screen view of the *iTunes* window:

☞ **Click Window**

☞ **Click Switch from Mini Player**

☞ **Close the *iTunes* window** 🐾 **13**

Now you can stop the program:

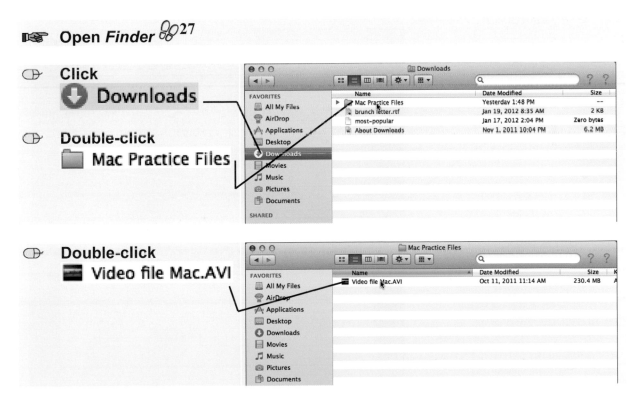

Click **iTunes**

Click **Quit iTunes**

# 6.17 Playing a Video File

In this example we will be using the video file from the *Mac Practice Files* folder. If you followed the steps in *section 6.3 Organizing Photos by Event* you will have copied this folder to the *Downloads* folder of your *Mac*. Here is how you play a video file:

☞ **Open** *Finder* 🐾²⁷

Click
**⬇ Downloads**

Double-click
📁 **Mac Practice Files**

Double-click
🎬 **Video file Mac.AVI**

The video will be opened in the *QuickTime Player* program:

You can play the video:

👆 **Click**

Here you can adjust the volume:

Here are the buttons to rewind or fast forward:

You can display the video on a full screen:

👆 **Click**

The video is displayed full screen:

Use the Esc key to return to the previous view:

⌨ **Press**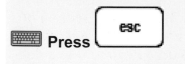

Now the video is displayed in a small window once more.

☞ **Close the window with the video file** 🦶¹³

To stop the program:

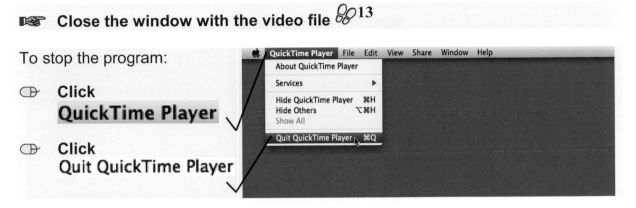

☞ **Click**
**QuickTime Player**

☞ **Click**
**Quit QuickTime Player**

In the next section you will learn how to play a DVD with *DVD Player*.

## 6.18 Playing a DVD

It is easy to play a DVD with the *DVD Player* program that comes with *Mac OS X*.

### ➥ Please note:

To carry out the actions in the following steps you will need to have a DVD, for example, a DVD with a movie or a TV series. If you do not have such a DVD, you can just read through this section.

When a DVD is inserted into the CD/DVD station, the *DVD Player* program opens and starts playing the DVD automatically. This is the default setting in *OS X*:

☞ **Insert a DVD into your computer's CD/DVD station**

The *DVD Player* program will open at once. If the program is opening for the very first time, you may see a window where you need to select the correct region code for your DVD player. For the USA and Canada it is region 1, for Europe it is region 2 and for Australia it is region 4.

☞ **If necessary, follow the onscreen instructions**

Now the *DVD Player* program will be started and you will see the opening scenes of the DVD. Almost every DVD has a built-in menu where you can select the languages for the subtitles, among other playback options. You can also use this menu to select a specific part of the DVD to view.

The DVD that is used in this example automatically displays the main menu, right after the copyright messages:

To play the movie:

☞  **Click** **PLAY MOVIE**

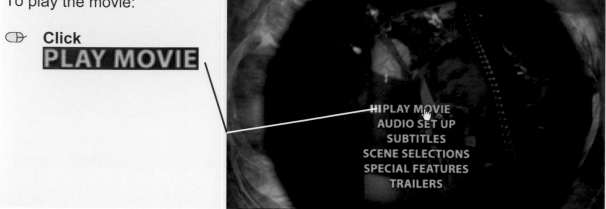

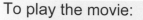 **Please note:**

The structure of the main menu can differ with each DVD. You may need to scroll through various menu options on your own DVD, before you reach the main menu or the subtitles settings.

The movie or TV episode begins:

While you are playing the video full screen, you will see a command bar at the bottom of the screen every time you move the pointer:

These are the functions of all the buttons:

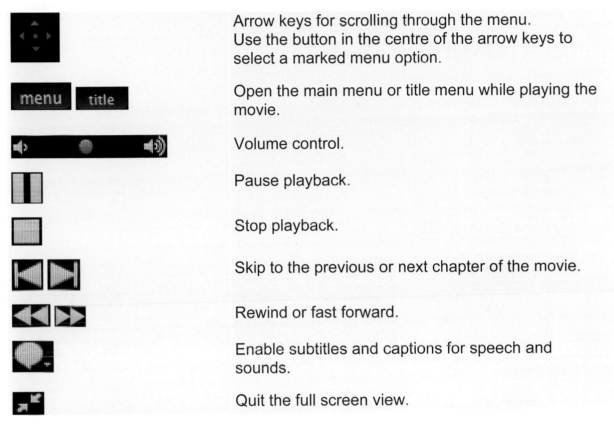

Arrow keys for scrolling through the menu.
Use the button in the centre of the arrow keys to select a marked menu option.

Open the main menu or title menu while playing the movie.

Volume control.

Pause playback.

Stop playback.

Skip to the previous or next chapter of the movie.

Rewind or fast forward.

Enable subtitles and captions for speech and sounds.

Quit the full screen view.

Now you can close the full screen view:

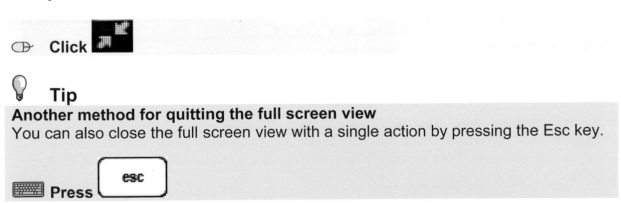

☞ **Click**

🔆 **Tip**

**Another method for quitting the full screen view**
You can also close the full screen view with a single action by pressing the Esc key.

⌨ **Press** esc

When the *DVD Player* window is minimized, you will see the control panel of the *DVD Player*, with similar buttons. To stop the DVD from playing altogether:

☞ **Click**

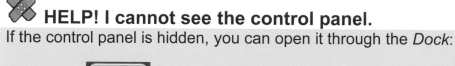 **HELP! I cannot see the control panel.**

If the control panel is hidden, you can open it through the *Dock*:

☞ **Click**

Now you can eject the DVD:

☞ **Click** eject

Stop *DVD Player*:

☞ **Click DVD Player**

☞ **Click Quit DVD Player**

In this chapter you have learned how to work with several of the *Mac*'s built-in programs: *iPhoto, iTunes, Quick Time Player* and the *DVD Player*. In the next chapter you will learn how to modify the settings of your computer according to your wishes.

## 6.19 Exercises

To be able to quickly apply the things you have learned, you can work through these exercises. Have you forgotten how to do something? Use the numbers next to the footsteps ₁ to look up the item in the appendix *How Do I Do That Again?* You will find the appendix at the end of this book.

## Exercise: Photo Editing

In this exercise you will repeat the actions necessary to edit a photo in *iPhoto*.

☞ Open *iPhoto*. ₇₆

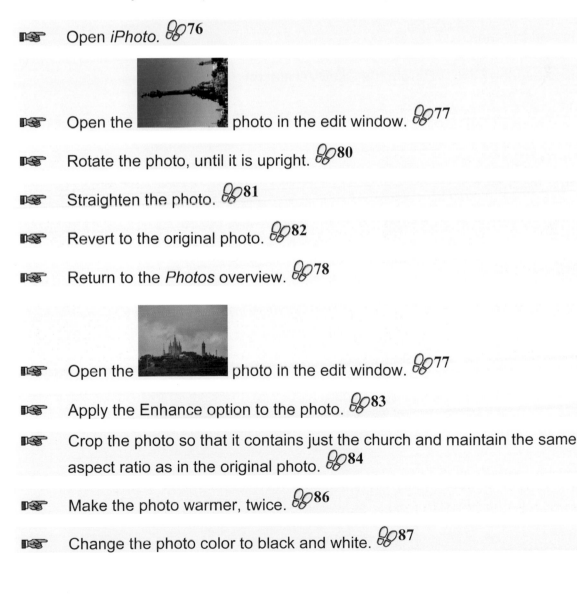

☞ Open the [photo] photo in the edit window. ₇₇

☞ Rotate the photo, until it is upright. ₈₀

☞ Straighten the photo. ₈₁

☞ Revert to the original photo. ₈₂

☞ Return to the *Photos* overview. ₇₈

☞ Open the [photo] photo in the edit window. ₇₇

☞ Apply the Enhance option to the photo. ₈₃

☞ Crop the photo so that it contains just the church and maintain the same aspect ratio as in the original photo. ₈₄

☞ Make the photo warmer, twice. ₈₆

☞ Change the photo color to black and white. ₈₇

☞     Return to the *Photos* overview. 🐾 78

☞     Stop *iPhoto*. 🐾 79

# Exercise: Import a CD in iTunes

In this exercise you are going to repeat the process of importing a CD into *iTunes*.

☞     Open *iTunes*. 🐾 88

☞     Insert a CD into the CD/DVD station.

☞     Import the music. 🐾 89

☞     Remove the CD/DVD from the CD/DVD station. 🐾 90

# Exercise: Play Music

In this exercise you are going to repeat the actions needed to play music.

☞     Play the music in *iTunes*. 🐾 91

☞     Play the songs in shuffle mode. 🐾 92

☞     Switch to the mini player. 🐾 93

☞     Return to the *iTunes* window. 🐾 94

☞     Close the *iTunes* window. 🐾 13

☞     Stop *iTunes*. 🐾 95

# Exercise: View a DVD

In this exercise you are going to repeat the actions needed to use the *DVD Player*.

☞ Insert a DVD into the CD/DVD station.

☞ Play the DVD in *DVD Player*. 🐾**96**

☞ Play the movie on a full screen. 🐾**97**

☞ Return to the previous view. 🐾**98**

☞ Stop *DVD Player*. 🐾**99**

# 6.20 Background Information

**Dictionary**

| | |
|---|---|
| **Crop** | Removing certain parts of a picture to focus attention on a particular area. |
| **DVD Player** | A program with which you can play DVDs. |
| **Event** | In the *iPhoto* program, photos are arranged by event. An event contains the photos you have made in a specific time period, for instance, during a wedding or a trip to the beach. You can order your photos and videos even further by merging or splitting up events and by changing the name of the events. |
| **Faces** | A library in *iPhoto* where the photos are sorted according to the people depicted in them. |
| **GPS** | Short for *Global Positioning System*. A space-based satellite navigation system that can determine your exact location on earth at any time. Among other devices, GPS is a built-in feature in most cell phones and nowadays also in digital cameras. |
| **iLife** | A collection of programs made by *Apple* with which you can create music, movies, digital photos, DVDs and websites. The *iLife* package includes the programs called *GarageBand*, *iPhoto*, *iMovie*, *iDVD*, *iTunes* and *iWeb*. |
| **Import** | Transferring digital photos from your digital camera or another device to your computer. Also refers to the transferring of music files from a CD, for example, to the *Mac*. |
| **iPhoto** | A program that lets you organize, save and edit digital photos. *iPhoto* is part of the *iLife* suite of software. |
| **iTunes** | A program that allows you to play CDs, import music from CDs or purchase music in the *iTunes Store*. The media files can be arranged by album, artist, playlist and more. Playlists can be burned to a disk, or transferred to an iPad, iPhone, iPod or other media player. |

*- Continue on the next page -*

| | |
|---|---|
| **iTunes Store** | An online store linked to *iTunes*. Here you can listen to audio fragments for free and download songs or albums for a fee. In the *iTunes Store* you can buy not only music, but games, movies, TV series, ringtones and more. |
| **Photo Loader** | An *Apple* program with which you can transfer photos from digital scanners or computers connected to your computer, or connected through a network, to your own computer. |
| **Places** | A library in *iPhoto* where the photos are organized by the place where they were taken. |
| **QuickTime Player** | The multimedia playback application included with *Mac OS X* that can play audio, MP3 music files, movies as well as many other file types. There is also a version for *Windows*. |
| **Red eye** | When you take a picture of a person and use flash, the light reflected off of the retina of the eyes may cause a red appearance on the eyes in the photo. |
| **Rotate** | Turn an image sideways to the left or right, usually a quarter turn. |
| **Scanner** | A device that converts a paper object into digital data, suited for use on a computer. |
| **SD card** | Short for *Secure Digital* card. A memory card about the size of a stamp, used by digital cameras and sophisticated cell phones to store data. |
| **Sepia** | A yellow/brown shade seen on old photographs. |
| **Shuffle** | Play tracks on a CD or in a playlist in random order. |
| **Slide show** | Displaying a series of pictures automatically on a full screen. |
| **Template** | A document containing standard data that can be used as a basis for a new document. For instance, *Mail* offers various templates for creating e-mail messages with sample texts, background images and space for your own photos. |

*Source: Apple Dictionary, Wikipedia*

# 6.21 Tips

### Tip

**Photo Loader**

Apart from *iPhoto, OS X* offers another program for importing photos from a digital camera or scanner (or other device with a camera): *Photo Loader*. This is how you open *Photo Loader*:

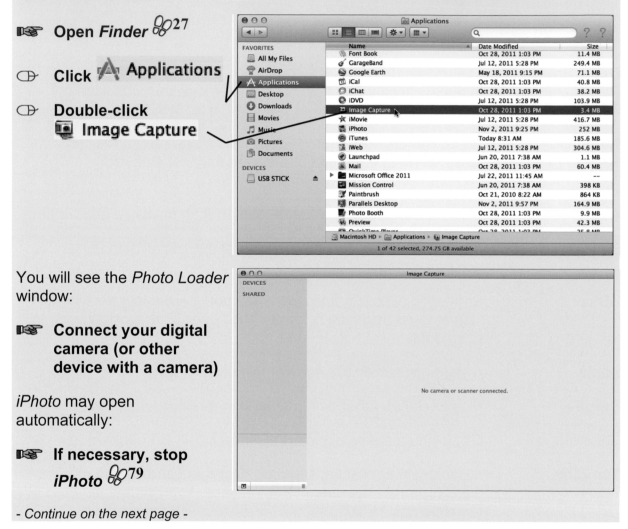

☞ Open *Finder* ⚘²⁷

☞ Click  **Applications**

☞ Double-click  **Image Capture**

You will see the *Photo Loader* window:

☞ **Connect your digital camera (or other device with a camera)**

*iPhoto* may open automatically:

☞ **If necessary, stop iPhoto** ⚘⁷⁹

- *Continue on the next page -*

With the [ **Import All** ] button you can import all of the photos:

You can also select specific photos and then select [ **Import** ].

By default, the photos are stored in the 🖼️ **Pictures** folder:
But if you prefer, you can always select another folder.

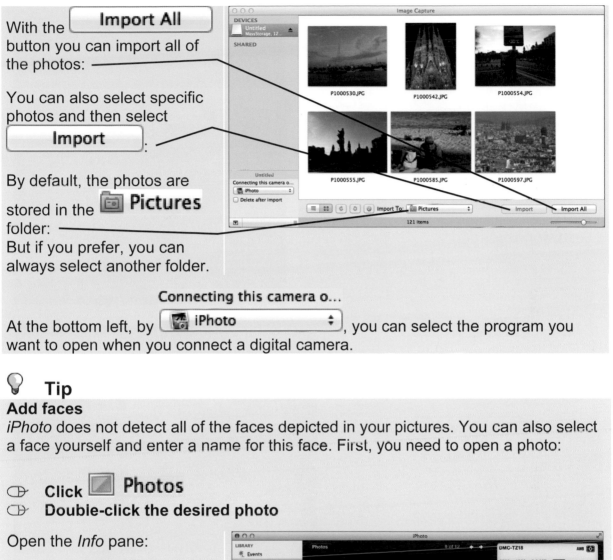

At the bottom left, by **Connecting this camera o...** [ 📷 **iPhoto** ⬍ ], you can select the program you want to open when you connect a digital camera.

💡 **Tip**

**Add faces**
*iPhoto* does not detect all of the faces depicted in your pictures. You can also select a face yourself and enter a name for this face. First, you need to open a photo:

☞ **Click** ▦ **Photos**
☞ **Double-click the desired photo**

Open the *Info* pane:

☞ **Click** ℹ️ **Info**

☞ **Click** **Add a face...**

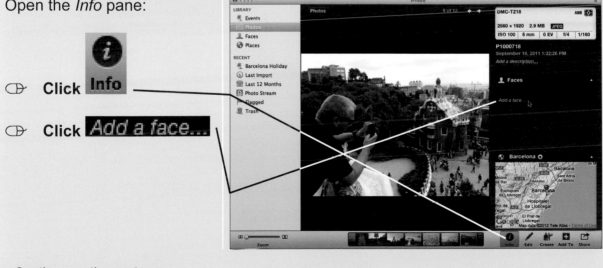

*- Continue on the next page -*

A square frame appears in the photo:

☞ **Click the frame and keep the mouse button/trackpad depressed**

☞ **Drag the frame over the face**

☞ **Release the mouse button/trackpad**

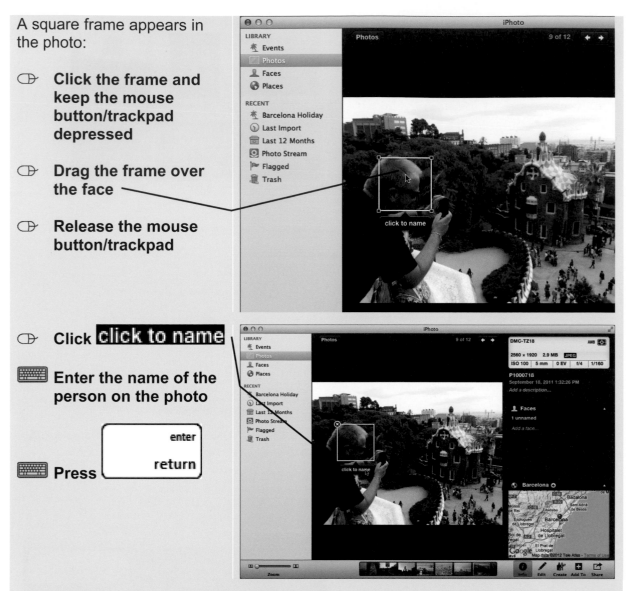

☞ **Click** **click to name**

⌨ **Enter the name of the person on the photo**

> enter
>
> return

⌨ **Press**

The person will be added to the *Clipboard*.

💡 **Tip**

**Automatic facial recognition**

After you have entered a number of names for various faces, you will notice that *iPhoto* is starting to recognize the persons in newly imported photos all by itself. This happens when you open 👤 **Faces**, or the *Info* pane for a photo. All you need to do is confirm that this is the right person.

## 💡 Tip

**Manually correct red eye**

When the eye is really red, *iPhoto* will be able to correct the red eye problem automatically. But if the red eye is made up of different shades of red, this will not always work. In this case, you can try to manually correct the red eye problem:

☞ **Uncheck the box** ✓ **next to** Auto-fix red-eye

The pointer will turn into a circle 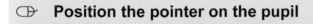 :

☞ **Position the pointer on the pupil**

If the pointer is too big or too small, you can use the slider in Size: ●──────── to adjust the size of the tool.

☞ **Click the first pupil**
☞ **Click the second pupil**

Now the red color is corrected.

☞ **Click** Done

## Tip

**Zoom in and zoom out**

In the *iPhoto* window you can use 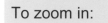 to zoom in and zoom out on the photo you are editing.

To zoom in:

☞ **Drag the slider in** 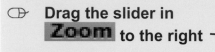 **to the right**

You will zoom in on the picture. In this small window you can see which part of the photo is displayed:

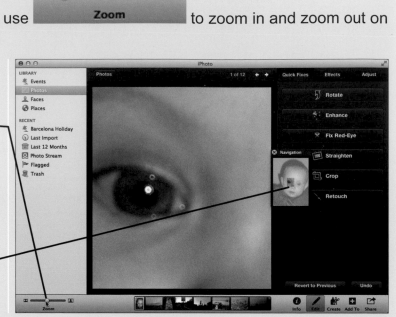

You can zoom out again by dragging the slider to the left.

## Tip

**Slide show**

In *iPhoto* you can also display your photos in a slide show. You can choose from various animated themes, each with its own soundtrack.

☞ **Click** 🌴 **Events**

☞ **Click an event**

☞ **Click** ▶ **Slideshow**

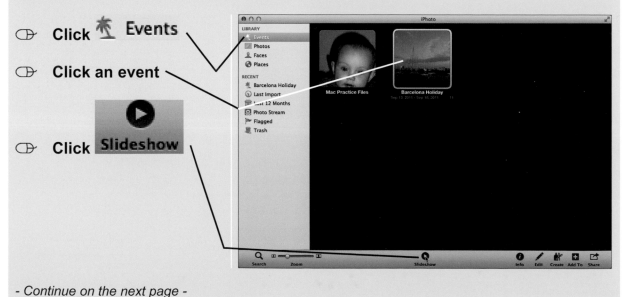

*- Continue on the next page -*

Before the slide show starts, you can select an animated theme:

☞ **Click an animated theme, for example**

☞ **Click** Play

The slide show begins. The photos will be displayed and you hear the music that goes with the theme.

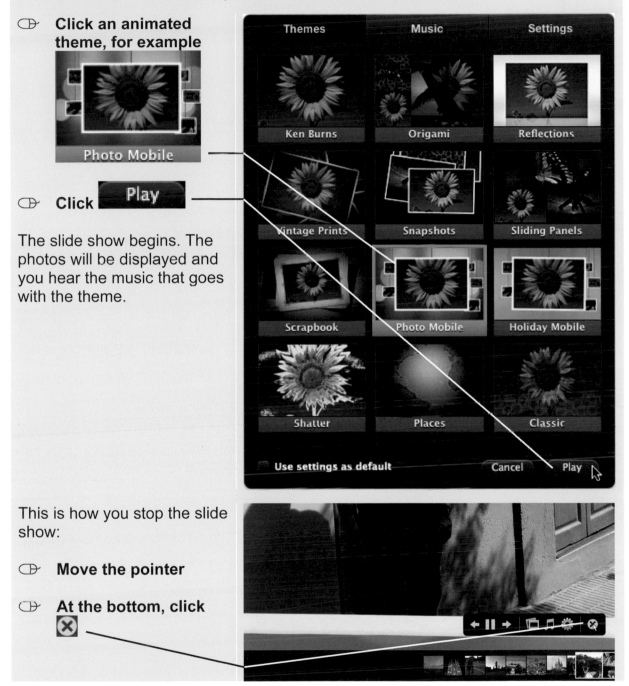

This is how you stop the slide show:

☞ **Move the pointer**

☞ **At the bottom, click** ☒

### 💡 Tip

**Use templates with photos**

In *Mail* you can easily send an e-mail message with a nice background and a photo, by using *templates*:

☞ **Open *Mail* ⚏⚏$^{63}$**

☞ **Open a new e-mail message ⚏⚏$^{58}$**

Open the templates pane:

⊕ **Click** [image]

You will see all sorts of templates for e-mails, suitable for several occasions:

⊕ Click **Photos**

⊕ **Click a template**

You can replace the text in the template by your own message. By adding your own photos, you can personalize your message and create an authentic, surprising and original e-mail. You can replace the photos in the template by dragging your own photos from *iPhoto* or *Photo Loader*:

☞ **Open *iPhoto* ⚏⚏$^{76}$**

⊕ **Click**  **Photos**

*- Continue on the next page -*

☞ **Position the pointer on a photo**

☞ **Keep the mouse button/trackpad depressed**

☞ **Drag the photo to one of the photos in the template**

☞ **Release the mouse button/trackpad**

Now the photo has been pasted into the template:

In this way you can replace all the photos.

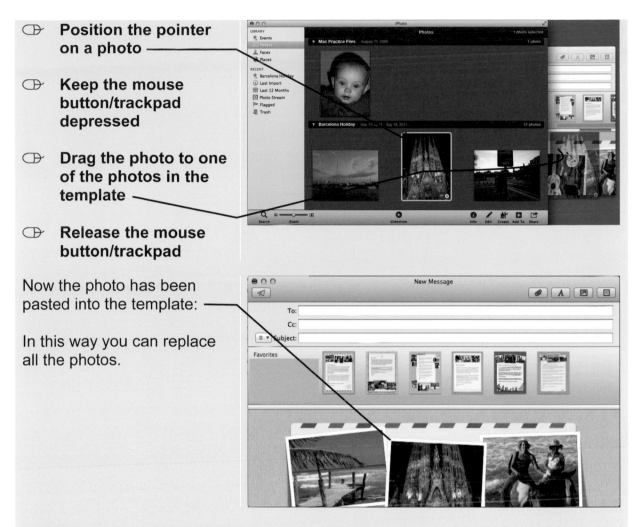

**Please note:** when you send a message with photos, bear in mind that there is a maximum size for sending photos. You might not be able to send very large photo files, or multiple photo files. Also take into account that the recipient's mailbox may overflow as a result of your e-mail.

### Tip

**Do not import all tracks**

If you do not want to import all the tracks, you can uncheck the boxes ✔ next to the tracks you want to skip.

### ☞ Insert a CD/DVD into the CD/DVD station

First, you need to close this window:

⊕ **Click**  No

For each track you do not want to import:

⊕ **Uncheck the box** ✔

Now you can import the selected tracks:

⊕ **Click** Import CD

# 7. Customizing Settings to Suit Your Needs

There are many components on your computer for which you can adjust the settings yourself, to suit your own needs and preferences. Changing the settings on your computer is worth the trouble. It can make difficult operations a bit easier and in the long term, it can also prevent harmful side-effects from occurring.
For instance, you can adjust the mouse in such a way that you can more easily work with it. This will prevent you from overburdening your wrist.

In this chapter you will read about a number of features on your computer that you can easily customize. We will pay special attention to the items that can be important for your motor skills, your eyesight and your sense of hearing.
You can freely experiment with these settings to discover whether the new settings are an improvement or not. Just give it a try. All the settings you have changed can easily be reset to their original status.

In this chapter you will learn how to:

- adjust the settings for the mouse and/or trackpad;
- change the wallpaper for your desktop;
- adjust the size of the icons;
- adjust the *Finder* window;
- change the sound settings.

# 7.1 Adjusting the Mouse and the Trackpad

To make it easier to use the mouse or the trackpad, you can adjust some of the settings. To change settings, you first need to open the *System Preferences* through the *Dock*:

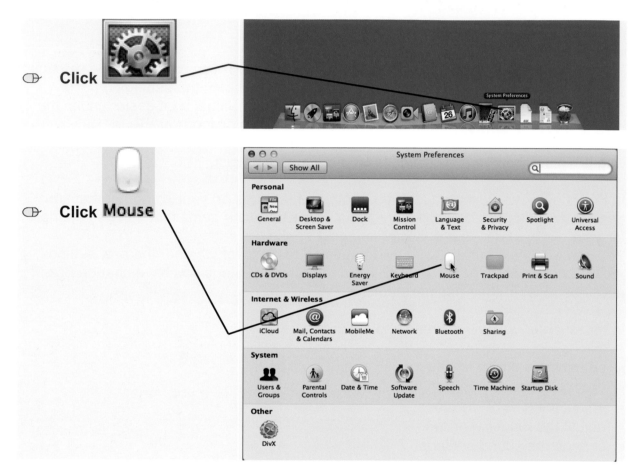

⊕  **Click**

⊕  **Click Mouse**

One of the settings you can change is the speed of the mouse. The mouse speed determines the relationship between the movement of the mouse across a work surface or mouse pad and the movement of the pointer on the screen.

- If the pointer has been set to *fast*, a very tiny movement of the mouse will suffice to move the pointer on the screen a long way.
- If the pointer has been set to *slow*, a big movement of the mouse is required to move the pointer on the screen over just a small distance.

For most people, the best setting for the mouse speed is when they move the mouse over an area the size of a CD case, the mouse on the screen moves from one corner of the screen to the other.

By **Tracking** you can drag the slider to the left (slow) or to the right (fast):

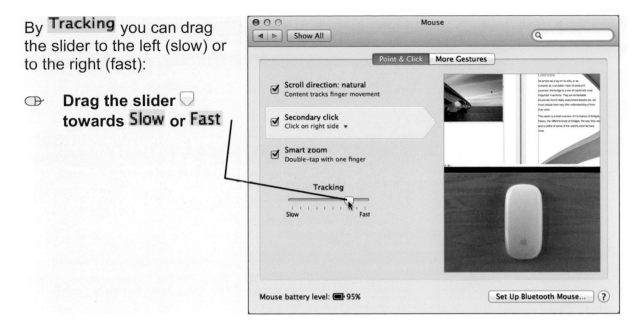

⏚ **Drag the slider** ▽
**towards Slow or Fast**

You can test the speed by moving the mouse across your desk. After you have set the preferred speed, you will return to the *System Preferences* overview:

⏚ **Click Show All**

You can adjust the same settings for a trackpad. This is how you do that:

⏚ **Click Trackpad**

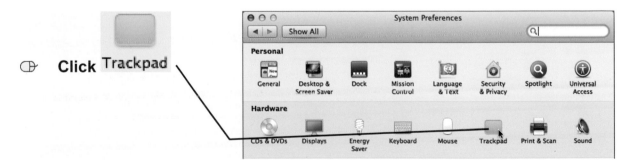

⊕  **Drag the slider** ▽
    **towards** Slow **or** Fast

To return to the *System Preferences*:

⊕  **Click** Show All

You can change even more settings, such as the size of the pointer and the scroll speed. You can do this in the *Universal Access* window:

⊕  **Click** Universal Access

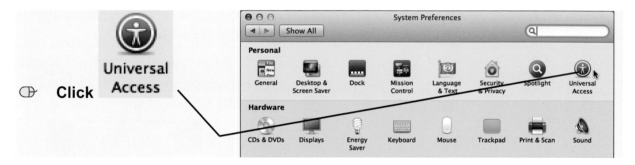

The pointer will be easier to see if you make it bigger. Here is how to adjust the size:

By Cursor Size::

⊕  **Drag the slider** ▽
    **towards** Normal **or**
    Large

In this example we have chosen a very large pointer, so you could clearly see the effect in this screenshot:

But of course you can select the size that works best for you.

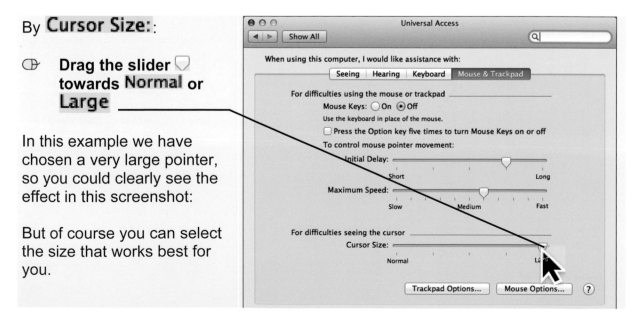

To adjust more mouse options:

⊕ **Click**

**Mouse Options...**

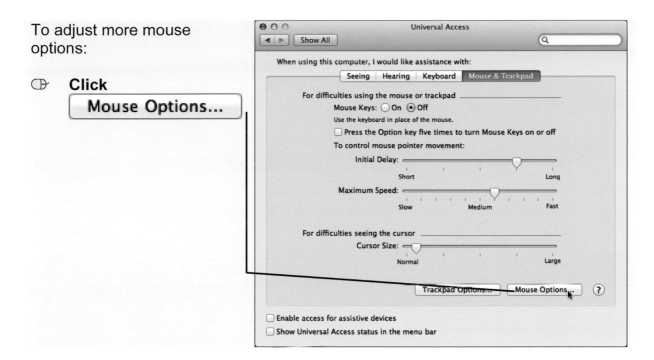

You can also change the double-click interval (the double-click speed) and the scroll speed. If you do not double-click fast enough, the computer will not recognize the two clicks as a double-click. Perhaps a different setting will make it easier for you to use the double-click. The scroll speed determines how fast you can scroll.

- Set the double-click interval to *slower* if double-clicking is difficult for you.
- Set the double-click interval to *faster* if you want to be able to double-click faster (as an experienced user).

This is how you change the settings:

By **Double-Click Speed** and **Scrolling Speed**.

⊕ **Drag the sliders** ▽

⊕ **Click** **Done**

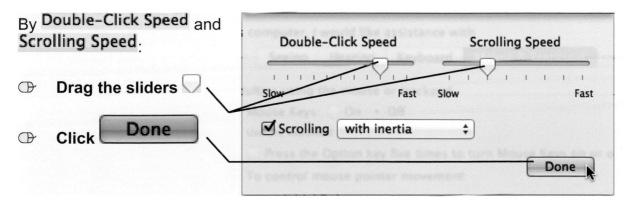

You will see the *Universal Access* window once more:

You can also change the trackpad options.

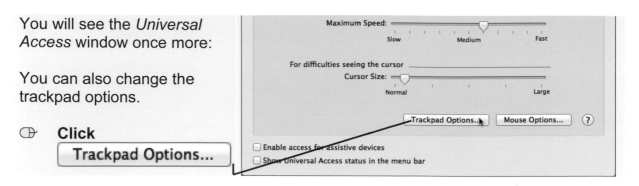

☞ **Click** ⬚ **Trackpad Options...**

For the trackpad, you can also adjust the double-click interval (the double-click speed) and the scroll speed:

By **Double-Click Speed** and **Scrolling Speed**.

☞ **Drag the sliders** ♡

☞ **Click** **Done**

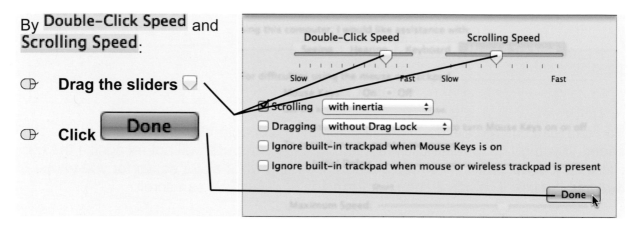

☞ **Show all options of the *System Preferences*** ⬚**100**

# 7.2 Changing the Desktop Wallpaper

A lot of people prefer working with a calm background on their computer desktop. But perhaps you think your wallpaper is boring and you would rather have a livelier background. It is very simple to select a different background:

☞ **Click** **Desktop & Screen Saver**

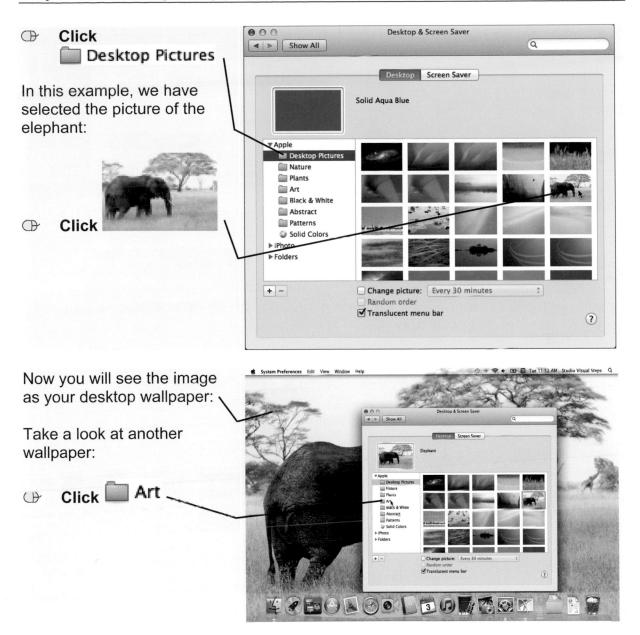

Click
📁 **Desktop Pictures**

In this example, we have selected the picture of the elephant:

Click

Now you will see the image as your desktop wallpaper:

Take a look at another wallpaper:

Click 📁 **Art**

In this example we have chosen a painting by Georges Seurat:

☞ **Click**

The new wallpaper will be displayed at once:

Apart from the set of standard wallpapers, you can also use one of your own photos as a wallpaper. Here is how to do that:

☞ **By Folders, click** ▶

☞ **Click** 🗔 **Pictures**

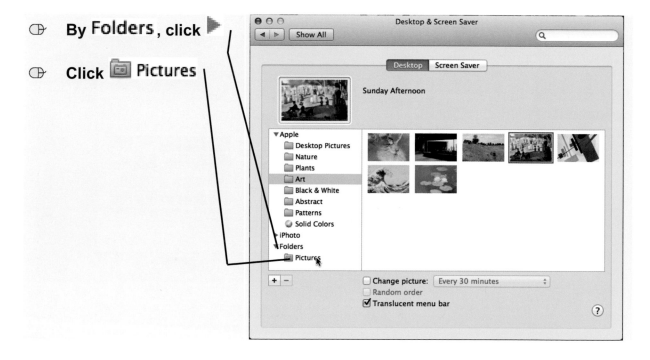

You will see the photos in the *Pictures* folder. In this case, it is a single photo, but you will probably see more photos on your own computer:

⊕ **Click the desired photo**

The photo will immediately be used as desktop wallpaper.

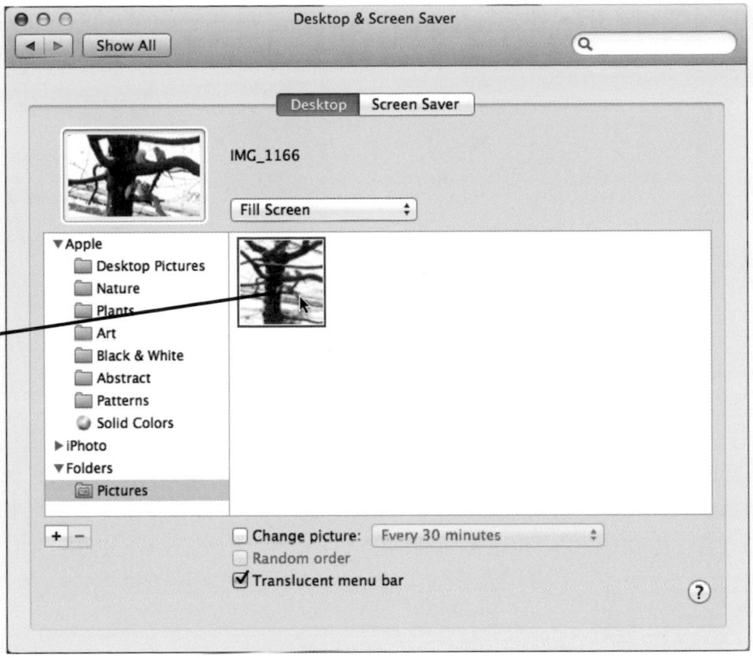

With the **Change picture:** option you can automatically change your desktop wallpaper after a set period of time. This is how you set these preferences:

⊕ **Check the box ☑ next to Change picture:**

You can select the time period for the wallpaper images to change:

⊕ **Click Every 30 minutes**

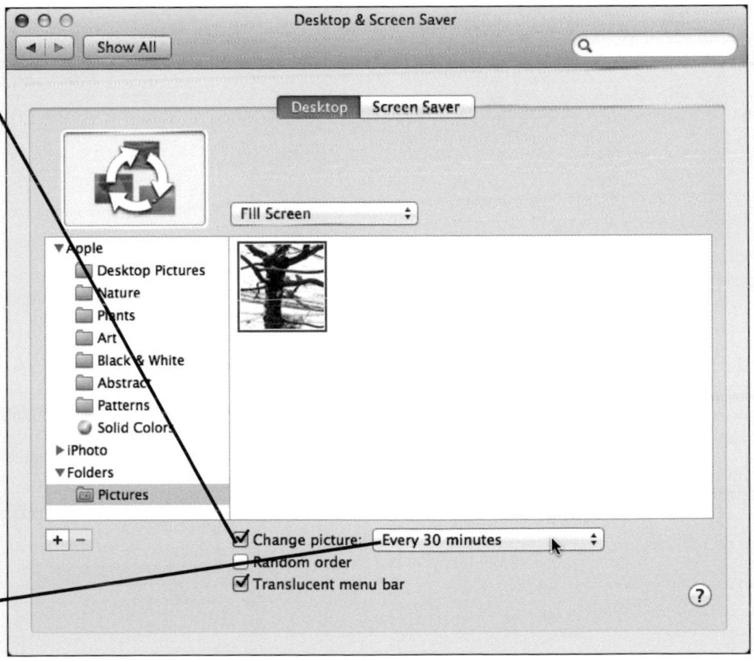

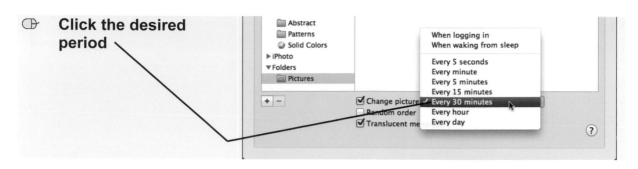

**Click the desired period**

# 7.3 The Screensaver

If you do not use your computer for a while, you can set a screensaver. This will prevent your screen from 'burning-in'. This burn-in may occur when the exact same frozen image is displayed on your screen for longer time periods. You can set your own screensaver. Many screensavers are not only useful, but also fun to watch.

**Click** Screen Saver

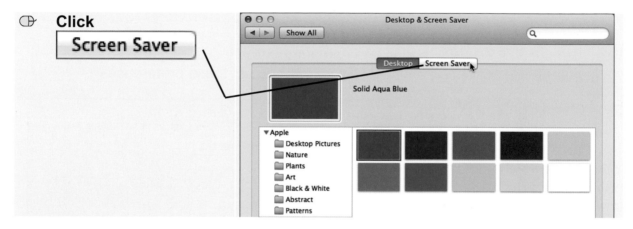

You are going to take a look at a couple of examples:

**Click an example, for instance,** Flurry

In the preview you can see what the screensaver will look like:

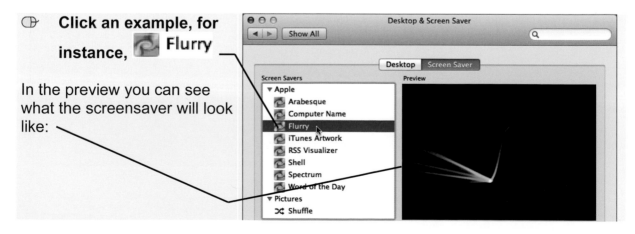

Now take a look at another example:

In the screensavers pane:

- ☞ **Scroll downwards**

- ☞ **Click** **Beach**

You will see a slide show of images that belong to the Beach topic.

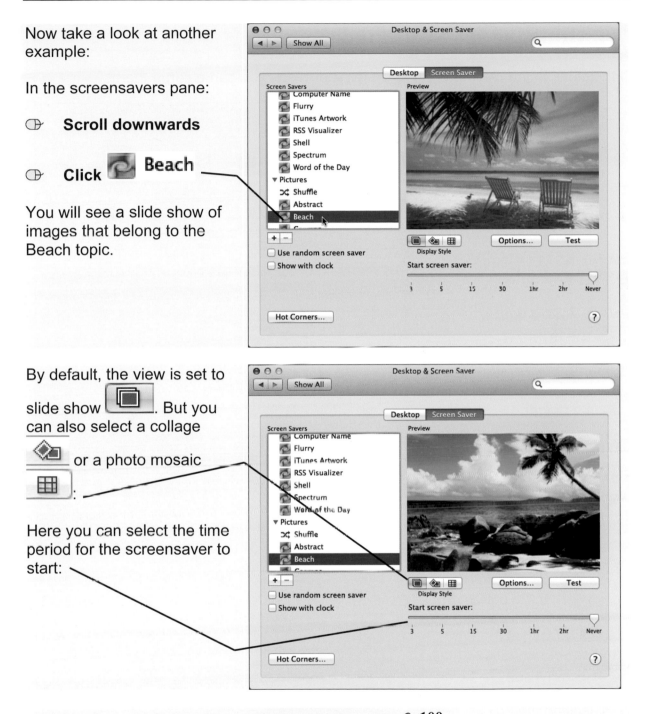

By default, the view is set to slide show . But you can also select a collage

or a photo mosaic

.

Here you can select the time period for the screensaver to start:

☞ Show all options of the *System Preferences* 𝒫𝒫**100**

# 7.4 Adjusting the Size of the Icons

If the icons in the *Dock* are too small for your taste, you can enlarge them.

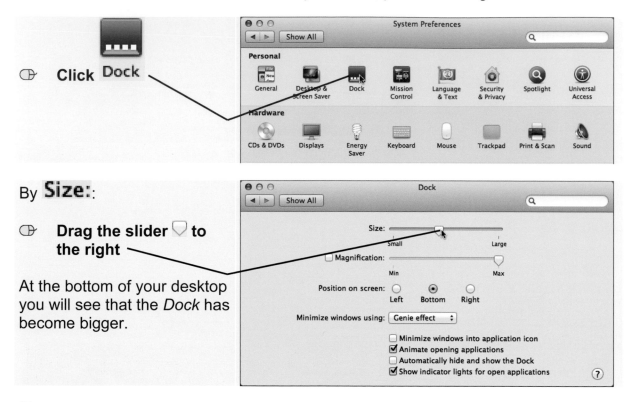

**Click Dock**

By **Size:**:

**Drag the slider ▽ to the right**

At the bottom of your desktop you will see that the *Dock* has become bigger.

**Please note:**

If the *Dock* is already taking up all of the space along the bottom of the screen, you will not be able to enlarge the *Dock* any further.

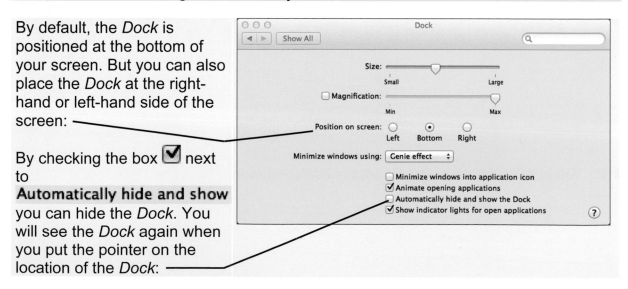

By default, the *Dock* is positioned at the bottom of your screen. But you can also place the *Dock* at the right-hand or left-hand side of the screen:

By checking the box ☑ next to **Automatically hide and show** you can hide the *Dock*. You will see the *Dock* again when you put the pointer on the location of the *Dock*:

## ☞ Show all options of the *System Preferences* ♘ 100

You can also enlarge the icons in the navigation pane of the *Finder*. You can change these settings in the *General* window of the *System Preferences*:

⊕   **Click** **General**

Now the *General* window will be opened. To clearly see the effect, you need to open the *Finder* window first:

⊕   **Click**

⊕   **Drag the *Finder* window, so as to view the navigation pane**

You will need to use the *System Preferences* window. You can bring that window back on top:

⊕   **Click the *System Preferences* window**

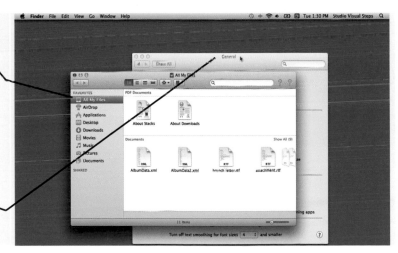

⊕ By Sidebar icon size:,
click [ Medium ⬍ ]

⊕ Click Large

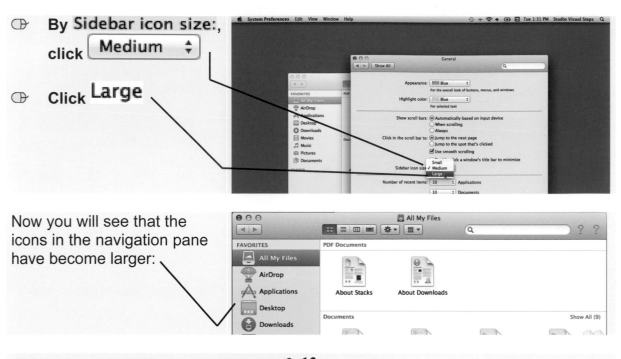

Now you will see that the
icons in the navigation pane
have become larger:

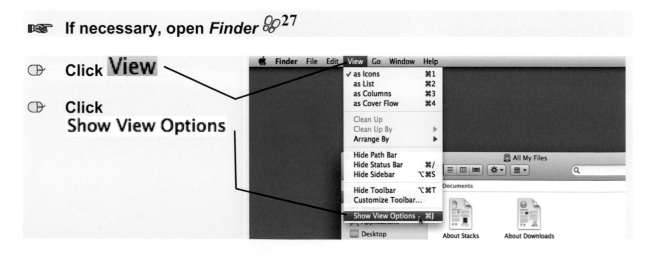

☞ Close the *System Preferences* 𝒫¹³

Now you have learned how to enlarge icons. In the next section you will learn how to
adjust some additional settings in the *Finder* window.

# 7.5 Adjusting the Finder Window

By default, the icons in the *Finder* window are displayed as small icons. But you can
change the size of the icons according to your own preferences. The *Finder* window
may still be open. If the window is closed:

☞ If necessary, open *Finder* 𝒫²⁷

⊕ Click View

⊕ Click
   Show View Options

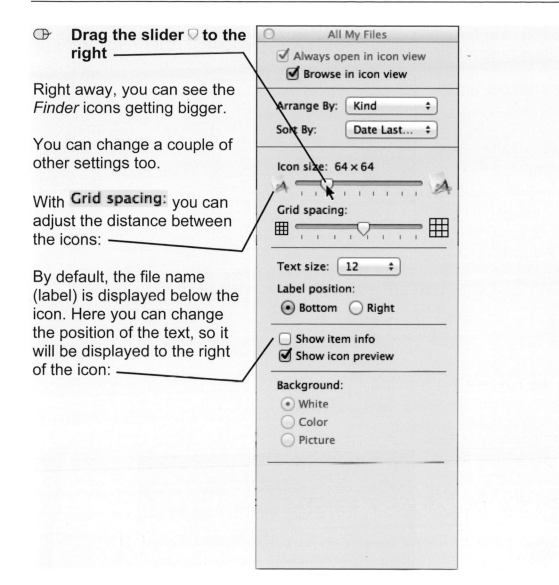

⊕ **Drag the slider ▽ to the right** ———

Right away, you can see the *Finder* icons getting bigger.

You can change a couple of other settings too.

With **Grid spacing:** you can adjust the distance between the icons: ———

By default, the file name (label) is displayed below the icon. Here you can change the position of the text, so it will be displayed to the right of the icon: ———

🖐 **Please note:**

When you make a change to the settings for the *Finder* window, those settings are only saved for the window that is currently open (in this case, the *All my files* folder).

When you open another *Finder* window, for instance the *Documents* folder, you will need to repeat the actions you just did once more. But once you have applied these changes, they will be saved whenever you close and open the window again. However, if you have select a different *view* in a *Finder* window, you will see a new set of viewing options available that can be set for that view.

If you find it difficult to read the file names (labels) below the icons, you can adjust the font size. Here is how you do that:

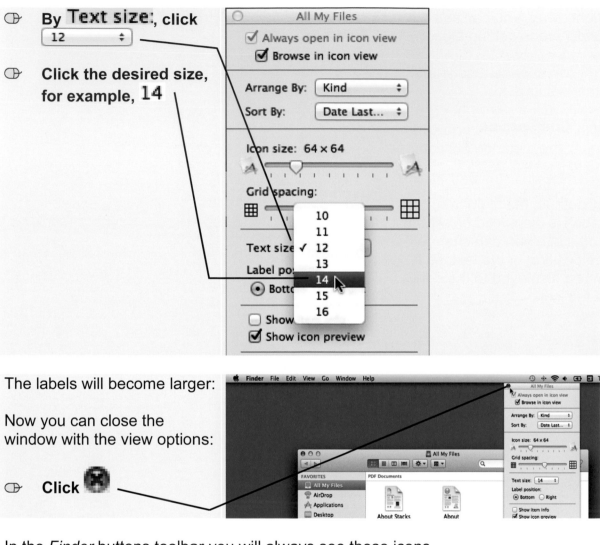

☞ By **Text size:**, click

☞ **Click the desired size, for example, 14**

The labels will become larger:

Now you can close the window with the view options:

☞ **Click** ✖

In the *Finder* buttons toolbar you will always see these icons

. But perhaps you do not know what they mean.

If that is the case, you can display the names of the icons. Here is how you do that:

⌨ **Press** control **(Control)**
**and keep this key**
**depressed**

☞ **Click a blank area in**
**the toolbar** ⟍

You will see a small menu:

☞ **Click** Icon and Text

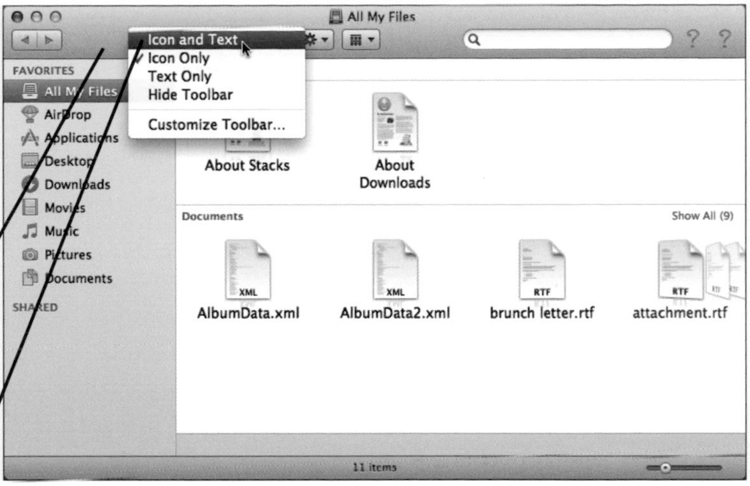

Now the names of the icons
have been added: ⟍

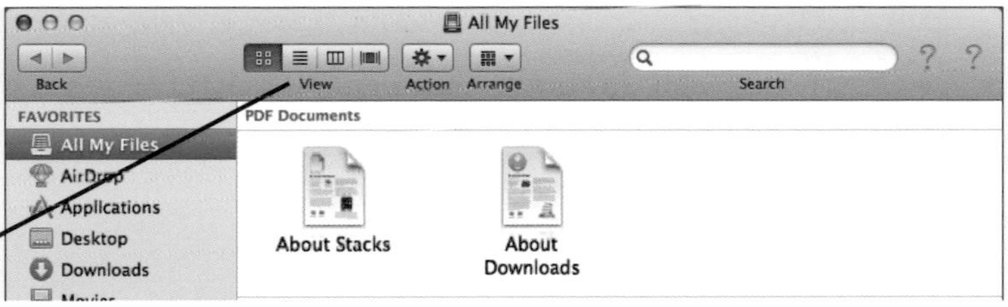

If you want to revert to just
displaying the icons:

⌨ **Press** control **(Control)**
**and keep this key**
**depressed**

☞ **Click a blank area in**
**the toolbar**

☞ **Click** Icon Only

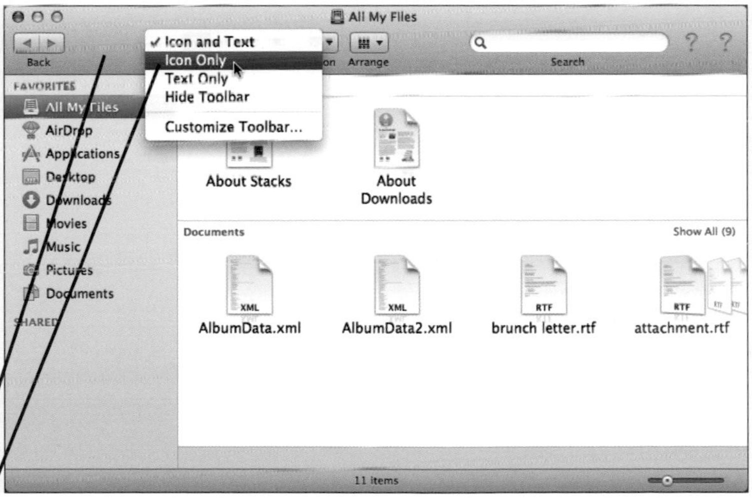

☞ **Close the** *Finder* **window** 👣**13**

# 7.6 Sound Settings

If you use a program in which audio tracks or sounds are played, it may sometimes be necessary to adjust the volume level. You can adjust the volume level with the volume buttons on your keyboard, and in the *System Preferences*. You can recognize the volume buttons on the keyboard by the images below:

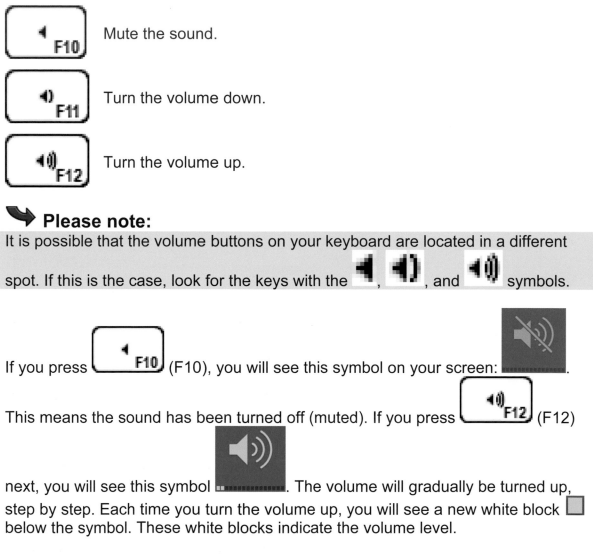

Mute the sound.

Turn the volume down.

Turn the volume up.

**➥ Please note:**

It is possible that the volume buttons on your keyboard are located in a different spot. If this is the case, look for the keys with the ◀ , ◀) , and ◀◊ symbols.

If you press ◀ F10 (F10), you will see this symbol on your screen: ▨ .

This means the sound has been turned off (muted). If you press ◀◊ F12 (F12) next, you will see this symbol ▨ . The volume will gradually be turned up, step by step. Each time you turn the volume up, you will see a new white block ▢ below the symbol. These white blocks indicate the volume level.

You can also adjust the volume settings in the *System Preferences*. Here is how to do that:

☞ **Open *System Preferences*** ℘ℓ75

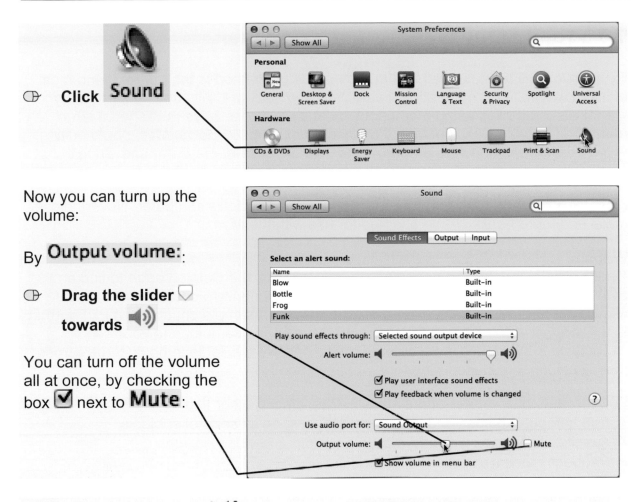

☞ **Click** Sound

Now you can turn up the volume:

By **Output volume:**.

☞ **Drag the slider** ▽

**towards** ◀))

You can turn off the volume all at once, by checking the box ☑ next to **Mute**:

☞ **Close all windows** ✇¹³

Now you have arrived at the end of this book. You have learned how to work with the *Mac*. Now you can start using your *Mac*.

If you want to learn more about the *Mac* and its programs, you can read and use the bonus chapters. On the web page **www.visualsteps.com/mac** you will find the following bonus chapters:

- *Bonus chapter 8 Basic Text Editing Operations*
  You can work through this chapter if you want to expand your basic knowledge of typing, selecting, cutting and pasting text.
- *Bonus chapter 9 Downloading Apps*
  Apps are programs that can be used on the *Mac*, iPad or iPhone.

# 7.7 Visual Steps Website and Newsletter

By now you will have noticed that the Visual Steps method is the quickest and most efficient way to learn more about computers and software. All books published by Visual Steps use this same method. In various series, we have published a large number of books on a wide variety of topics, including *Windows*, *Mac*, photo editing, video editing, free software programs such as *Skype, Google Earth* and *Google Maps* and many other topics.

Most titles are suited for and written for users of a *Windows* computer. Nevertheless, more and more books will be adapted for use with the *Mac*.

### Website
On the **www.visualsteps.com** website you can click the Catalog page to find an overview of all the Visual Steps titles, including an extensive description. Each title allows you to preview the full table of contents and a sample chapter in a PDF format. In this way, you can quickly determine if a specific title comes up to your expectations. All titles can be ordered online and are available in bookstores across the USA, Canada, United Kingdom, Australia and New Zealand.

Furthermore, our website offers many extras, among other things:
- free computer guides and booklets (PDF files) on all sorts of subjects;
- specific web pages with information on photo and video editing;
- frequently asked questions and their answers;
- information on the free Computer Certificate that you can acquire at the certificate's website **www.ccforseniors.com**;
- a free notify-me service: receive an e-mail as soon as a new book is published.

### Visual Steps Newsletter
Do you want to keep abreast of all the Visual Steps publications? Then you can subscribe to the free Visual Steps Newsletter (no strings attached), which is sent to you by e-mail.

The Newsletter is sent about twice a month. You will receive information about:
- the latest titles and previously published books;
- special offers and discounts;
- new, free computer booklets and guides;
- contests and questionnaires.

As a subscriber to the Visual Steps Newsletter you have immediate access to the free booklets and guides at **www.visualsteps.com/info_downloads**

# 7.8 Background Information

**Dictionary**

| | |
|---|---|
| **Apps** | *Apps* stands for applications. These are programs you can install on your *Mac*, iPad or iPhone. |
| **Desktop** | The working space on a computer screen. When you open a program, it will appear on the desktop. |
| **Desktop wallpaper** | The background for a desktop, usually one of the wallpapers included in the *Mac* software, but it can also be a uniform color or a digital photo from your own collection. |
| **Dock** | A component in *Mac OS X* with which you can open programs. By default, the *Dock* is positioned at the bottom of the screen. It contains icons for many of the programs installed on the computer. |
| **Screensaver** | An animated image or pattern that appears on the screen when the mouse or keyboard has not been used for a longer period of time. The *Mac* offers a number of different screensavers. You can choose the one you like best. |
| **System Preferences** | In *System Preferences* you can view and change the settings for the computer. The sections in the window have been divided into categories, such as Dock, Sound, Mouse and General. |

*Source: Apple Dictionary, www.apple.com, Wikipedia*

# 7.9 Tips

### Tip

**Quickly open the Sound window**

In the *Sound* window you can adjust the volume of your computer sounds. You can quickly open this window with the Alt key and the volume key:

 **Press** and keep this key depressed

**Press one of the volume keys**

### Tip

**Quickly maximize the Dock**

In this chapter you have learned how to adjust the size of the *Dock* through the *System Preferences*. But you can also change the settings in the *Dock* itself. For example, you can quickly enlarge the *Dock*. This is how you do it:

At the bottom right in the *Dock*:

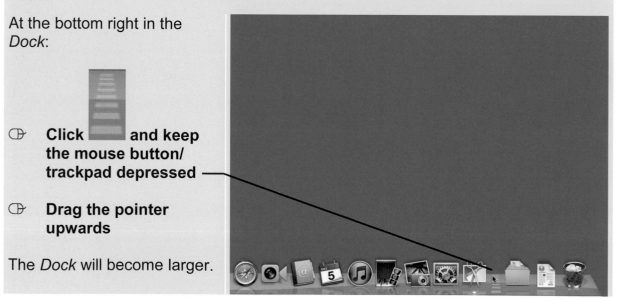

⊕ **Click** and keep the mouse button/ trackpad depressed

⊕ **Drag the pointer upwards**

The *Dock* will become larger.

## Tip

**Quickly enlarge the icons in the Dock**

You can enlarge the icons if you position the pointer on the *Dock*. This way, you will be able to see the icons better. This is how you do it with the Control key:

**Press** `control` **and keep the key depressed**

**Click**

You will see a small window:

To enlarge the icons:

**Click**
**Turn Magnification On**

**Position the pointer on an icon, for example**

You will see that the icons have become larger:

# iPad for SENIORS

### iPad for SENIORS
*Get started quickly with the user friendly iPad*

**Author**: Studio Visual Steps
**ISBN**: 978 90 5905 108 9
**Book type**: Paperback
**Number of pages**: 296
**Accompanying website**:
www.visualsteps.com/ipad

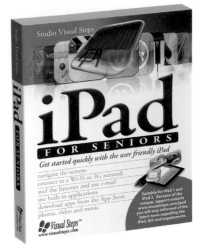

This comprehensive and invaluable guide will show you how to get the most out of your iPad. The iPad is a very user friendly, portable multimedia device with endless capabilities. Use it to surf the Internet, write e-mails, jot down notes and maintain your calendar.
But that is not all you can do with the iPad by far. With the Apple App Store you can choose from hundreds of thousands of applications (apps). Many apps can be downloaded for free or cost practically nothing. This practical tablet computer offers apps to allow you to listen to music, take and view photos and make video calls. Perhaps you are interested in new recipes, horoscopes, fitness exercises, news from around the world or podcasts? You can even use it to view the place where you live in Google Street View. There is literally an app to do almost anything.
With *iPAD FOR SENIORS* you can learn how to take complete advantage of this technology. Before you know it, you won't believe you ever lived without an iPad and your world will open up and become a lot bigger!

**You will learn how to:**
- navigate the screens
- connect to a Wi-Fi or 3G network
- surf the Internet and use e-mail
- use built-in applications
- download apps from the App Store
work with photos, video and music

# Appendix A. How Do I Do That Again?

The actions and exercises in this book are marked with footsteps: 🐾1
In this appendix you can look up the numbers of the footsteps and read how to execute certain operations.

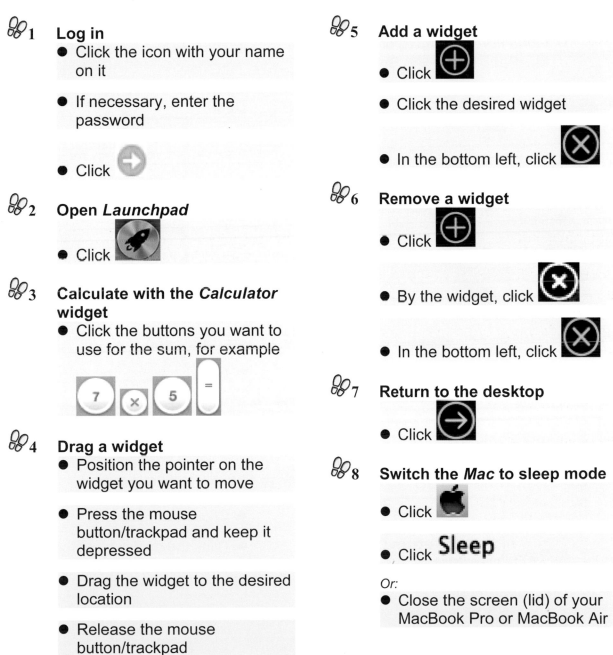

🐾1 **Log in**
- Click the icon with your name on it
- If necessary, enter the password
- Click ➡

🐾2 **Open *Launchpad***
- Click 🚀

🐾3 **Calculate with the *Calculator* widget**
- Click the buttons you want to use for the sum, for example
  7 × 5 =

🐾4 **Drag a widget**
- Position the pointer on the widget you want to move
- Press the mouse button/trackpad and keep it depressed
- Drag the widget to the desired location
- Release the mouse button/trackpad

🐾5 **Add a widget**
- Click ⊕
- Click the desired widget
- In the bottom left, click ⊗

🐾6 **Remove a widget**
- Click ⊕
- By the widget, click ⊗
- In the bottom left, click ⊗

🐾7 **Return to the desktop**
- Click ➡

🐾8 **Switch the *Mac* to sleep mode**
- Click 🍎
- Click **Sleep**

*Or:*
- Close the screen (lid) of your MacBook Pro or MacBook Air

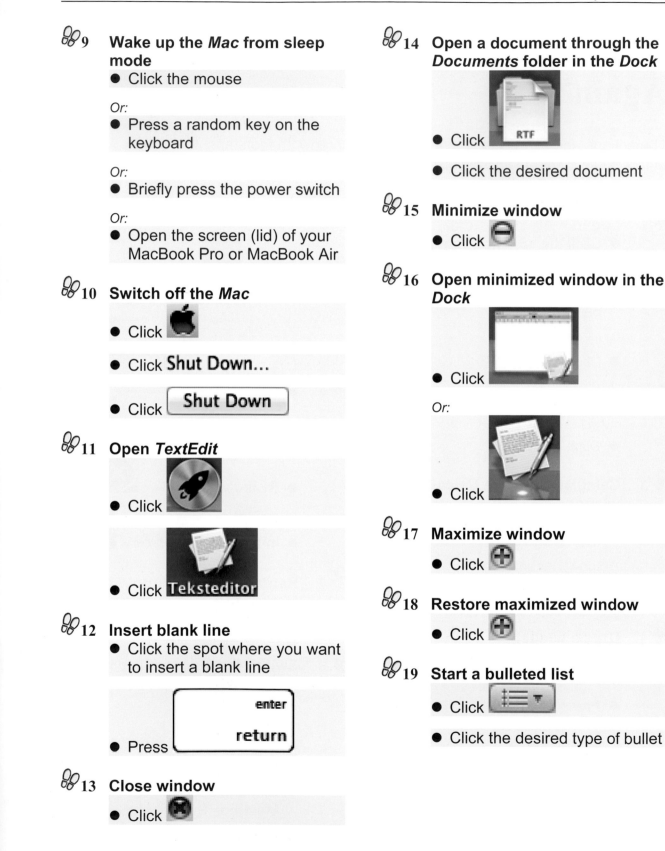

9  **Wake up the *Mac* from sleep mode**
- Click the mouse

*Or:*
- Press a random key on the keyboard

*Or:*
- Briefly press the power switch

*Or:*
- Open the screen (lid) of your MacBook Pro or MacBook Air

10  **Switch off the *Mac***
- Click 
- Click Shut Down...
- Click Shut Down

11  **Open *TextEdit***
- Click 
- Click Teksteditor

12  **Insert blank line**
- Click the spot where you want to insert a blank line
- Press  enter / return

13  **Close window**
- Click 

14  **Open a document through the *Documents* folder in the *Dock***
- Click  RTF
- Click the desired document

15  **Minimize window**
- Click 

16  **Open minimized window in the *Dock***
- Click 

*Or:*
- Click 

17  **Maximize window**
- Click 

18  **Restore maximized window**
- Click 

19  **Start a bulleted list**
- Click 
- Click the desired type of bullet

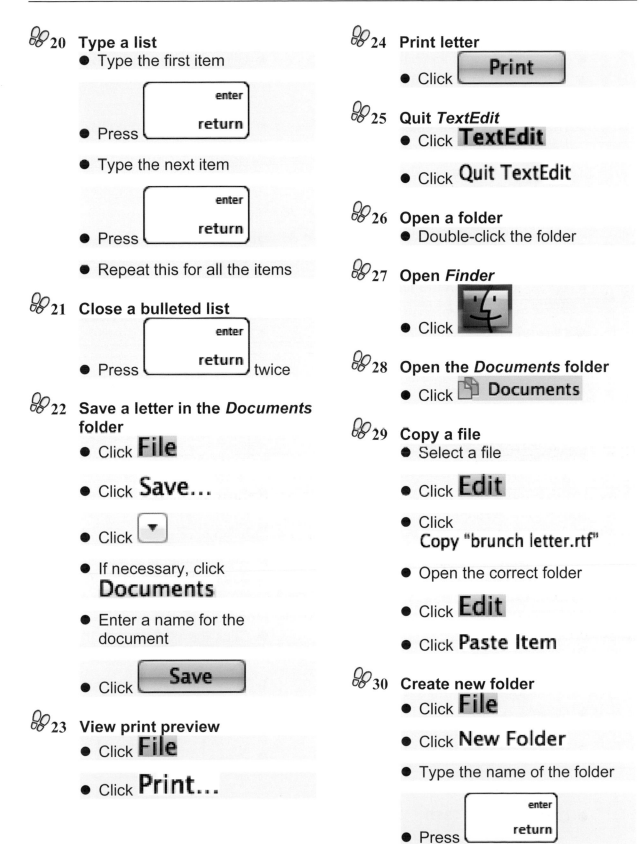

**20  Type a list**
- Type the first item
- Press [enter / return]
- Type the next item
- Press [enter / return]
- Repeat this for all the items

**21  Close a bulleted list**
- Press [enter / return] twice

**22  Save a letter in the *Documents* folder**
- Click **File**
- Click **Save...**
- Click [▼]
- If necessary, click **Documents**
- Enter a name for the document
- Click **Save**

**23  View print preview**
- Click **File**
- Click **Print...**

**24  Print letter**
- Click **Print**

**25  Quit *TextEdit***
- Click **TextEdit**
- Click **Quit TextEdit**

**26  Open a folder**
- Double-click the folder

**27  Open *Finder***
- Click

**28  Open the *Documents* folder**
- Click **Documents**

**29  Copy a file**
- Select a file
- Click **Edit**
- Click **Copy "brunch letter.rtf"**
- Open the correct folder
- Click **Edit**
- Click **Paste Item**

**30  Create new folder**
- Click **File**
- Click **New Folder**
- Type the name of the folder
- Press [enter / return]

**31  Move a file**
- Click the file and keep the mouse button/ trackpad depressed

- Drag the file to the desired folder

*As soon as the folder is opened:*
- Release the mouse button/trackpad

**32  Change the name of a file/folder**
- Click the name of the file or folder

- Click the name of the file or folder once more

- Type the new name

- Press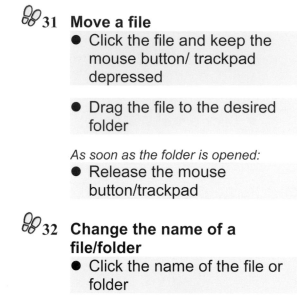

**33  Move a file/folder to the *Trash Bin***
- Select the file

- Click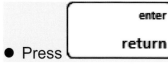

- Click **Move to Trash**

**34  Open the *Trash Bin***

- Click

**35  Empty the *Trash Bin***

- Click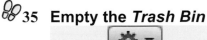

- Click **Empty Trash**

**36  Copy a file to USB stick**
- Click the file and keep the mouse button/ trackpad depressed

- Drag the file to the USB stick in the navigation pane
*As soon as the USB stick is displayed:*
- Release the mouse button/trackpad

**37  Disconnect USB stick**
- By the USB stick in the navigation pane, click ⏏

**38  Zoom in with the keyboard**
- Simultaneously press

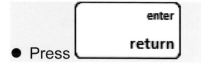 (Command) and

(+)

**39  Return to previously web page**
- Click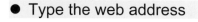

- Repeat this, until you see the desired web page

**40  Open a website**
- Click the address bar three times

- Type the web address

- Press

 **41  Open *Safari***

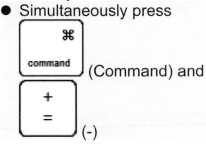

- Click

 **42  Zoom in**
*With the Magic Mouse:*
- Tap the Magic Mouse twice in rapid succession

*With the (Magic) trackpad:*
- Tap the (Magic) trackpad with two fingers, in rapid succession

*With the keyboard:*
- Simultaneously press

⌘ command (Command) and

+ = (-)

- Repeat this until you see the web page in the desired size

 **43  Scroll downwards**
*With the Magic Mouse:*
- Drag your finger upwards a bit over the Magic Mouse

*With the (Magic) trackpad:*
- Drag two fingers upwards over the trackpad

*With the scroll wheel:*
- Turn the scroll wheel away from you

**44  Scroll upwards**
*With the Magic Mouse:*
- Drag your finger downwards a bit over the Magic Mouse

*With the (Magic) trackpad:*
- Drag two fingers downwards over the trackpad

*With the scroll wheel:*
- Turn the scroll wheel towards you

 **45  Zoom out**
*With the Magic Mouse:*
- Tap the Magic Mouse twice in rapid succession

*With the (Magic) trackpad:*
- Tap the (Magic) trackpad twice with two fingers, in rapid succession

*With the keyboard:*
- Simultaneously press

⌘ command (Command) and

− ‑ (-)

- Repeat this until you see the web page in the desired size

 **46  Open a link**
- Click the link

 **47  Open a link in a new tab**

⌘ command (Command)

- Keep (Command) depressed

- Click the link

- Release 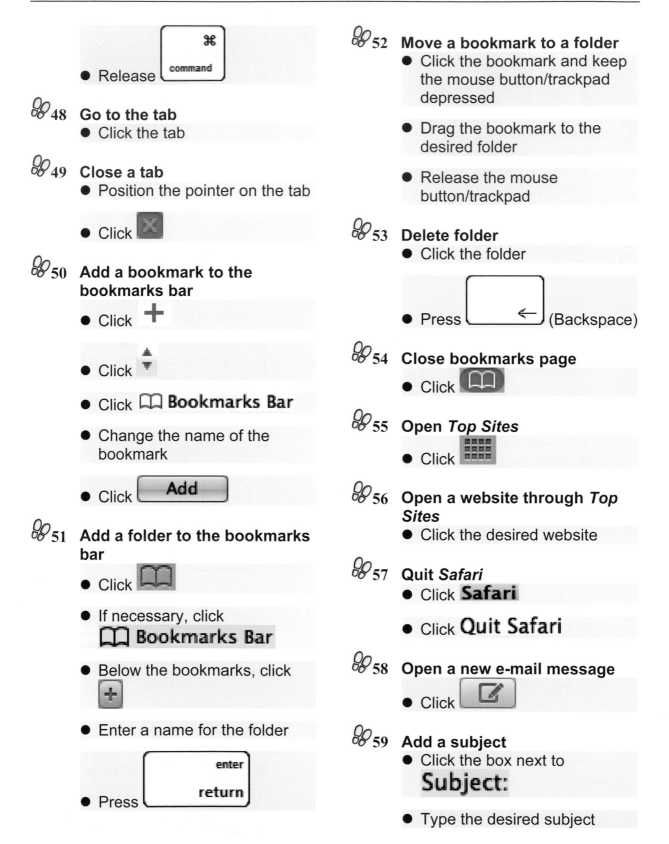 ⌘ command

**48  Go to the tab**
- Click the tab

**49  Close a tab**
- Position the pointer on the tab

- Click ⊠

**50  Add a bookmark to the bookmarks bar**
- Click **+**

- Click ⬍

- Click 📖 **Bookmarks Bar**

- Change the name of the bookmark

- Click **Add**

**51  Add a folder to the bookmarks bar**
- Click 📖

- If necessary, click 📖 **Bookmarks Bar**

- Below the bookmarks, click **+**

- Enter a name for the folder

- Press ⏎ enter return

**52  Move a bookmark to a folder**
- Click the bookmark and keep the mouse button/trackpad depressed

- Drag the bookmark to the desired folder

- Release the mouse button/trackpad

**53  Delete folder**
- Click the folder

- Press ⟵ (Backspace)

**54  Close bookmarks page**
- Click 📖

**55  Open *Top Sites***
- Click ▦

**56  Open a website through *Top Sites***
- Click the desired website

**57  Quit *Safari***
- Click **Safari**

- Click **Quit Safari**

**58  Open a new e-mail message**
- Click ✎

**59  Add a subject**
- Click the box next to **Subject:**

- Type the desired subject

**60 Add a message**
- Click the big blank area
- Type your message

**61 Send an e-mail**
- Click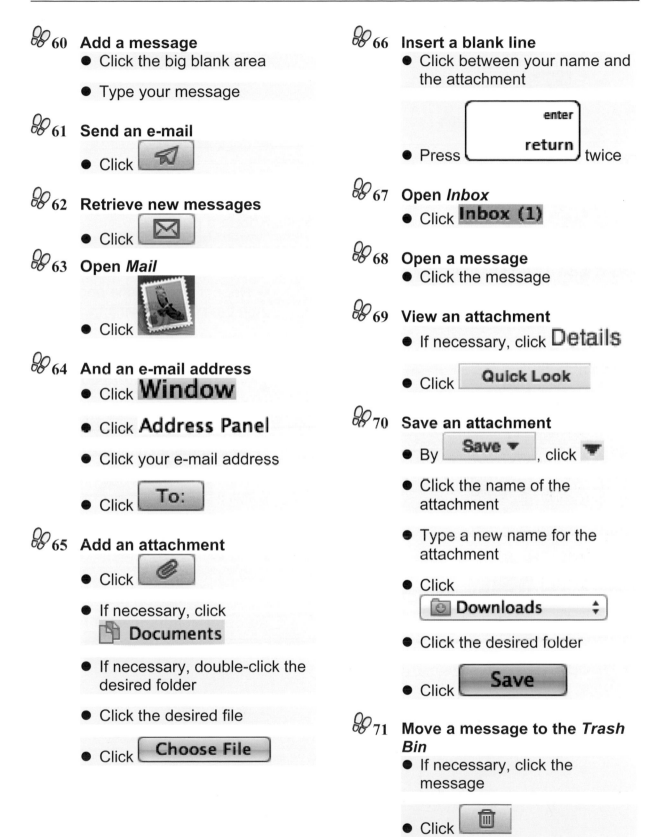

**62 Retrieve new messages**
- Click

**63 Open *Mail***
- Click

**64 And an e-mail address**
- Click **Window**
- Click **Address Panel**
- Click your e-mail address
- Click **To:**

**65 Add an attachment**
- Click
- If necessary, click **Documents**
- If necessary, double-click the desired folder
- Click the desired file
- Click **Choose File**

**66 Insert a blank line**
- Click between your name and the attachment
- Press [enter return] twice

**67 Open *Inbox***
- Click **Inbox (1)**

**68 Open a message**
- Click the message

**69 View an attachment**
- If necessary, click **Details**
- Click **Quick Look**

**70 Save an attachment**
- By **Save ▼**, click ▼
- Click the name of the attachment
- Type a new name for the attachment
- Click **Downloads ↕**
- Click the desired folder
- Click **Save**

**71 Move a message to the *Trash Bin***
- If necessary, click the message
- Click

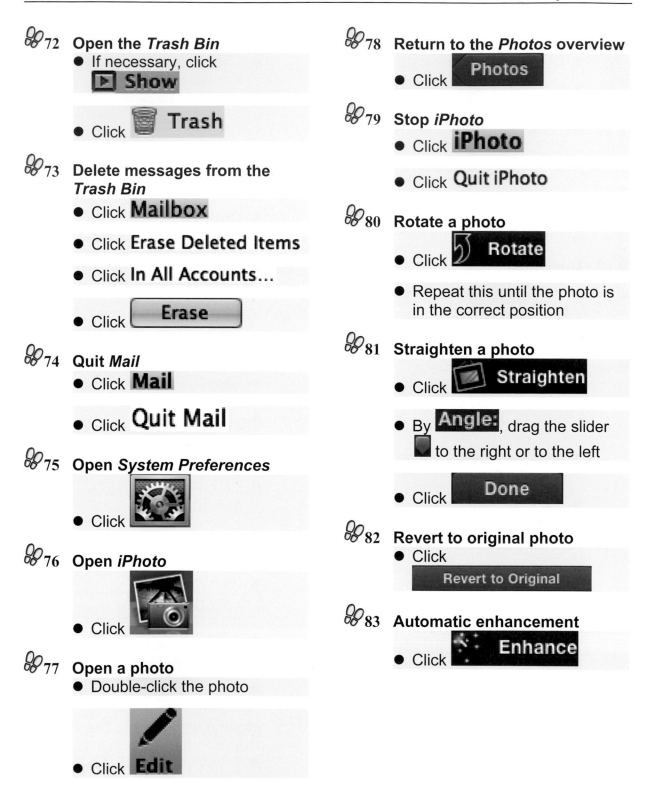

**72** **Open the *Trash Bin***
- If necessary, click
  ▶ **Show**
- Click 🗑 **Trash**

**73** **Delete messages from the *Trash Bin***
- Click **Mailbox**
- Click **Erase Deleted Items**
- Click **In All Accounts...**
- Click **Erase**

**74** **Quit *Mail***
- Click **Mail**
- Click **Quit Mail**

**75** **Open *System Preferences***
- Click

**76** **Open *iPhoto***
- Click

**77** **Open a photo**
- Double-click the photo
- Click **Edit**

**78** **Return to the *Photos* overview**
- Click **Photos**

**79** **Stop *iPhoto***
- Click **iPhoto**
- Click **Quit iPhoto**

**80** **Rotate a photo**
- Click **Rotate**
- Repeat this until the photo is in the correct position

**81** **Straighten a photo**
- Click **Straighten**
- By **Angle:**, drag the slider to the right or to the left
- Click **Done**

**82** **Revert to original photo**
- Click **Revert to Original**

**83** **Automatic enhancement**
- Click **Enhance**

**84 Crop a photo**

- Click 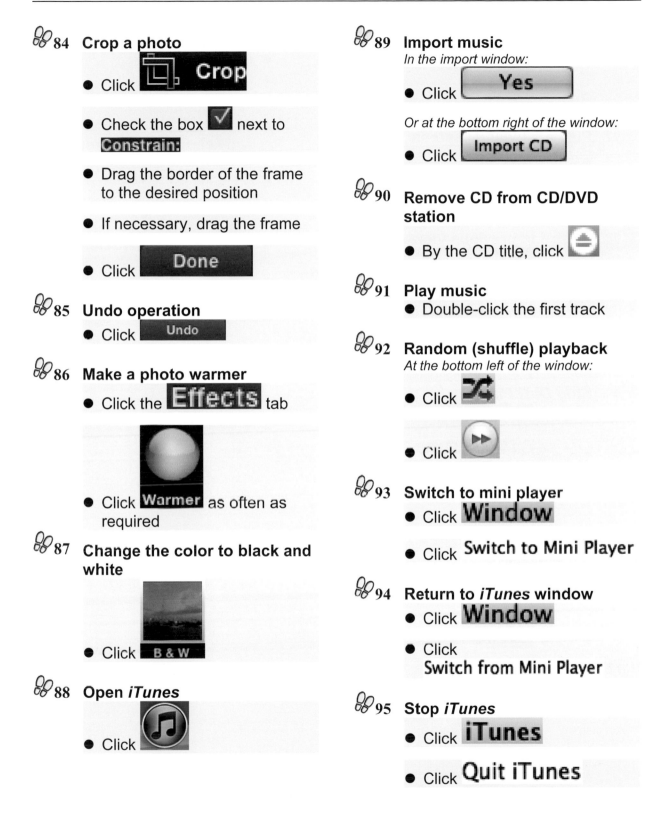 **Crop**

- Check the box ✅ next to **Constrain:**

- Drag the border of the frame to the desired position

- If necessary, drag the frame

- Click **Done**

**85 Undo operation**

- Click **Undo**

**86 Make a photo warmer**

- Click the **Effects** tab

- Click **Warmer** as often as required

**87 Change the color to black and white**

- Click **B & W**

**88 Open *iTunes***

- Click

**89 Import music**

*In the import window:*

- Click **Yes**

*Or at the bottom right of the window:*

- Click **Import CD**

**90 Remove CD from CD/DVD station**

- By the CD title, click ⏏

**91 Play music**

- Double-click the first track

**92 Random (shuffle) playback**

*At the bottom left of the window:*

- Click 🔀

- Click ⏩

**93 Switch to mini player**

- Click **Window**

- Click **Switch to Mini Player**

**94 Return to *iTunes* window**

- Click **Window**

- Click **Switch from Mini Player**

**95 Stop *iTunes***

- Click **iTunes**

- Click **Quit iTunes**

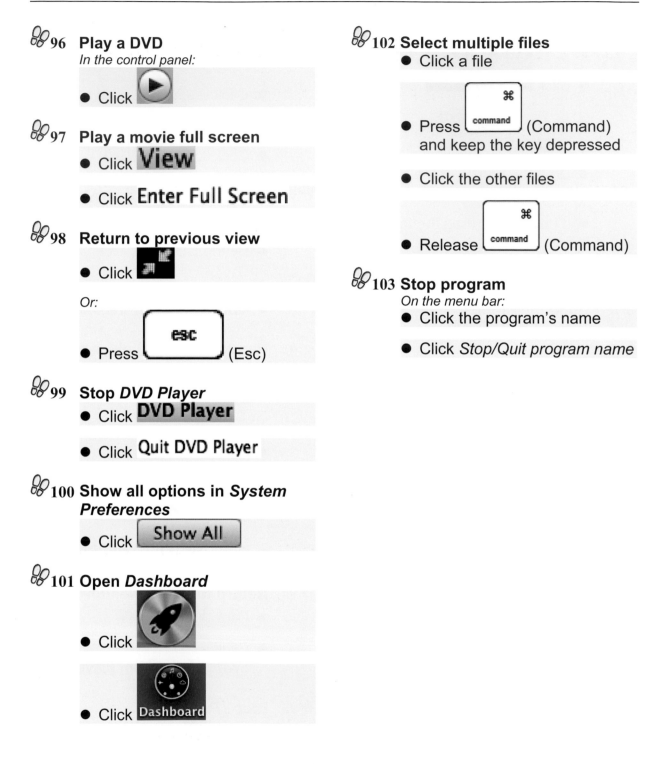

**96  Play a DVD**
*In the control panel:*
● Click ▶

**97  Play a movie full screen**
● Click **View**

● Click **Enter Full Screen**

**98  Return to previous view**
● Click ▣

*Or:*

● Press **esc** (Esc)

**99  Stop *DVD Player***
● Click **DVD Player**

● Click **Quit DVD Player**

**100  Show all options in *System Preferences***
● Click **Show All**

**101  Open *Dashboard***
● Click 🚀

● Click **Dashboard**

**102  Select multiple files**
● Click a file

● Press **⌘ command** (Command) and keep the key depressed

● Click the other files

● Release **⌘ command** (Command)

**103  Stop program**
*On the menu bar:*
● Click the program's name

● Click *Stop/Quit program name*

# Appendix B. Opening Bonus Chapters

On the website accompanying this book you will find the following bonus chapters:

- *Bonus Chapter 8 Basic Text Editing Operations*
- *Bonus Chapter 9 Downloading Apps*

These are PDF files. This is how you open the files from the website that goes with this book:

☞ **Open** *Safari* ∂∂⁴¹

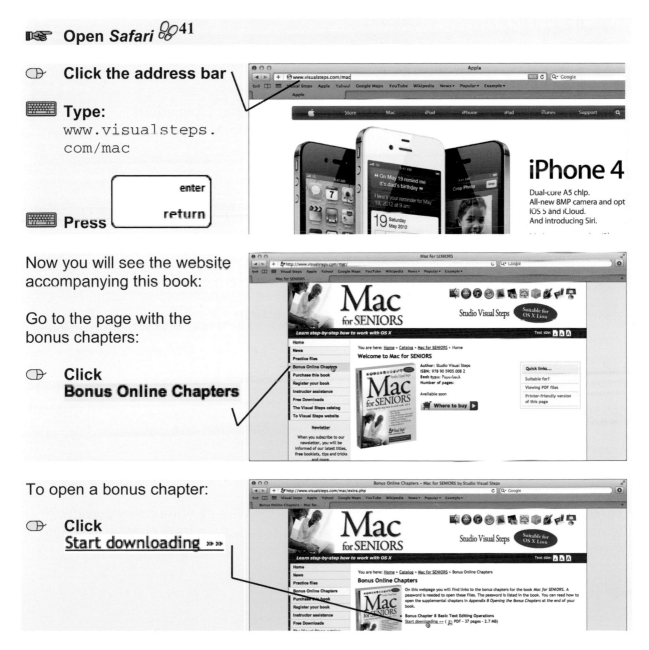

**Click the address bar**

**Type:**
www.visualsteps.
com/mac

**Press** enter / return

Now you will see the website accompanying this book:

Go to the page with the bonus chapters:

☞ **Click**
**Bonus Online Chapters**

To open a bonus chapter:

☞ **Click**
**Start downloading** »»

The PDF files are password protected. To open the PDF files, you need to enter the password first:

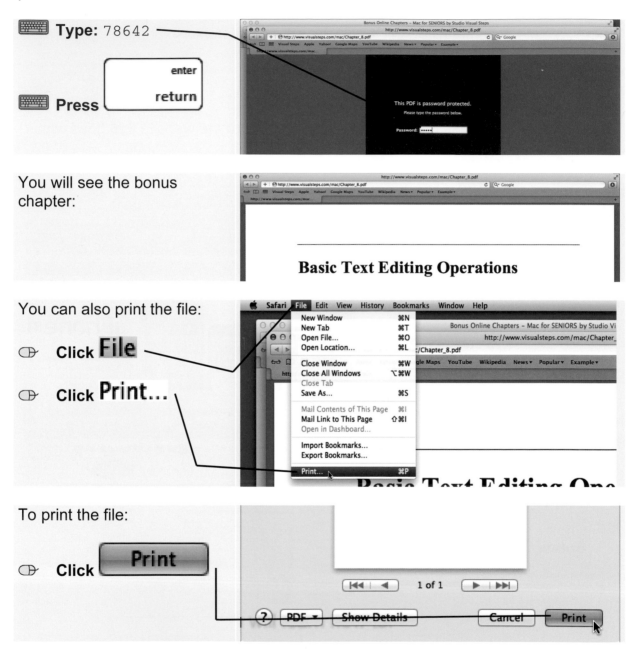

Type: 78642

Press enter / return

You will see the bonus chapter:

**Basic Text Editing Operations**

You can also print the file:

☞ Click **File**

☞ Click **Print...**

To print the file:

☞ Click **Print**

You can work through this bonus chapter in the same way as you have worked with the chapters in this book. After you have read or printed the bonus chapter, you can close all the windows.

☞ **Close all windows** ᵍ13

# Appendix C. Downloading the Practice Files

If you want to follow the examples in *Chapter 6 Photos, Videos and Music*, you will need to use a few of the practice files. You can download these practice files from the website accompanying this book.

☞ **Open *Safari* ⟨⟨41**

☞ **Open the www.visualsteps.com/mac/practice.php web page ⟨⟨40**

The web page with the practice files will be opened:

⬚ **Click**
  **Mac Practice Files**

The practice files will be downloaded right away.

In the top right of your window, the ⬇ indicates the progress of the download operation:

You can take a closer look at the progress bar:

⬚ **Click** ⬇

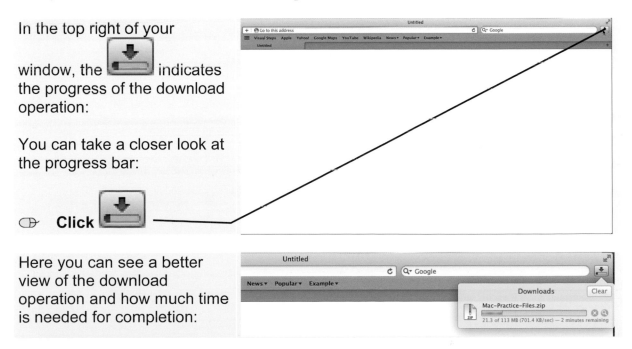

Here you can see a better view of the download operation and how much time is needed for completion:

The files have been downloaded. The folder with the practice files will be stored in the *Downloads* folder on the *Mac*. Now you can delete the folder from this list. If you do this, the folder will only be deleted from the download list; the actual files will still remain in the *Downloads* folder.

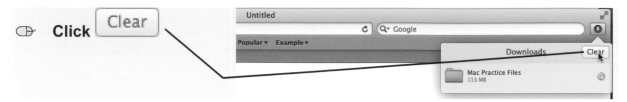

Now you can stop *Safari*:

☞ **Stop *Safari*** 🦶⁵⁷

If you want to use the practice files in *iPhoto*, you will need to import these files into the program. This is how you do that:

☞ **If necessary, open *iPhoto*** 🦶⁵⁷

The practice files have been stored in the *Downloads* folder:

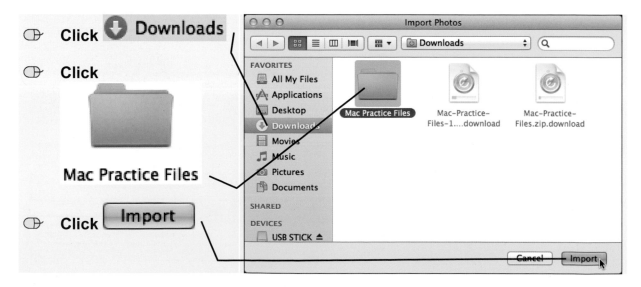

Now the photos have been imported into *iPhoto*. You can find them in the Recent group with the heading

Last Import.

The video file from the *Mac Practice Files* folder has also been imported, but is not needed in *iPhoto*:

You can remove this file from *iPhoto*:

☞ **Click the video file**

☞ **Drag the file to**
   **Trash**

Now the video file has been moved to the *Trash Bin*. This is how you empty the trash:

☞ **Right-click** **Trash**

☞ **Click**
   **Empty Trash**

☞ **Click** OK

Please note: You can still work with the video file later on in another program. It is still stored in the *Mac Practice Files* folder, within the *Downloads* folder.

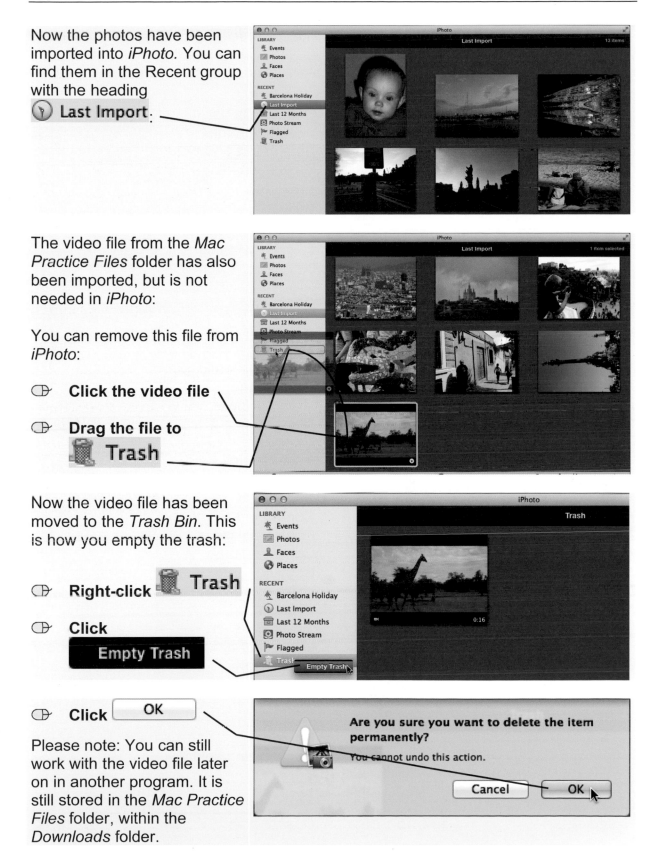

Are you sure you want to delete the item permanently?

You cannot undo this action.

Cancel    OK

# Appendix D. Index